Odd Fellows Manual

Modern Guide to the Origin, History, Rituals, Symbols and
Organization of the Independent Order of Odd Fellows

LOUIE BLAKE SAILE SARMIENTO, J.D.

Editor: Cyril Jaymes Plantilla
Layout and Cover Design: Louie Blake Saile Sarmiento
Cover photo: John Badillo and Eric Fuertes

International Research Society
on Fraternal Societies

Full Color Edition: ISBN 978-1-7338512-5-1
Black and White Edition: ISBN 978-1-7338512-8-2
Published in the U.S.A.

Contents

"The true effort to revitalize Odd Fellowship should be to educate and inform its members. Knowledge leads to confidence; confidence leads to enthusiasm; enthusiasm leads to commitment; commitment leads to pride; and these all collectively leads to organizational success."

Dedication and Acknowledgement

This book is dedicated in memory of former authors of Odd Fellows' history books and manuals, namely: James Ridgely, Aaron Burt Grosh, Theodore Ross, Thomas Beharrell, Thomas Andrews, L. Hamel Cooke, Paschal Donaldson, Charles Brooks, Elvin James Curry, Joseph Powley, Henry Leonard Stillson and Donald Smith. The work of these brothers has been one of the major bases of my writings. And to my fellow 21st century Odd Fellows' historians and authors – Peter Sellars, Dave Rosenberg, Daniel Weinbren and Kjell-Henrik Hendrichs - who work tirelessly to research, study, write and publish new books and articles about Odd Fellowship even without the support of Grand Lodges and the Sovereign Grand Lodge. We do this not for profit or personal gain but to help preserve and uplift our Order. It is our modest hope that our writings will be helpful in bringing the Independent Order of Odd Fellows into the future.

To my grandparents, parents, family and true friends whose support have been the fuel for my successes. To The Sovereign Grand Lodge of the Independent Order of Odd Fellows for giving me the opportunity to profoundly study and experience Odd Fellowship – especially to Sovereign Grand Secretary Terry Barrett and Past Sovereign Grand Masters Donald Smith, Paul Cuminale, Charles Renninger, Harry Lohman, Delmar Burns and George Glover III. To Past Grand Sire Harald Thoen of Norway, Grand Sire Erling Stenholdt Poulsen of Denmark and Jane Nelson of the Manchester Unity Oddfellows. Also, to John Cain+, Stacey Layne, Suzie Robertson+, Brenda Nelson, Walker Houchins and Amy-Ruth Hallet who provided all the moral and social support during my stay at the International Headquarters in Winston-Salem, North Carolina. To John Badillo and Eric Fuertes of the Three Links PHL for recreating and taking pictures of the traditional lodge collar regalia used in this book.

Most importantly, to all active members - present and future - who are true and loyal to the principles of Odd Fellowship!

Always in FL&T

Member Information

Name: _____

Lodge Name: _____

Lodge Address: _____

Contact #: _____

Junior Lodge / Theta Rho Girls' Club / United Youth Group / PM Cadet Corps

Date Initiated: _____

Odd Fellows Lodge

Date of Initiatory Degree: _____

Date of Degree of Friendship: _____

Date of Degree of Love: _____

Date of Degree of Truth: _____

Date of Grand Lodge Degree: _____

Rebekah Lodge

Date of Rebekah Degree: _____

Date of Rebekah Assembly Degree: _____

Encampment / Ladies Encampment Auxiliary

Date of Patriarchal Degree: _____

Date of Golden Rule Degree: _____

Date of Royal Purple Degree: _____

Date of Grand Encampment Degree: _____

Patriarchs Militant / Ladies Auxiliary Patriarchs Militant

Date of Patriarchs Militant / LAPM Degree:_____

Preface

The aim of this **Odd Fellows Manual and Modern Guide** is to create a 21st century reference book highlighting the essentials of the Independent Order of Odd Fellows. This book hopes to acquaint potential candidates, members and leaders with a straight-forward approach of its origin and history; philosophy and purposes; degrees, teachings and symbols; organizational structure, officers, regalia and jewels of office. But this does not aim to teach the rituals itself or any of its signs and passwords. In addition, this does not also aim to supplant the Code of General Laws but only to emphasize some of the generally accepted rules within the IOOF.

Membership education and mentoring are very important prerequisites for a successful and growing non-profit organization. But when I first joined in 2009, there was almost nothing new about the Independent Order of Odd Fellows except old history books and manuals that were quite hard to find. There was also minimal online presence except a one paragraph entry on Wikipedia that tells almost nothing about its history and its purposes. Further, there was no active presence on social media websites nor a single YouTube video explaining the Odd Fellows. What the IOOF had at that time was the old Sovereign Grand Lodge and some of the Grand Lodges' websites that needed updates.

At the beginning of 2009, I volunteered to create and manage several Facebook pages and social media groups as well as YouTube videos. I realized the importance of using free online platforms to share modern infographics on the topic of Odd Fellowship. I also worked on adding more information on Wikipedia, including the first list of famous members. Since then, most of the information I wrote, created and uploaded online have been re-shared and re-used by many members across the world. The social media platform has become the primary venue where people can ask questions and where members can answer queries. Many members, lodges and Grand Lodges eventually followed and took advantage of online tools. Fortunately, these online tools have been helpful in reviving lodges and instituting new ones.

I was appointed as Public Relations Coordinator and member of both the Revitalization Committee and Communications Committee of the Sovereign Grand Lodge from 2012-2015. In a span of three years, I was lucky enough to have full access of all journals, history books, manuals, rituals, unwritten work and artifacts at the international headquarters. This gave me the opportunity to read everything written about Odd Fellowship from cover-to-cover. Further, I launched an online survey to conduct a SWOT Analysis of the IOOF that was participated by exactly 2,120 members from all over North America, Latin America, Europe, Australia and Southeast Asia. With the help of the Sovereign Grand Secretary and several members, I also had the chance to visit nearly a hundred lodges and several Grand Lodges in the United States and Canada to observe their workings. With this background, I learned many of the needed organizational changes and improvements that may help bring the IOOF into the future.

I have since passed-on to others the responsibility of managing IOOF social media and promoting Odd Fellowship due to the demands of my law studies and career. I now prefer working behind the scenes and living a secluded and peaceful life. But helping Odd Fellowship does not stop with social media marketing. The survey study I conducted in 2012 showed that majority of the respondents are in agreement that Odd Fellowship lacked the needed modern literature to educate and mentor its members. Similar fraternal organizations, like Freemasonry, have long benefited from thousands of published research studies and books that are easily accessible through online bookstores and outlets. On the other hand, Odd Fellowship have long suffered from a lack of up-to-date information and literature. Irrefutably, the last history book, manual and guide about the IOOF was published more than 100 years ago. A lot about the IOOF has already changed. The focus and purposes of the organization has evolved. The rituals, symbols, regalia and Code of General Laws have been amended and revised through the years. With modern technology, access to historical documents has also become easier. Furthermore, a lot of new evidence is coming out to light which calls for a need to re-visit and re-write the origins and history of Odd Fellowship. The claims of past writers can already be easily confirmed or debunked. This suggests that most of the manuals and books published many years ago have become outdated although not completely obsolete. This book will attempt to fill the gap. Lastly, it is my hope that my books will encourage others to write and publish more up-to-date literature about Odd Fellowship.

Ethics of Odd Fellowship

Odd Fellows believe in a Supreme Being. Their thoughts and actions are based on healthy philosophical principles. They know that life here on earth is temporary. They are aware of the vanity of earthly things, the frailty and inevitable decay of human life, and the fact that wealth has no power to stop the certainty of eventual death. They start by asking the question, "How am I going to live my life?" Then, they work towards the improvement and elevation of their character: to fight against their human weaknesses and to live responsibly.

Odd Fellows are advocates of genuine FRIENDSHIP, the strongest bond of fraternity that teaches goodwill and harmony. They never look at people with prejudiced eyes nor base their judgment on outward appearances. They support the idea that all people regardless of race, gender, nationality, religion, political affiliation, social status, rank and station in life are brothers and sisters. They do not take undue advantage of their power or the weaknesses of those around them. They are humble in a way that they never boast about their 'self.' They know and accept their individual strengths and weaknesses and keep away from badmouthing people and making unreasonable allegations. In this way, they promise never to slander a brother or sister but will defend his or her well-being, advise him or her for his or her best, and will help his or her family in times of need.

Odd Fellows are enactors of unfettered LOVE, the basis for all life's ambitions, service to others, and family. They work for goodwill between humankind, understanding between classes of the community and peace between nations. They fight against selfishness, the natural human weakness that hampers the will to do what is good. They feel jointly responsible for their fellowmen and are prepared to give attention and help wherever and whenever help is needed. They know the application of sympathy, sincerity, unselfishness, and generosity. They accept the fact that nothing is perfect but believe that they have an obligation to contribute in making the world a better place to live by "visiting the sick, relieving the distressed, educating the orphans, and burying the dead."

Odd Fellows are pursuers of inflexible TRUTH, the standard by which they value people and the foundation of their fraternity. They adhere to equality, justice, and righteousness. They are honest not just in words but also through deeds and actions. They will never defraud their lodge, but will prevent unlawful use of its funds and property, and strive at every occasion to promote its welfare. They see searching for the truth as searching for clarity in the sense of their individual lives. Oftentimes, they think before they speak and act. They know that before they start doing something, they can make the choice what to do, can think it over, and consider whether the choice was the right one. They believe that making good and well-considered choices is called "behaving in a responsible way."

Archive section at the International Headquarters of The Sovereign Grand Lodge of the Independent Order of Odd Fellows in Winston-Salem, North Carolina, U.S.A.

Introduction

Evolving from the traditions of the English craft guilds and journeymen associations, the name Odd Fellows (also spelled as Oddfellows) refers to a number of fraternal orders, friendly societies and service organizations whose origin goes back on or before the year 1700s. There are four remaining major *Affiliated Orders* existing in more than 30 countries today, namely:

- Grand United Order of Oddfellows (GUOOF), established in 1798;

- Independent Order of Oddfellows Manchester Unity (IOOFMU), established in 1810;

- Independent Order of Odd Fellows (IOOF), established in 1819;

- Caledonian Order of Odd Fellows (COOF), established in 1827.

This branch, the Independent Order of Odd Fellows (IOOF), was established on April 26, 1819 in Baltimore, Maryland, USA, by Thomas Wildey and four members from England. The IOOF is also known as the *"Three Link Fraternity"*, referring to its *"Triple Link Chain"* symbol which represents its motto: "Friendship, Love and Truth."

Fraternal order vis-à-vis a friendly society

The first fraternal lodges came into being sometime between the 1600s and 1700s, when remnants of the medieval guild system were taken over and reshaped to meet the needs of new mercantile society. Freemasonry, which allegedly evolved out of stonemasons' craft guilds, and Odd Fellowship, which has its roots in journeymen's associations of the late Middle Ages, are two of the very few fraternal orders to have survived up until today from this earliest period.

A fraternal order (also known as fraternal organization or fraternity) is a form of social and community organization. It is an organized society of men or women or both, associated together to foster camaraderie and unity; dedicated to the moral, social and charitable goals; and have secret initiation rituals, signs, grips and symbols. A friendly society, on the other hand, is a mutual association for providing life and health insurance and old-age pension benefits to members. Many friendly societies take the form of a fraternal order.

There is little distinction between the fraternal orders and friendly societies. Both are associations where members consider each other as "brothers" and "sisters" belonging to one "family." Both teach principles and values through allegory, symbols, rituals and ceremonies. Both also have social, moral and charitable or mutual-benefit goals. What makes the two different is that friendly societies offer clear and guaranteed set of financial benefits while fraternal orders only provide assistance as an act of altruism or charity. The GUOOF and IOOFMU still provide life and health insurance benefits for its members while the IOOF is more focused on the social and moral development of its members.

Non-sectarian and Non-political

Odd Fellowship is *non-sectarian* because it is not a religion nor is it exclusively allied with or against any particular religion or religious sect. Membership is open to all regardless of religion, sect or creed. In fact, the Odd Fellows is composed of people from various religions who are only united by a belief in a Supreme Being. Odd Fellowship is *non-political* because it is not affiliated with any political party nor does it claim any access to political and government power. It is an organization composed of people from different political inclinations and affiliations.

Odd Fellowship have long promoted religious and political tolerance and understanding within their Lodge rooms. Their membership consists of people representing different religious denominations and political backgrounds. Their Lodge rooms were and still are considered neutral grounds where religious and political debates are discouraged during meetings and official events. This is mainly for the purpose of promoting unity and harmony while preventing disharmony and conflict between members.

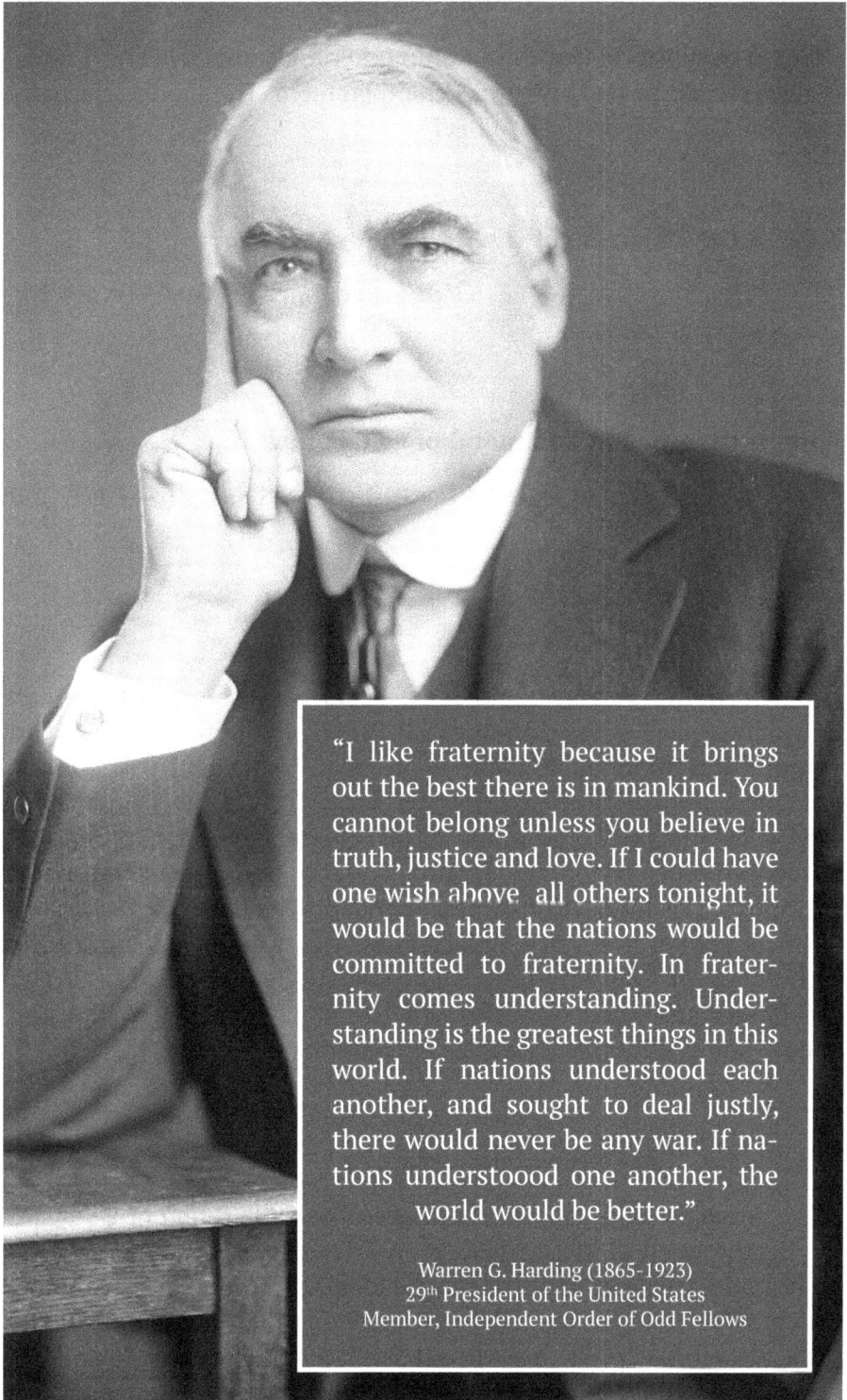

"I like fraternity because it brings out the best there is in mankind. You cannot belong unless you believe in truth, justice and love. If I could have one wish above all others tonight, it would be that the nations would be committed to fraternity. In fraternity comes understanding. Understanding is the greatest things in this world. If nations understood each another, and sought to deal justly, there would never be any war. If nations understoood one another, the world would be better."

Warren G. Harding (1865-1923)
29th President of the United States
Member, Independent Order of Odd Fellows

What is the Motto of Odd Fellowship?

The motto of Odd Fellowship is "Friendship, Love and Truth," as represented by its three links chain emblem. The motto is usually abbreviated by members as "FL&T".

What is the Objective of the Odd Fellowship?

The objective of the IOOF is "To Improve and Elevate the Character of Mankind."

What is the Ancient command of Odd Fellowship?

To Visit the Sick, Relieve the Distressed, Bury the Dead and Educate the Orphan.

What is the Odd Fellows Creed?

Genuine Friendship, which hears all things, believes all things, hopes all things, endures all things, is the first step toward progress and personal enrichment, and the teachings of Temperance, Prudence, and Justice. Love is the basis for all life's ambitions, service to humanity, and more family oriented. Truth, the imperial virtue, promotes economic stability, equality under law, freedom of enterprise, the highest of ethical standards, and lasting peace, the ultimate goal of fraternity. Universal Brotherhood of man under the Fatherhood of God is imperative to the survival of the World, and can be accomplished only through the practice of fellowship and understanding among all peoples and nations.

What is the Odd Fellows valediction?

I am an Odd Fellow! I believe in the Fatherhood of God, and the Brotherhood of Man; I believe in Friendship, Love and Truth as basic guides to the ultimate destiny of all mankind. I believe my home, my church or temple, my lodge, and my community deserve my best work, my modest pride, my earnest faith, and my deepest loyalty, as I perform my duty "to visit the sick, relieve the distressed, bury the

A Neutral Ground

An Odd Fellows Lodge is a neutral ground where debates about religion and politics are discouraged. A Lodge is a place for:

Photo from Odd Fellows of San Fernando, 2013.

- Character improvement

- Sincere friendships, mutual-respect and understanding

- Benevolence and charity

- Proper decorum, teamwork and leadership training

Members are encouraged to set aside their personal, political, religious or racial disputes behind. Within the walls of an Odd Fellows Lodge, there shall only be genuine Friendship, Love and Truth.

dead, and educate the orphan" and as I work with others to build a better world because in spirit and in truth, I am, and must always be, grateful to my Creator, faithful to my Country, and fraternal to my fellow man; I am an Odd Fellow!

Do I know anyone in history who is an Odd Fellow?

As an institution, Odd Fellowship was built by the great middle class to serve the needs of ordinary people at a time when government social services were almost inexistent. Thus, majority of its members belonged to the working-class because they are the ones who needed assistance from the lodges during hard times. But even though the organization does not make any special efforts to attract "famous" people, thousands of notable individuals in history joined the Odd Fellows. Just to name a few:

- George IV, King of the United Kingdom (1820–1830)

- Winston Churchill, Prime Minister of the United Kingdom (1951-1955)

THE WHITE HOUSE
WASHINGTON

January 9, 1939

Dear Brother Gaskill:

The one hundred twenty years that have elapsed
since the founding of the Odd Fellowship in America afford
a broad perspective on which to view the accomplishments
of our Order in this country.

Its record is a noble one told in terms of true
brotherhood among men; the relief of sickness and distress;
the care of the widow; the education of the orphan and
the promotion of good will and good citizenship wherever
our far-flung subordinate lodges have been established.

In the hope that our fraternity will in the years
that lie ahead ever uphold its splendid humanitarian ideals,
I send fraternal greetings and good wishes.

Very sincerely yours,

Franklin D. Roosevelt

Mr. Burton A. Gaskill,
Grand Sire,
Sovereign Grand Lodge of the I.O.O.F.,
506 Guarantee Trust Building,
Atlantic City, New Jersey.

President Franklin Roosevelt's letter to Grand Sire Burton Gaskill in 1939. President Roosevelt was a member of Hyde Park Lodge No. 203 of the Independent Order of Odd Fellows in New York. The introduction of Social Security System and National Health Insurance are some of the ideas Roosevelt introduced by way of the *New Deal*, which he allegedly patterned from the system of financial benefits previously offered by Odd Fellowship. Photo courtesty of The Sovereign Grand Lodge, IOOF

Prince Bertil, Duke of Halland in Sweden, desired membership in a lodge that bore the name of his friend, Folke Bernadotte, and was initiated as a member of the Independent Order of Odd Fellows in Sweden on May 22, 1950. Photo from public domain

- Stanley Baldwin, Prime Minister of the United Kingdom (1923-1929; 1935-1937)

- Andrew Fisher, Prime Minister of Australia (1908-1909, 1910-1913, and 1914-1915)

- George Houstoun Reid, Prime Minister of Australia, (1904–1905)

- Joseph Cook, Prime Minister of Australia (1913-1914)

- William Massey, Prime Minister of New Zealand (1912–1925)

- Gustaf VI Adolf, King of Sweden (1950-1973)

- Prince Bertil of Sweden, Duke of Halland (1912–1997)

- John Alexander Macdonald, Prime Minister of Canada (1867-1873)

- Ulysses S. Grant, President of the United States (1869–1877)

- Rutherford Hayes, President of the United States (1877–1881)

- William McKinley, President of the United States (1897–1901)

- Warren Gamaliel Harding, President of the United States (1921–1923)

- Franklin Delano Roosevelt, President of the United States (1933–1945)

Where can we find Odd Fellows Lodges?

As of writing, there are four existing Orders of Odd Fellows, namely: Grand United Order of Oddfellows Friendly Society, Independent Order of Oddfellows Manchester Unity Friendly Society,

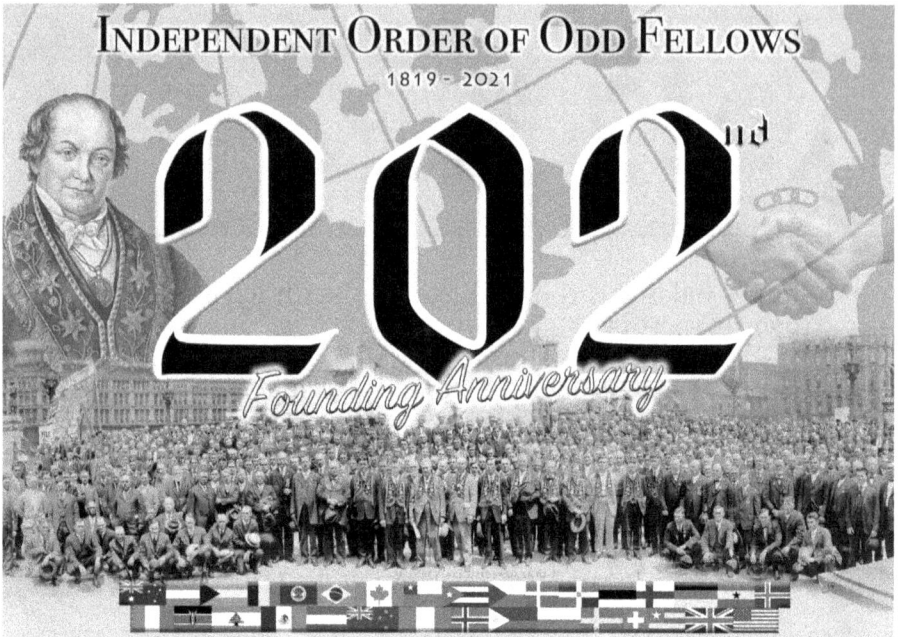

INDEPENDENT ORDER OF ODD FELLOWS
1819 - 2021
202nd Founding Anniversary

Independent Order of Odd Fellows and Caledonian Order of Odd Fellows with approximately 600,000[1] members belonging to 10,000 Odd Fellows Lodges located in the following countries:

1. Australia
2. Bahamas and Turks Island
3. Belgium
4. Belize
5. Brazil
6. Canada
7. Chile
8. Cuba
9. Czech Republic
10. Denmark
11. Dominican Republic
12. Estonia
13. Finland
14. Germany
15. Ghana
16. Iceland
17. Italy
18. Kenya
19. Lebanon
20. Mexico
21. Netherlands
22. New Zealand
23. Nigeria
24. Norway
25. Philippines
26. Poland
27. Puerto Rico
28. South Africa
29. Spain
30. Sweden
31. Switzerland
32. Togo
33. United Kingdom
34. United States

Philosophy and Purpose

As an organization, the Independent Order of Odd Fellows aims to provide a framework that promotes personal and social development. Lodge degrees and activities aim to improve and elevate every person to a higher, nobler plane; to extend sympathy and aid to those in need, making their burdens lighter, relieving the darkness of despair; to war against vice in every form, and to be a great moral power and influence for the good of humanity. For members, the degrees in Odd Fellowship emphasizes a leaving of the old life and the start of a better one, of welcoming travelers, and of helping those in need.[1] Today, the general purposes of the Independent Order of Odd Fellows can be summarized into three:[2]

- **Improving Character (ethical):** To improve and elevate the character of humankind by teaching and promoting the principles of Friendship, Love, and Truth; Faith, Hope, and Charity; and Universal Justice, as exemplified in the degrees of initiation and practiced in real life;

- **Making Friends (fraternal):** To promote goodwill and understanding among people and nations through the principle of universal fraternity, holding the belief that all men and women regardless of race, nationality, religion, social status, gender, rank and station are brothers and sisters;

- **Helping People (humanitarian):** To help make the world a better place to live by aiding each other in times of need and by volunteering in or organizing charitable activities and projects that would benefit the less fortunate, the children, the youth, the elderly, the community and the environment in every way possible, guided by our ancient command: *"to visit the sick, relieve the distress, bury the dead and educate the orphan"*.

What is Odd Fellowship?

Odd Fellowship is a philosophy of life which have as its object the elevation of character, morally, intellectually, socially, physically, recognizing mankind's individual helplessness and great need of cooperation in all the affairs of life. It requires all its members to aid, assist, and protect each other, to visit the sick, relieve the distressed, bury the dead, and protect the widow and orphan. It teaches the Fatherhood of God and the brotherhood and sisterhood of mankind; it strives to breakdown the artificial barriers that separate mankind from his or her fellowman, and places upon all an equality, as members of one great family.[3] According to a pamphlet by The Sovereign Grand Lodge, Odd Fellowship is:

First – It is an organization, because it is a systematic union of individuals in a body whose officers, committee, and members work together for a common end.

Second – It is a philosophy of life, because we follow certain standards of living, govern our thoughts and conduct according to the principles of practical wisdom; and are lovers of the vision of truth.

Third – It is a unified effort to promote that philosophy, because we are organized in communities throughout the World, in Grand Jurisdictions, and a Sovereign Grand Body. This affords an opportunity for counsel, assimilation of wisdom and application and extension to others.

Fourth – It is an obligation everyone owes to others, because all are created equal and governed by the laws of our Creator. The principles and purposes to which we have all obliged ourselves must be upheld both within and without the Order if civilization is to survived the forces of evil and destruction.

Fifth – It is the teaching and application of Friendship, Love and Truth; of Faith, Hope and Charity; and of Universal Justice, because these are the principles of our doctrine; the basis for thought and action which will create peace and harmony among people and lead us toward our ultimate goal.

What do Odd Fellows do today?

The early Odd Fellows Lodges were first set up to protect and care for their members and communities at a time when there was still no social security system, national health insurance, service clubs and modern-day charitable institutions. The aim was and still is to provide help to their members, their families and their communities when they need it, along with the purpose of developing friendships and improving moral character through the principles taught in the degrees of initiation, which usually includes mystic signs of recognition, symbols, dramatic plays and lectures.[4]

During the 18th to early 20th centuries, lodges served dual purposes: (1) A particular system of morality designated in its Ritual, and (2) a particular system of insurance against the misfortunes arising from sickness and death.[5] The system of insurance had already been taken over by modern institutions such as Social Security System and commercial insurance companies. The Manchester Unity Oddfellows and Grand United Order of Oddfellows in the United Kingdom still provide some kind of insurance benefits, but most lodges under the IOOF already stopped doing so.

The Odd Fellows of today is a worldwide ethical, humanitarian and social network composed of people, of good character, who meet at least once a month to enjoy each other's company and assist each other in times of need. Through membership fees, annual dues and other fundraising efforts, lodges are also involved in various charitable projects in a local, national and international level. The activities of Odd Fellows in modern times are three-fold: *ethical* (improving character), *fraternal or social* (making friends) and *charitable* (helping people).

Ideally, an Odd Fellows Lodge is an avenue for fellowship in all its forms: from character improvement through the teachings of the degrees of initiation; to discussion of ideas; to professional and social networking; to hanging out and just having clean fun; to collaboration on creative and constructive projects; all with an eye not only on our own satisfaction but on what we might offer to the community at large.

Is Odd Fellowship a Secret Society?

No. A secret society is an organization which conceals its membership, has secret meeting places, and their purposes or aims are hidden or unknown to the public. The Independent Order of Odd Fellows has a very public agenda to promote and do not claim any secret knowledge to conceal from the public.

As an organization, the aim of Odd Fellowship is only the improvement and elevation of human character by instilling to each member practical and benevolent values, and by encouraging its members to exemplify these principles into actions through: character improvement, tolerance and understanding between people from different racial, political and religious backgrounds, and human compassion through mutual-assistance in times of need and participation in local, national and international charities.

By far the larger portion of its ritual is in print and is known to hundreds of thousands.[6] The teachings, principles, symbols and their meanings have been published in many books written by Odd Fellows during the 1800's and these books are available in many public libraries and a handful can be accessed online. The constitutions and by-laws of Grand Lodges and lodges, which embody the principles of the organization, and contain the rules and regulations which govern their meetings and all operations, are also accessible to the public. Most lodges own buildings with signage "I.O.O.F." or "Odd Fellows." Furthermore, members freely wear Odd Fellows emblem in public.

True, it possesses an unwritten and unspoken signs, passwords and grips known only to the membership. These, however are unimportant to outsiders because it serves simply the purpose of mutual recognition between members. The purpose of such privacy does not differ from that of manufacturing companies, banking institutions or churches. Corporations, literary societies, churches, sports clubs and even married couples have or ought to have secrets or information that they consider confidential and do not freely share with those that do not belong within their circle. When these associations meet to transact their own private business, none but members are admitted; and the reason for this is that the information are of concern to nobody else. Will you be willing to give your bank account password and PIN to just anyone? Will you share with strangers your spouse's or best friend's secrets? No! It's an honor code.

Is Odd Fellowship a religion or cult?

No. Odd Fellowship is not a religion or cult. It is a moral rather than a religious organization.[7] The religious world is divided into many sects, each intent upon the promotion of is peculiar plans and interests, and of consequence wanting in that unity of action so essential in every secular institution to the securement of those great results which illustrate the triumph of benevolence and charity.[8]

A fundamental principle of Odd Fellowship is toleration of all religions. It professes to be predominantly a system of toleration in religion and politics. It is more inclusive than any single religious organization and is represented by almost all faiths, all races, and all stations in life. Membership is comprised of people from all social, economic, political and religious backgrounds. In the Odd Fellows Lodge, Muslims, Christians, Jews, Hindu and many others meet as equals and consider themselves "brothers" and "sisters" with Friendship, Love and Truth as the common ground.

But Odd Fellowship is not a religion and a lodge is not a church. A lodge does not aim to usurp the place of the church. The business of the church is to save mankind, to lift them up, and make them better in every conceivable way. As compared to religion, Odd Fellowship does not promise spiritual salvation. A lodge does not ordain priests or ministers, save souls, preach sermons, encourage confession of sins, conduct baptism, or hold Mass. Members meet in the lodge room not to worship but only for the purposes of "mutual counsel, the relief of the distress and the elevation of human character."[9]

Odd Fellowship does not have a fight against the church; rather it does have interests in common with the church. The work that lodges do is rooted in universal religious doctrines that can be found in scriptures and tenets of the many religions in which the people of this world find hope and the meaning of life.[10] One of which is the Golden Rule "Do unto others as you would have them do unto you." So, although Odd Fellowship is not a church, not a religion, it was created based on religious principles.[11] Its mission supports the idea of mutual responsibility encouraged by almost all religions:

- To feed the hungry

- To give drink to the thirsty

- To clothe the naked

- To relieve the prisoner

- To shelter the homeless

- To visit the sick

- To bury the dead

- To care for the widow and orphan

Some of the best people in church and public life are connected with Odd Fellowship, and will testify gladly to its good qualities and splendid work.[12] A number of priests and ministers actually joined and took active part in the Odd Fellows as early as 1842.[13] In fact, a number of religious leaders have held high positions within Odd Fellowship. These people have not found in the Bible and other religious texts that disapproved Odd Fellowship. Odd Fellowship does not have a principle or a lesson that will make people less Christian or less religious. The initiation, instruction, lectures, and obligations have a tendency to inculcate a veneration for religion and the higher and nobler things of life. A person cannot be initiated into the degrees of Odd Fellowship without becoming a better person, without holding the Bible, Qur'an or the Book of Sacred Law of his church in greater reverence, and without appreciating the goodness and greatness of the Supreme Being with a higher degree of intelligence.

Is there a religious ban against Odd Fellowship?

There is no Papal Bull or religious condemnation against Odd Fellowship. Canon 1374 of the *Code of Canon Law of 1983* forbids Catholics from joining societies which plot against the Church. Odd Fellowship does not plot against any church. As an institution, it respects all recognized religions, and encourages its members to faithfully support the religion of their choice. It conforms to "law, religion, and sound morality, and does not permit anything contrary to the allegiance we owe to or country, or the duty we owe to ourselves."[14] Membership requires "no sacrifice of your opinions, no change in your relations to the state and no loosening of the obligations, which you owe to the laws and institutions under which you live."[15] To become a member, one must "be grateful to his or her creator, faithful to his

The Bishop of Lincoln, Rev. Dr. King, together with the Mayor, W.W. Richardson, and a political candidate, W. Crosfield, were admitted as members of the Machester Unity Independent Order of Odd Fellows in 1892.
Photo from the *Illustrated London News*, March 12, 1892.

or her country, and fraternal to his or her fellowmen."[16] At present, Odd Fellowship have members who are practicing and retired priests, pastors, rabbis, imams, etc.

Many people now live in secular countries where the State is neutral in matters of religion and people are free to choose their religion without fear of government or church persecution. However, secular organizations and clubs were not yet widely acceptable at the time when Odd Fellowship was first founded. A lot of the freedoms that people enjoy today such as freedom of religion and worship were not yet acceptable to the Church. Historically, religious neutrality was believed to go against the Churches' belief in a one absolutist religion. Primarily because Odd Fellowship is open to anyone regardless of religious affiliations and its similarities with Freemasonry, it did met opposition from the clergy especially the Roman Catholic Church. During the 19th century, there were priests, reverends and ministers who tried to discredit Odd Fellowship usually using baseless accusations and absurd exposés. But there were also a number of well-known ministers at that time who were very active Odd Fellows and

On top of the Roman Catholic Church in Cebu, Philippines, is the all-seeing-eye surrounded by twelve stars, symbolizing the eye of God watching through the twelve tribes of Israel. Photos by the Author, 2015.

The All-seeing-eye

Many people fear this symbol because of conspiracy theories on the so-called influence of Freemasonry and the Illuminati in global politics. But the All-seeing-eye, or the Eye of Providence, actually symbolizes the omniscient eye of God who continually watches over our thoughts and actions. This is not a symbol exclusively used by the Freemasons or the Illuminati but was widely and generally used by churches and many ancient societies stretching back thousands of years ago. In fact, the ancient Egyptians, Assyrians, Jews, and Christians have used the eye as a symbol of their God. Among Christians, the Holy Scriptures provide, "The eye of the Lord is in every place, beholding the evil and good" (Prov. XV.3) and "The Eye of the Lord runs to and fro throughout the whole earth, to show himself strong in behalf of them whose heart is perfect toward him" (2 Chron. XVI 9).

have sincerely defended the goodness of the institution such as Rev. A.B. Grosh, Rev. I.D. Williamson, Rev. J.W. Henley, Rev. C.E. Sayre, Rev. D.W. Bristol, and Rev. T.G. Beharrell.

As soon as the religious bigotry and intolerance declined during the 20th century, many religious leaders in democratic and free countries began to accept secular organizations as the norm. A number of priests, bishops and rabbis from different religious sects have become members and some even held leadership positions in the Odd Fellows.[17] In 1974, it was eventually clarified that Catholics were not forbidden to join Odd Fellows Lodges and that the Odd Fellows did not fall under the ban regarding Freemasonry. That affiliation with the Odd Fellows is not punishable by ex-communication. In the changing spiritual context of the times, the Catholic Church has left prejudicial attitude in the past and was seeking cooperation with men of goodwill and that there is no justification for any ban. It was unjustified to impose a clerical ban on a Catholic regarding membership, or to cast doubt on his loyalty to his faith because of his membership in the Independent Order of Odd Fellows. Several bishops opined that if a Catholic is interested in joining the Odd Fellows, he will not be excommunicated nor have to fear any other advantages as far as the church is concerned so long as he continuous to perform his religious duties as a Catholic.[18]

In 1973, Reverend Monsignor Titian Miani, a Roman Catholic Priest, became the first Roman Catholic Priest to become a member of the IOOF in the United States when he joined Scio Lodge No.102 in Linden, California.[19] Reverend Leo Dennis Burns became the first Roman Catholic Priest to serve as the Grand Master of the IOOF Grand Lodge of Ontario in 1992 and Sovereign Grand Chaplain of the Sovereign Grand Lodge. Several pastors and ministers representing different religious denominations have also served as the Sovereign Grand Master of the Independent Order of Odd Fellows.

Is Odd Fellowship a part of Freemasonry?

No. Odd Fellowship and Freemasonry are not the same. Odd Fellowship is not and has never been a masonic organization. Since its inception, it has been a completely separate organization. Rather, both organizations appear to have common roots and were influenced by early forms of fraternal associations such as "guilds, journeymen's associations, religious confraternities, and village youth brotherhoods".[20]

Modern Freemasonry and Odd Fellowship both emerged in England during the 1700s and both their rituals attained stability

Although the Odd Fellows and Freemasons are completely separate organizations, confusion sometimes happen because of similarities in some symbols and regalia. Many people also held membership in both ancient fraternities. As a result, it is quite common to see the emblems of both fraternal organizations engraved on gravestones and merchandise In some towns, the Odd Fellows and Freemasons share the same building to save costs of maintenance, utility bills and taxes. Photo by the author, 2012.

during the 1800s. From an outsider's perspective, both organizations share some similarities in customs and symbols like the all-seeing eye and the skull and cross-bones. But from an insider's perspective, one will find so many differences both in their teachings, symbols, organizational structure, titles, design and focus.

But Odd Fellowship should not be viewed as a competitor or rival of Freemasonry. Holding membership in both fraternities is quite prevalent and still is common even until today. The first documented person to be a member of both fraternities was King George IV (1762-1830), who was initiated as an Odd Fellow in 1780 and as a Freemason in 1787. The list includes Albert Pike (1809-1891); 17th U.S. Vice President Schuyler Colfax Jr. (1823-1885); 29th U.S. President Warren Harding (1865-1923); 32nd U.S. President Franklin Roosevelt (1882-1945); former British Prime Minister Sir Winston Churchill (1874 –1965); 14th U.S. Chief Justice Earl Warren (1891-1974) and over a thousand more others.

𝔊𝔥𝔢 𝔑𝔞𝔪𝔢

Why the name Odd Fellows?

Through the years, there had been many theories that attempted to explain the name. There is no absolute answer but the widely accepted beliefs today, as passed from generation to generation, are derived from any or a combination of a number of explanations.

Fellows from Odd Trades

A number of historians and researchers today widely accept that the origin of English fraternal orders and friendly societies can be traced from the various craft guilds and journeymen associations that existed in England at the beginning of the Middle Ages.

A *guild* is an association of workers usually belonging to a particular trade and organized to protect and care for their members and families at a time when there was still no welfare state, trade unions or National Health Service. Usually, guilds were composed of workers belonging only to the same trade or craft such as masons,

It is asserted that there were other crafts not strong enough to establish a craft guild of their own so a combination of these "fellows" representing "odd" jobs, joined forces to form their own trade association and called themselves "Odd Fellows." Illustration by Asher Alpay as commissioned by the author, 2015.

The Prologue to *The Canterbury Tales*, written by Geoffrey Chaucer between 1387 to 1400, mentioned an association of journeymen belonging from different trades having a fellowship at an Inn:

> It happened that in that season on one day,
>
> In Southwark at the Tabard Inn as I lay
>
> Ready to go on my pilgrimage
>
> To Canterbury with a very devout spirit,
>
> At night had come into that hostelry
>
> Well nine and twenty in a company
>
> Of various sorts of people, by chance fallen
>
> In fellowship, and they were all pilgrims,
>
> Who intended to ride toward Canterbury

Journeymen associations existed during the 17th century as some kind of deviation from the guild system. In contrast with the guilds which accepted only those practicing the same craft, journeyman associations consisted of tradesmen from an assortment of trades or crafts. They also have an elaborate initiation rite in which a young journeyman who joins the association will go through a system of degrees intended to test courage and loyalty and to ascend into hierarchy within the association. Sparce evidence do show that the early Odd Fellows practiced lesser-known crafts or trades that were not big enough to form their craft guild. For example, Thomas Wildey practiced the craft of coach spring-making.

gardeners, carpenters, cabinet-makers, and so on.

In smaller towns and villages, however, there were too few people practicing the same trade to form a guild of their own. Hence, a group of "*fellows*" from a mixture of trades such as tinkers, tailors, smiths, dyers, bakers, merchants and what-not workers joined forces to form an *omnium gatherum* or a brotherhood from an assorted or "*odd*" collection of workers, hence, the name "Odd Fellows." Some historians suggest that the term Odd Fellows was a description of a *type* of guild or association rather than the actual title, nearly all of which adopted the name of a chosen Patron Saint or a religious title.

Ordinary People Doing Good Deeds

During the 18th century England, people were facing a lot of challenges. Life was tough, often lawless and desperate. There were still no social security programs and national health insurance, so people who fell upon hard times found very little help or resources available to them. Being out of work even temporarily could mean that an individual's family was not only going to go hungry but may starve to death. Medicine was still crude. There were a lot of sickness, orphaned children, widowed mothers and many could not afford to pay a decent burial for the dead. Morally, people were given over to selfishness and indifference. There was still a huge gap between the rich and the poor. Many people fended only for themselves, living without much care for others.

However, a group of ordinary people from different trades and walks of life deviated from the trends of those times and found it necessary to group together into a fraternity for social fellowship and mutual-relief. Because it was rather peculiar or "odd" to see a group of ordinary people helping one another, coming to each other's aid and offering social relief to those in need, they were labeled as "Odd Fellows". Because of the appropriateness of the name, those engaged in forming these associations accepted it. When legally incorporated, the title "Odd Fellows" was purportedly adopted. The benevolence, charity and fraternalism of the organization continue up until today and somehow support this story.

Traditionally, Odd Fellows take an oath promising to visit sick members and help the widows and orphans of their deceased members. From *The Odd Fellows' Offering*, 1847.

Lodge that opened its door to working people

There was a time when most fraternal orders and clubs in England were the purview of the elite, the nobility and the upper classes. Another suggestion is that the Odd Fellows got its name because they were the first Lodge or club that opened its doors to working class people. The group theoretically deviated from that trend when it accepted laborers as a reaction to the "*crushing burdens imposed on laborers by the aristocracy of a dissipated, semi-despotic government*", thus, they were the "Odd Fellows".

Sworn Brothers

Historical linguistics, on the other hand, suggest the possibility that "odd" is a corruption of the word "ad" or "oath".[1] One of the prominent features of the guilds and early lodges was taking an "ad and wed" – oath and pledge. It is probable that the name Odd Fellows was derived from "ad fellows" or "oath fellows", meaning "sworn brothers".[2] Since its inception members of the Odd Fellows take firm promises or oaths upon joining.

Etymological Perspective

What is certain is that the word "Odd" in Odd Fellows was not intended to mean "weird" or "foolish". The word "Odd" originally meant "noted", "remarkable", "different" or "out of the ordinary." The word "Fellow" has not changed at all, it still means a member of a society or group, where persons are banded together for the common good or their common interest.

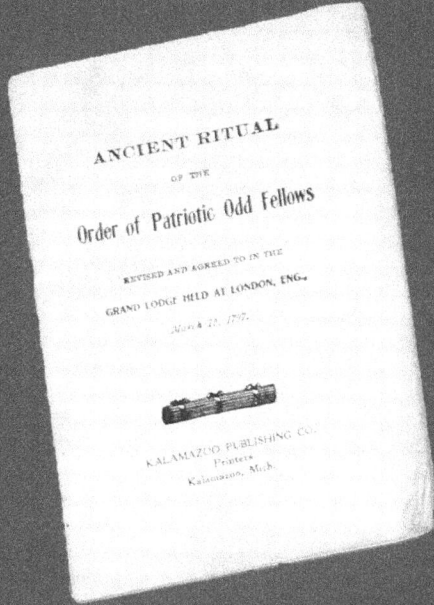

The oldest surviving written explanation of the name can be found in the revised rituals of the Order of Patriotic Odd Fellows in 1797. In the White or Covenant Degree, the Vice Grand Master says,

> ...But I tell you, brother, it is this that contracts our sphere of usefulness. It fills the world with sects and parties, who are each one saying, mentally, give place – my opinions are superior to yours; but you, as an Odd Fellow (which really means that you are singled out from the general mass with a desire for true knowledge), should look beyond the surface, and view with a friendly eye, all mankind.[1]

This suggests that the name "Odd Fellows" was intended to be a commendable title for people who believed in the ideas of social unity, religious tolerance, benevolence, and charity which were believed to be "out of the ordinary" at that time.

Hand-painted Odd Fellows' leather apron showing some of the early symbols used by Odd Fellowship: heart-and-hand, all-seeing-eye, dove, hour-glass, three links chain, serpent, axe, globe and beehive. The early purposes of Odd Fellowship were the propagation of the principles of "Benevolence and Charity."

Which among these explanations is true?

The origin of the name remains a mystery probably because the explanation may have meant differently across time and interpreted differently by various members. Except for the explanation found in the 1797 ancient ritual, other explanations were passed on among members from generation to generation only by word-of-mouth. But whatever the true reason may have been, the unusual name has been the object of public curiosity, criticism and even ridicule for more than 200 years.

Origin and Early History

The origin of Odd Fellowship is full of mystery and speculation. Undeniably, the date of the exact founding of the first Odd Fellows Lodge is already lost in the fogs of antiquity. The early Odd Fellows had originated in obscurity as it was not yet popular to claim any public attention of its early operations. Record keeping was also not given much importance in the past. In addition, many of the early documents were destroyed as a result of government regulations aimed at suppressing fraternal orders during the late-1700s.

Surviving documents and new research studies by various historians and scholars do suggest that the early Odd Fellows did not originate from one source. They are a result of mergers of various independent social groups, box clubs, guilds and friendly societies in England that realized the need to unite into one singular organization.

LEGENDARY HISTORY

The symbolic or mythical history of Odd Fellowship narrates that this Order was first established by exiled Israelites in Babylon sometime in 587 BC, when many banded together into a brotherhood for mutual support. The fraternity is said to have continued among the Jewish legion of the Roman Army during the reign of Nero about 55 A.D. Some twenty-four years later, Titus Caesar, observing the singularity of their notions, their camaraderie and their uncanny ability to recognize each other by signs even at night, called them Odd Fellows. As a pledge of friendship, Titus Caesar also presented them a charter, engraved on a plate of gold, bearing different emblems - such as the sun, moon, stars, the lamb, the lion, the dove and other emblems of mortality. It is claimed that this legend was the basis for the *Royal Arch of Titus Degree* of the Order of Patriotic Odd Fellows during the 1700s. Others claimed that the Order was first founded in 1452 by five French knights who met at Bull and Mouth Inn in London and established the "Grand Lodge of Honour." Members took a solemn oath of mutual support and promised to act with justice among all men. Collections were made during meetings for a common fund out of which payments would be made if there is a member in need. Of course, both stories can never be proven.

Historians have noted that there was a revival of interest in the romantic and chivalric image of medieval Orders of Knighthood such as the Knights Templar during the mid-late 1700s. The Napoleonic campaign in Egypt further sparked a worldwide enthusiasm for the revival of ancient mysteries and esoteric wisdom. Many of the early historians – both from Freemasonry and Odd Fellowship – claimed some link with medieval knights and ancient and mystic societies. Some Feemasons claim some link with the medieval Knights Templar while some Odd Fellows claim a link with other chivalric groups. These unsubstantiated claims are often the result of the confusion and the reason why many members of Freemasonry and Odd Fellowship fail to separate legend from factual history. Many of these fanciful theories of origin had already been dismissed by many masonic and odd fellow historians as fictional or symbolic rather than factual. During the 19th century, notable Odd Fellow historian Theo A. Ross asserted that:

> "Odd Fellowship does not seek a veiled origin in the misty shades of the past to surround it with the false glamour that arises from the belief in the doctrine of *omne ignotum pro magnifico*. This age of enlightenment has emaciated us from the gross credulity of the past. Antiquity bears with it no passport of truth or goodness."

CRAFT GUILDS AND JOURNEYMEN ASSOCIATIONS

A number of historians and researchers widely accept that the origin of English fraternal orders and friendly societies can be traced from the various craft guilds and journeymen associations which existed in England and its environs at the beginning of the middle Ages. The historical connections are manifest in the rituals, terminology and functions shared by both the guilds and fraternal orders. In England, organizations and clubs with benefit systems took the form of the guilds or livery companies and reach back to the middle Ages.

A craft guild is a benevolent association of mutual-help that usually consisted of craftsmen belonging to the same trade or living in the same neighborhood. They were sworn brotherhoods that had

A medieval Master Baker and his apprentice. From public domain

binding oaths to support one another in times of adversity and back one another in trade ventures alongside with their religious and ceremonial role. Meetings involved proper decorum and wearing of regalia such as chains of office, special robes and so on. They charged entrance fees and indulged in feasting and merry-making. Usually, the structure and degrees are the following: Apprentice, Fellow or Journeyman, and then Master.

Many craftsmen joined forces and formed their individual guilds or trade fraternities. In fact, there were more than one hundred early guilds in England alone during the middle Ages. The Fraternity of Butchers, for example, owned a meeting Hall as early as year 975 and has charters dating back in 1605 and 1637. A record dating 1345 shows that the Fraternity of Gardeners petitioned the Lord Mayor to sell produce in front of the church of St. Austin. The earliest surviving record of Gardeners Lodge in Scotland dates back in 1676. The Worshipful Company of Carpenters has charters dating 1477, 1558, 1560, and 1607 and controlled the craft with religious and charitable aims. There is a reference to the "Masters of the mysteries" of the Fraternity of Cooks, Pastelers and Piebakers from 1312 to 1438.

Similarly, the early Odd Fellows presumably began as a craft guild or journeymen association in England. While major trades like the Butchers, Masons, Gardeners or Farmers were large enough to form their own individual guilds, smaller trades did not have enough numbers. As a result, people from smaller trades or those who exercised unusual, miscellaneous or odd trades joined forces to form their own trade association. In those days, the term Odd Fellows would be a description of a type of guild or journeymen association rather than the actual title because nearly all of which adopted the name of a chosen Patron Saint or a religious title. The *Prologue to The Canterbury Tales, written by Geoffrey Chaucer between 1387 and 1400*, describes a group of such Guildsmen from different trades who belonged to a single guild:

> Well nine and twenty in a company of *various sorts* of people, by chance fallen in fellowship, and they were all pilgrims, who intended to ride toward Canterbury.

Operative and Speculative Lodges

At the beginning, these guilds and journeymen associations were exclusive only to artisans who literally practiced a specific craft. However, some guilds eventually admitted noblemen who did not practice their craft. The guild of Weavers, for example, originally consisted of members of the craft when they were founded in 1155 but they later admitted sons of members and noblemen. The guild of Merchant Taylors, on the other hand, admitted King Edward III as a member after they had lent him money to pay his wars. The Worshipful Company of Mason's book of accounts mentioned a lodge of "*Accepted*" masons in 1620 and 1621. This is the earliest reference to the masons accepting people not practicing their trade or craft. It was advantageous for the guilds to admit aristocrats because they would increase the social prestige of their association. This apparently resulted into a split in the membership: (1) *operative* (those that regulate and practice the trade or craft as a profession) and (2) *speculative* (those that use the trade or craft only for social, moral and mutual-benefit purposes).

Decline of the Guild System

During the reign of Queen Elizabeth I, the Statute of Apprentices was passed and this took the responsibility for apprenticeship away from the guilds. The nature and scope of work was also chang-

Order of Ancient Free Gardeners

The Guild of Gardeners can be traced back to the 14th Century England. The earliest surviving record of a Free Gardeners Lodge in Scotland dates back in 1676. Many of these lodges eventually evolved into friendly societies by the 1700s. Their emblem is a square and compass with a pruning knife in the center as a representation of "the simplest tool of gardening." They have three degrees of initiation: *Apprentice*, *Journeyman* and *Master Gardener*. Like many other 18th century fraternal orders, they use collars and aprons as regalia which they probably adopted from the customs of the craft guilds.

By the 20th century, the Free Gardeners had become almost extinct. Today, there are still few remaining lodges in Australia, Belgium, England, France, Philippines, Scotland, and South Africa.

ing; thus, the role of the guilds and journeymen associations eventually went into a decline. This removed an important form of social and financial support among ordinary workers. It is asserted that the operative lodges survived as *Livery Companies* while speculative lodges adapted to the changing times by evolving into *Fraternal Lodges* or social clubs with a combination of social, moral and charitable or mutual-benefit functions. By the 18th century, there seems to be a number of these fraternal orders and friendly societies with guild-

There are more than 100 livery companies in London, comprising ancient and modern trade associations and guilds. Almost all of which are styled the '*Worshipful Company of...*' their respective craft, trade or profession. Similar to many fraternal orders, livery companies also have a passion for dressing up in unusual robes, for participating in arcane ceremonies and use titles for many of their officers such as: Past Master, Master, Deacon, Warden, Steward, Almoner, Chaplain, etc. Photo from public domain, 1930.

like names that were formed in England and Scotland: Order of Free Masons, Order of Free Gardeners, Order of Free Carpenters, Order of Free Fishermen, Order of Free Colliers, Order of Odd Fellows, Order of Foresters, Order of Mechanics, Order of Shepherds, etc.

EARLY BOX CLUBS OR FRIENDLY SOCIETIES

There is strong evidence to suggest that Odd Fellowship really is "an outgrowth of English Friendly Societies which were mutual associations formed for the payment of monetary benefits in times of incapacity for work due to sickness or injury, or death."[13] The first of these groups emerged in England as "a number of independent lodges or clubs comprised mostly of working-class people who were not rich, not royalty, and whose very lives depended on each other

The early Odd Fellows started as a form of *box club* or *friendly society* in England with philosophical, social and charitable purposes. These clubs held their meetings and initiations inside pubs or taverns. Similar to the Livery Companies, the Odd Fellows dress-up in unusual robes when performing their arcane ceremonies. Illustration published by Bentley and Co., 1789.

if ever one of their members got sick, became disabled, lost a job or died."[14] Like cooperatives and labor unions, they would contribute some of their hard-earned wages to a common fund which they could use for unfortunate times such as sickness, losing a job or death of a member.[15] By uniting themselves, they were able to build up funds to aid each other, their families and their communities in times of need.

Such groups were also called as *box clubs* and had been in existence in England and nearby countries since the early 1600s. These clubs held their meetings in a specific pub or tavern where men could join and pay a fee, and the funds collected are placed in a box to be used whenever a member needs some financial assistance. These box clubs were later known as friendly societies. The first known use of the term friendly society was in 1684. Daniel Defoe in his book, *Essay on Projects*, wrote about friendly societies in 1697 and defined them as "a number of people entering into a mutual compact to help one another in case any disaster or distress fall upon them, and emphasized the contributory nature of these societies as a way to lower the poor rates and raise the self-respect of working people."[16] He recommended the creation of these societies as "a means to prevent the general misery and poverty of mankind and at once secure the country against beggars, parish poor, almshouses, and hospitals." Other advocates shared the desire to use friendly societies to decrease the cost of poor relief. During the 18th century, a number of these clubs developed in virtually every English town and village.

Self-Institution

The early friendly societies followed the ancient usage of *self-institution*. This meant that any person can gather at least five people to form a Lodge without need of approval from any national association. A group of individuals can form their own lodge by asking for a charter or dispensation from an older lodge. But they had no Grand Lodge of any kind; they were all independent and separate lodges. Each lodge was presided by a Noble Grand Master and governed itself according to their own rules, traditions and practices. These lodges differed from place to place. They had rituals and customs unique to themselves and these rituals evolved from time to time. Noting the absence of any regulation by a higher organization, each lodge independently developed their own degrees, oaths, teachings, symbols, interpretations and secret signs.

Hence, there were actually so many clubs or lodges that were not formally connected with each other. They gave no benefits apart from helping widows and deceased members. The only one thing they had in common was a traveling assistance given to their members who were traveling in search of work. If a member enters into a similar lodge in another town, he is given a traveling password and a certificate to show to the lodge. He is then given assistance in terms of food and lodging. That money would then be reimbursed by one lodge to another. Unfortunately, they got into trouble between lodges in reclaiming money so some lodges decided to form a Grand Lodge for better administration.

Mergers, Acquisitions and splits

The Order of Odd Fellows seems to be an amalgamation of these numerous small and independent lodges and clubs in England that eventually decided to unite themselves to form a larger and more organized association. Fragmentary surviving records, newspaper accounts and artifacts do prove that the early Odd Fellows Lodges began to spread in England sometime on or before 1730 when various independent friendly societies or lodges united to form an affiliated order or a regional organization usually designated as a "Unity."

George IV, while Prince of Wales, was initiated into a Lodge of Odd Fellows in 1780.

It is asserted that the first Order of Odd Fellows was a result of amalgamation of these numerous self-instituted independent friendly societies and benefit clubs that eventually realized the need to federate themselves into a regional association for better coordination. Historical accounts demonstrate individual clubs that eventually organized themselves into a regional organization or later merged with existing *Affiliated Orders* and adopted the name *Odd Fellows*. Presumably, the first of the affiliated groups was the *Ancient Order* which had at least nine associated lodges by 1748. An *Improved Order* was successively formed as a schism from an earlier organization but little is known about this group.[18] During the mid-1700s, some lodges in southern England further split and formed the *Order of Patriotic Odd Fellows*.[19] The existence of the Patriotic Order is proven by their *Revised Rituals* as approved by their Grand Lodge on March 12, 1797.

Ancient and Honourable Order of Bucks

Some historians have noted the existence of the *Most Antient and Honourable Society of Bucks*. This society was formed in a London tavern sometime not later than 1722 and flourished between 1770 and 1802. The framework and purposes of the said organization described seems to indicate a link between the ancient guilds and the early Lodges of Odd Fellows, or at least, show that it existed along the same

Crest of the Most Antient and Honourable Society of Bucks. Some historians assert that the Bucks eventually merged with other societies such as the Odd Fellows. From public domain

line under a different name.

The presiding officer is called "Most Noble Grand," the same title used by the Independent Order Odd Fellows in its installation ceremony up until 1832. The next officers were a Senior and Junior "Vice Grand." The "bundle of sticks" was used as a symbol for teaching unity. Furthermore, one of the principal emblems was three bucks' heads with antlers joined together, as if forming the three links emblem of the Odd Fellows. The activities of this society included innocent mirth and good fellowship, one of the prominent characteristics of the early Lodges of Odd Fellows. This "Ancient Order" began to decline after 1780.

Surviving newspaper accounts would suggest that the name Odd Fellows gained public attention at least by the 1780s. However, their popularity and growth were hampered when the British government passed laws that banned all friendly societies in the United Kingdom. When fear of revolution began to fade, a number of surviving lodges merged into one singular organization. In 1802, there is a reference to the Ancient Order as the "United Order", the name "Buck" having been disused. Whether this was the Ancient Order that eventually merged with the Patriotic Order, it could no longer be ascertained.

Grand United Order of Odd Fellows

On January 8, 1798, the *Ancient Order* and the *Patriotic Order* entered into a merger as the *Grand United Order of Oddfellows* (GUOOF).[23] The *Gentleman's Magazine of 1798* mentioned that the Original United Lodge of Odd Fellows consisted of 50 lodges, 39 of them in London and its environs. Finding the Ancient Ritual unsuited to the new order of things, the GUOOF made great changes in the lectures. It was also during this period when the Order allegedly abandoned all political and religious disputes and committed itself to promoting the harmony and wel-

Seal of the Grand United Order of Oddfellows Friendly Society.

Pour forth that sweet
Virtue of Charity

GRAND UNITED LODGE
OF ODD FELLOWS
Instituted at Northfleet
KENT.
1799.

Unity with all, envy with none

Friendship & Benevolence

Brothers attentive stand,
Whilst our most Noble Grand,
Gives you the Charge,
The Bond of Society,
Is Friendship and Harmony,
Honour and Secrecy,
Will us Unite.

SONG.

Brothers you have nought to fear,
Momus's Court is here,
Love, Mirth, and Joy,
Loyalty here abounds,
Whilst Mirth our Evenings crown,
Let every Voice resound,
Long Live the King.

Prepare, prepare, your Rights prepare,
Loud, loudly ring, the echoing air,
In solemn pace, proceed around,
Where Order is with Pleasure Crown'd,

At the time of the merger, there were 50 lodges affiliated with the Grand United Order of Odd Fellows based in London and its environs.

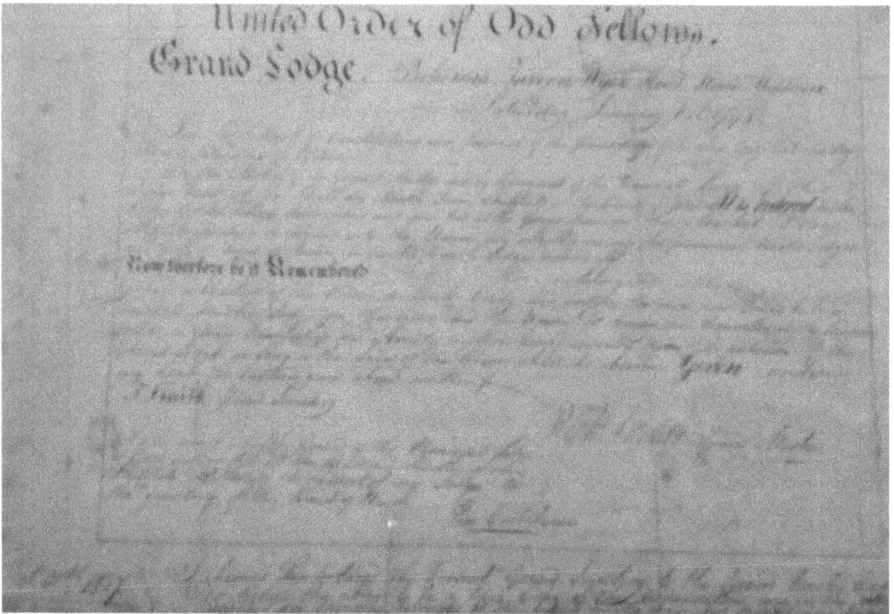

A bond of union to establish Amicable Lodge, in Sheffield, dated January 6, 1798, and signed by the Grand Master and the Grand Secretary on behalf of a meeting of the Grand Lodge of the United Order of Odd Fellows is displayed at the GUOOF headquarters in the United Kingdom today. Photo courtesy of Neil Robinson, 2014.

fare of its members.

Sometime in 1803, the GUOOF claimed to be the "Grand Lodge of England" and assumed authority over all Odd Fellows Lodges in the United Kingdom. This failed when some Odd Fellows Lodges in Manchester area seceded and formed the Independent Order of Odd Fellows Manchester Unity.[1]

Regardless of the secession, the GUOOF Friendly Society still continued and even chartered predominantly black lodges in the United States in 1843.[2] The GUOOF still exists today with approximately 50,000 members and some 1,000 lodges in Africa, Australia, Cuba, Dominican Republic, Grand Turks, Netherlands, New Zealand, West Indies, United Kingdom, and the United States of America.[3]

Why are there very few surviving records of the early Odd Fellows?

When the *French Revolution of 1789* occurred, it became the opinion of the English government that large gatherings of common people were plotting against the monarchy. Undeniably, England at

During the 18th up to the early-19th centuries, all lodges and clubs in England held their meetings and initiations inside pubs or taverns. Shown is a satirical illustration of "Making a Sailor an Odd Fellow" in 1806. Illustration published by T. Tegg Cheapside, 1806.

A satirical illustration in 1808 featured a Society of Odd Fellows from Downing Street, complaining to John Bull for the loss of their Lodge cash and accounts. Illustration published by Thomas Rowlandson, 1808.

Circa 1794 Provincial or Conder token that bore the name "Odd Fellows." Several of these tokens have the "heart and hand" symbol on the obverse side - the oldest symbol popularly used by Odd Fellowship until today. From the collection of the author

that time was full of radical protests. There was a propaganda war between radical advocates of political and economic reform and the loyalist defenders of the status quo. The government at that time was probably apprehensive about the ideas of democracy reaching to the working classes. Freedom of association and freedom of speech among common people were still not widely acceptable during that era. Using spies and informers, the government tried to infiltrate and investigate any potential threat to parliamentary monarchy. The government eventually passed legislations to manage this growing domestic unease and to made sure that English people will not follow the example of the French who waged a revolution against their monarchy in 1789.

The English government first responded by passing the *Rose Act of 1793* which required such societies to register, given that they conform with the government's scrutiny of how they should be organized. This was followed by the *Treasonable and Seditious Practices Act of 1795*, which banned people from speaking or printing grievances or anything against the government together with the *Seditious Meetings Act of 1795*, which banned meetings of more than fifty people. The *Unlawful Oaths Act of 1797* further illegalized oath-taking and various other methods in any society or association. Subsequently, the *Corresponding Societies Act of 1799* made merger and communication between Lodges and clubs illegal. Ultimately, the *Unlawful Societies Act of 1799* made membership in almost all fraternal orders and friendly societies a criminal offence.

Through lobbying by aristocrats and Dukes who were members, the Freemasons were eventually exempted from the ban. This is one reason why many of their early records remained intact. All other fraternal orders like the Odd Fellows tried to apply for a similar exemption but to no avail. As a result, many of the early Odd Fellow Lodges were closed while some went underground and developed secret ciphers and codes for their meetings. This also meant that many of the early documents were deliberately destroyed to avoid identification and arrest and undoubtedly one reason why very few records and artifacts survived today. Fragmentary surviving records and artifacts do tell us that the early Odd Fellows' existed in the early-mid 1700s.

Surviving Fragmentary Records and Artifacts

Among the few surviving documentations and relics of early Odd Fellows Lodge activities in the 18th century are the following:

1736 – The *Loyal Rose of Sharon Lodge* was first self-instituted in Hathersage, Derbyshire, on January 29, 1736. This lodge later affiliated with the Manchester Unity Independent Order of Odd Fellows in 1836.

1748 – A minutes of meeting and rules of *Aristarcus Lodge No.9 of the Most Antient and Noble Order of Odd Fellows*, which met at Globe Tavern, London on March 13.

1750 – Records possessed by the Loyal St. Olives Lodge that proved that the lodge was in existence in London as far back as 1750, discovered when it transferred dispensation under the Manchester Unity Independent Order of Odd Fellows in 1822.

1775 - A lodge of the Union Order of Odd Fellows existed in Derby.

1780 - George IV, while still Prince of Wales, was initiated into a lodge of Odd Fellows that held its meeting in a private house at Grosvenor Street, in West England.

1788 – A song written by James Montgomery starts with the line, "When Friendship, Love, and Truth abound among a band of brothers."

1789 – Bentley and Co. published a satirical depiction of a meeting night of a Club of Odd Fellows, drawn by English artist and caricaturist Samuel Collings.

1790 – The *Public Advertiser* issue on July 27 mentioned a "Grand Original Lodge of Odd Fellows."

1793 – The *Morning Chronicle* issue of July 20 mentioned the celebration of the union of the "United Order of Odd Fellows" and the "Imperial Order of Odd Fellows."

1794 - Provincial or Conder tokens bearing the name Odd Fellows dating back to 1794-1795 have survived and are in the hands of several collectors today.

1796 – The *Lloyd's Evening Post* issue of February 17 mentioned "a Society of Odd Fellows with a Vice Grand, a Most Noble Grand and a Secretary."

1797 – The *True Briton* issue on December 4 mentioned a "Society of Odd Fellows" in Gravesend. The Revised Ritual of the Patriotic Order of Odd Fellows was adopted on March 12. The Oddfellows' Magazine of 1838 included a picture of a medal presented to the Secretary of the Grand Independent Order of Odd Fellows, 1796-1797.

1798 – The *Morning Post* and *Gazetteer* issue of January 16 mentioned "a meeting of the Loyal and Constitutional Third Lodge of Odd Fellows" in Birmingham. The Whitehall Evening Post issue of April 7 mentioned the "Town Lodges of the United Order of Odd Fellows." The Gentleman's Magazine of 1798 mentioned that the "Original United Lodge of Odd Fellows consisted of 50 lodges, 39 of them in London and its environs." An Amicable Bond of Union of the Grand United Order of Odd Fellows in London was signed on January 6.

1799 – The *General Evening Post* issue of March 7 mentioned

"Odd Fellows, Free and Easy and the Jolly Friars," which met at the Goose and Gridiron tavern in London.

1800 – The *Star issue* of May 19, Lloyd's Evening Post issue of June 25, and the Caledonian Mercury issue of June 30 recorded that Hadfield confessed that he was a member of the Odd Fellows Society.

1806 – T. Tegg Cheapside published a caricature entitled Making a Sailor an Odd Fellow, on December 1.

1808 – The journal, *Odd Fellows Miscellany*, was first published in London.

1811 – The *Dictionary of the Vulgar Tongue* provided a definition of Odd Fellows as "a convivial society: the introduction of the 'Noble Grands' arrayed in royal robes is well worth seeing at the price of becoming a member."

Circa 1795 Provincial or Conder tokens that bore the name "Odd Fellows." It is asserted that these tokens were created to advocate for civil liberties and as a protest against the suppression of people's "freedom of association" when fraternal orders and friendly societies were banned by the English monarchy from the late-1700s up to the early 1800s. From the collection of the author.

Rise of the Manchester Unity

Independent Order of Odd Fellows Manchester Unity

In 1810, the Naylor's Amalgamated Society and Prince Regent Lodge of Odd Fellows in Salford merged to form the Lord Abercrombie Lodge No. 1. This lodge focused on the purpose of mutual relief for its members.[1] It asserted that this lodge was convivial, political and charitable in the beginning and, on their merger, the benevolent aspect became the principal aim. This new feature resulted in membership growth and financial strength that other lodges in Manchester area eventually followed.

Seal of the Independent Order of Oddfellows Manchester Unity Friendly Society.

Due to miscommunication and discontentment, six lodges in Manchester area declared "independence" from the GUOOF and organized themselves as the *Independent Order of Odd Fellows - Manchester Unity (IOOFMU)* in 1813.[2] The Manchester Unity eventually elected their own Grand Lodge officers in 1814, and further revised and stabilized the Odd Fellows ritual at the beginning of 1817.

At first, all lodges were located within or near Manchester area. But with their improved system, they were able to influence other independent lodges and associations throughout the United Kingdom to join their Unity (including small benefit clubs not named Odd Fellows). In just a few years, they also chartered lodges in Canada and the first successful Odd Fellows Lodge in the United States.

1808	1809
Robert Naylor formed a social and benevolent club known as *Naylor's Amalgamated Society,* which met at the Ropemakers Arms in Salford, Manchester, England.	A member from London named "Bolton" became a resident of Manchester and was able to get a dispensation from London to form *Victory Lodge of Odd Fellows*.

The Manchester Unity Oddfellows have always promoted international brotherhood regardless of race, nationality, and social status. Photo taken during the Annual Movable Conference of the Manchester Unity in 1910. Photo courtesy of Manchester Unity Oddfellows.

By 1845, there were Manchester Unity-affiliated lodges in every English county and were established in Ireland, Scotland, Germany, New Zealand, Australia and other parts of the kingdom. In 1860, lodges were opened in South Africa, South America and Istanbul. As membership grew, Manchester Unity eventually registered with the government and complied with regulations to avoid persecution.[3] Ultimately, the Manchester Unity became the largest Odd Fellows organization in the United Kingdom. The peak of membership was sometime in 1922 when IOOFMU had about 2 million members.[4]

1813	1814

A convention of past and present officers of all lodges of Odd Fellows in and around Manchester was held and the name, *Independent Order of Odd Fellows Manchester Unity*, was officially adopted.

A *Grand Committee* was formed and a Grand Master was elected. The Manchester Unity also issued the first IOOFMU Lecture Books on January 14, 1814.

Why the name Independent Order?

The word Independent was used to emphasize that these lodges declared "independence" from an older Order of Odd Fellows.

Were there other Orders of Odd Fellows in the United Kingdom?

Secession did not stop with the Manchester Unity. The government suppression against friendly societies as well as other socio-political factors during the early-mid 19th century developed to further schisms that led to the creation of more than thirty-four (34) different affiliated Orders of Odd Fellows, just to name a few:[2]

- Grand United Order of Odd Fellows

- Independent Order of Odd Fellows, Manchester Unity

- Nottingham Ancient Imperial Order of Odd Fellows

- Ancient Noble Order of Odd Fellows, Bolton Unity

- British United Order of Odd Fellows

- Improved Independent Order of Odd Fellows, London Unity

- Albion Order of Odd Fellows

- Independent Order of Odd Fellows, Kingston Unity

- National Independent Order of Odd Fellows

- Ancient Independent Order of Odd Fellows, Kent Unity

1817	1820
Facing problems of lack of uniformity and having issues with local travel relief, IOOF Manchester Unity further revised the "old" ritual ceremonies and proceeded to standardize the degree work for their lodges.	The *Duke of York Lodge* of the IOOF Manchester Unity chartered *Washington Lodge No.1* in Baltimore, Maryland, and gave the members there the authority to charter other lodges in North America.

- Independent Order of Odd Fellows, Wolverhampton Unity

All these affiliated Orders developed their own rituals, signs and passwords although there remained some similarities in terms of the general principles, regalia and symbols. The passage of welfare state, national health insurance, as well as other social changes, resulted to the decline of membership in all fraternal orders and friendly societies during the mid-late 20th century. A number of these groups eventually closed while others merged with the Manchester Unity.

At present, Manchester Unity is an international friendly society with autonomous Grand lodges in the United Kingdom, Australia and New Zealand.[5] There are also those termed as *Overseas Districts* or *Branches* attached to the mother organization in the United Kingdom and operating in the North America, Central and South America, and the Mediterranean area.[6] As of writing, there are approximately

100th anniversary medallion belonging to Sir John Falstaff Lodge of the Loyal Ancient and Independent Order of Odd Fellows founded in 1799. From the collection of the author.

309,000 members in the United Kingdom and several thousands in Australia, Gibraltar, Guyana, Malta, Natal, New Zealand, Otago, Dominican Republic, Transvaal, South Africa and some in the United States and Canada.[7] At least 50,000 are fraternal members while the rest are beneficial members.

Pendant belonging to the defunct Grand Lodge of the Nottingham Imperial Union of Odd Fellows, United Kingdom.

Independent Order of Odd Fellows

There were a number of self-instituted Odd Fellow Lodges in the United States and Canada. Masonic author Robert Macoy noted that Odd Fellowship was first introduced in the United States as early as 1799, at which time a lodge was self-instituted in Connecticut.[1] A lodge also made appearance in Baltimore in 1802 and New York in 1806.[2] However, these self-instituted lodges were short-lived. The leaders of these early lodges never attempted to form a state or national association nor were these lodges granted a dispensation or charter by a parent English Order.

Because of charter relationship with the Manchester Unity Oddfellows in England, Thomas Wildey is revered as founder of Odd Fellowship on the North American continent when he and four other members from England instituted Washington Lodge No.1 in Baltimore, Maryland, on April 26, 1819. This lodge was given a dispensation by the Duke of York's Lodge of the Manchester Unity on February 1, 1820 as the *Grand Lodge of Maryland and the United States* of the Independent Order of Odd Fellows (IOOF) with the power to grant a Warrant or Dispensation to others lodges in the continent.[3] The formal organization of the Grand Lodge on February 22, 1821[4] helped unite a number of self-instituted Odd Fellows Lodges across North America and made the IOOF into a national association. Lodges in Philadelphia, New York, and Boston made efforts for a general union and applied for charter from the Grand Lodge. By 1823, the Grand Lodge of Massachusetts, Grand Lodge of New York and the Grand Lodge of Pennsylvania were instituted.[5]

1799	1802
Masonic historian, Robert Macoy, asserted that Odd Fellowship "was introduced into the United States as early as 1799, at which time a lodge was constituted in Connecticut."	John Duncan, who was a charter member of Washington Lodge No.1 in 1819, was initiated in a Lodge of Odd Fellows in Baltimore in 1802.

On January 15, 1825, the *Grand Lodge of the United States* (now known as The *Sovereign Grand Lodge*) became a separate entity from the Grand Lodge of Maryland. This structure provided the IOOF in the United States a democratic and united system under one acknowledged head.[6]

Who is Thomas Wildey?

Thomas Wildey, revered as the founder of the IOOF in the United States.

Thomas Wildey (1782-1861) is revered as the founder of the Independent Order of Odd Fellows in North America. He was born in London, England, on January 15, 1782.[7] He was a craftsman by profession who practiced the trade of couch spring-maker. At age 21, he joined the Odd Fellows Lodge No.17 in London and became a Past Grand at the age 23.[8] Three years after, he was instrumental in organizing Morning Star Lodge No.38 in another city in England which he was also elected as presiding officer and became a Past Grand.[9]

He migrated to the United States in 1817. In 1819, Wildey was elected as the first Noble Grand of Washington Lodge No.1.[10] He was unanimously elected as the first Grand Master when the Grand Lodge of Maryland and the United States was created in 1821.[11] He then served as the first Grand Sire of the IOOF when the Grand Lodge of the United States (now known as The Sovereign Grand Lodge) became a

1806	1815
Shakespeare Lodge No.1 was instituted in New York on December 23, 1806. The lodge dissolved in 1812 and was revived in 1818. Other lodges were also instituted in Philadelphia and New York through the efforts of Shakespeare Lodge.	Two Odd Fellows lodges existed in Halifax, Canada, as early as 1815.

separate organization in 1824, composed of representatives from all over North America.

Who were the first five members of Washington Lodge No.1?

The five original members were Thomas Wildey, John Welch, John Duncan, John Cheatham and Richard Rushworth.[12]

In 1818, Thomas Wildey met John Welch who was also an Odd Fellow from England. After spending time, they discussed the possibility of establishing an Odd Fellows lodge in Baltimore. But the ancient usage established a rule that a minimum of five people is needed to institute a lodge. They needed to find at least three more members, so they advertised their plans of forming a lodge in the *Baltimore American* on February 13, 1819.

John Duncan and John Cheatham responded and attended the first meeting. The two proved themselves to be worthy members and were duly qualified. They still needed one more member but private search left them unsuccessful. Again, they advertised in the *Baltimore American* on March 27, 1819. Finally, Richard Rushworth responded to the second advertisement and proved himself to be a worthy member. They cross-examined each other and all four were believed to be affiliated with the Odd Fellows in England. John Duncan claimed to have been initiated in an Odd Fellows Lodge then-existing in Baltimore in 1802, which presumably closed at the onset of the War of 1812. But Duncan was also able to prove himself

1816	1817
Prince Regent Lodge of Odd Fellows was instituted in New York but eventually disbanded or became unheard of.	*Massachusetts Lodge No. 1* was self-instituted in Boston. The lodge later affiliated with the IOOF and received a charter from the Grand Lodge of Maryland and the United States on March 20, 1820.

as Odd Fellow through the ancient password, sign, and grip.[13]

They met again on April 26, 1819, this time at the *Seven Stars Tavern* in Baltimore, Maryland, and self-instituted *Washington Lodge No.1*. Within one month, they aligned their work towards the Independent Order of Oddfellows Manchester Unity (IOOFMU) and took the initiative to obtain a charter. *Abercrombie Lodge* in Manchester issued them a dispensation but this never reached them. Through John Crowder, who visited Baltimore in 1819, the lodge finally received a charter from the *Duke of York Lodge* in Preston, England, in 1820. This gave them the authority to charter other lodges in the continent.

Who are the Rebekahs?

During this period, women were not yet allowed to own property, go to school, practice a profession, vote, hold public office, or join fraternal organizations. The Independent Order of Odd Fellows started to deviate from this trend when a resolution to extend fraternal care and protection to women was passed by the Grand Lodge of the United States in 1845.

> Resolved: That it is expedient for this Grand Lodge to adopt some measure by which wives of Odd Fellows may be enabled to make themselves known to members of the Order and prove themselves when among strangers.

This further improved when the Independent Order of Odd Fellows became the first international fraternal organization to officially accept women on its adoption of the "Rebekah Degree" on September 20, 1851. This degree was written by Schuyler Colfax, who later became the Vice President of the United States from 1869 to 1873.

In 1856, the Rebekahs were permitted to organize for promoting the cause of benevolence.[14] By September 25, 1868, the Rebekah Lodges were given full freedom to elect and vote for their own set of officers, collect fees and dues, and organize their own philanthropic projects.[15] With their example and success, many other fraternal organizations also opened their doors to women by establishing auxiliary groups for females. This was way ahead of

Dispensation of Washington Lodge No.1 under "the Grand Lodge of Maryland and the United States of America" granted on February 1, 1820 by the Duke of York Lodge of the Independent Order of Oddfellows Manchester Unity Friendly Society in Preston, United Kingdom. Photo by the author.

Vice-President Schuyler Colfax in Odd Fellows' regalia. He joined the South Bend Lodge No. 29 of the Independent Order of Odd Fellows in Indiana. He is regarded as author and founder of the Rebekah Degree in 1851. Photo courtesy of The Sovereign Grand Lodge, IOOF.

Rebekahs in collar regalia. Photo courtesy of Ruby Rebekah Lodge No.52, 1900.

the times, noting that the USA only recognized women's rights and suffrage in 1920.

Separation from Manchester Unity

In 1834, six farm laborers known in history as the *Tolpuddle Martyrs,* were arrested for taking an oath of secrecy and were sentenced to seven years' imprisonment. The verdict shocked many fraternal orders in England.[16] As a result, Manchester Unity Odd Fellows abolished their oaths and simplified their initiations for fear of a backlash against their organization.[17] In 1839, both the IOOFMU in the United Kingdom and the IOOF in North America revised their ceremonies and initiation rituals with disastrous results.[18]

The changes made were radical in nature, so that Manchester Unity members who visited lodges in North America found it difficult to pass the necessary tests and were denied admission in lodges. This eventually led to the official separation of the two affiliated orders in 1843.[19] What was not clearly understood by the Odd Fellows in North America during this period was the objection by the British government against fraternal orders and friendly societies.[20] As mentioned earlier, the reason was fear that these groups were plotting against the English King, so any association that wanted to remain in existence was required to register with the government or close down.

To register, the IOOFMU had to dispense with certain ways by which they conducted their ceremonies, particularly in giving degrees of initiation and in administering the oath of membership. They had to revise their degrees from dramatic form to purely lectures.[21] It had been often erroneously alleged that the IOOF in the United States absolved their allegiance and affiliation with the Manchester Unity Odd Fellows because the latter granted dispensation to an African-American Lodge in New York City. However, the Manchester Unity IOOF in the United Kingdom never chartered a lodge for black men. It was the Grand United Order of Oddfellows that did, and the year 1843 was just a mere coincidence.

Inter-fraternal Recognition with the Manchester Unity

In 1854, the IOOF Manchester Unity made overtures for the re-establishment of reciprocal relations with the IOOF in the United States. The Grand Lodge of the United States expressed its willingness provided the Manchester Unity adopt the work and usages practiced by the IOOF.[22] In 1876, another movement for the restoration of friendly relations between the IOOF and the IOOFMU began but also made little progress.[23] The experiences during World War I and World War II played an important role in making the two organizations realize the importance of a friendly relationship. In 1944, a committee was formed to explore possibilities for more friendly ties between the two Affiliated Orders.[24]

But owing to the big differences in the degrees of initiation, finances, and general method of operations, the possibility of an organic union is remote, if not impossible.[25] Both affiliated orders were able to create a system that would allow inter-visitation without need for departure from any of the well-established operations and organizational structure of either organization. This was done by adopting an *inter-fraternal sign of recognition*.

Who are the Grand United Order of Odd Fellows in America and Jurisdiction?

During the 19th century up to the mid 20th century, it was

publicly unacceptable for white and black Americans to comingle in the same school, church, comfort room or fraternal order. Historically, many countries passed laws that implemented racial segregation. Thus, the IOOF was obligated not to accept blacks as members especially in the United States where racial segregation laws were enforced. This was not confined to the IOOF alone. This was the rule even in other fraternal orders such as Freemasonry. There were even self-instituted lodges of white men in Pottsville, Pennsylvania, and vicinity operating under the name Grand United Order of Odd Fellows that were also constrained not to accept black members due to racial prejudice.[26]

So, in 1843, African-Americans formed *Philomathean Lodge No. 646* in New York. This Odd Fellows lodge was granted a dispensation by the *Grand United Order of Odd Fellows* (GUOOF) of England through the effort of Peter Ogden who was already a member of *Victoria Lodge No. 448* in Liverpool.[27] The GUOOF of the United States eventually became the Odd Fellows' association for black or colored men. Many of the founding members of the GUOOF lodges in the United States were known abolitionists and civil rights activists including John C. Bowers, who served as the Grand Master of the GUOOF of Pennsylvania.

The GUOOF membership in North America reached approximately 400,000 during its peak in the 1920's. The GUOOF of America and Jurisdiction opened lodges in Africa, Costa Rica, Cuba, Barbados, Bermuda, British Honduras, Dominican Republic, Haiti, Jamaica, Netherlands, Nicaragua, Liberia, St. Kitts, Virgin Islands, and West Indies. Just recently, there had been a revival of lodges under the GUOOF in the United States.

Who is Peter Ogden?

Peter Ogden is revered as the founder of the Grand United Order of Odd Fellows in America. He was of African ancestry and was born in the West Indies. Working as a steward of the S.S. Patrick Henry, he had the opportunity to travel to different countries and was initiated as

Peter Ogden, founder of the GUOOF in the United States.

an *Odd Fellow in Victoria Lodge No. 448* under the Grand United Order of Odd Fellows in Liverpool.[28]

When he settled in the United States, he persuaded a group of African-American men belonging to the *Philomathean Society* to affiliate with the *Grand United Order of Oddfellows* in the United Kingdom which gladly accepted men regardless of skin color. Through the efforts of Ogden, a dispensation was granted for the Philomathean Lodge No. 646 in New York, and he became their first Most Noble Grand.

Who are the Household of Ruth?

In 1857, Patrick H. Reason led the successful efforts to officially create a female group affiliated with the Grand United Order of Odd Fellows known as the Household of Ruth. Membership in the Household is open only to females. Although in smaller numbers today, this female branch of the GUOOF still exists in the United States, Canada, Cuba, Bahamas, Africa, etc.

Is there inter-fraternal relationship between the IOOF and the GUOOF?

Currently, there is no official inter-fraternal relationship or amity between the GUOOF and the IOOF except in Australia. But both Orders have always respected each other's co-existence without any competition, hostility and conflicts. In fact, a handful of people today are members of both the IOOF and GUOOF.

Although the GUOOF and IOOF members were historically separated by racial segregation laws imposed in many countries' years ago, newspaper accounts and journal of proceedings documented instances when the two groups exchanged correspondences and assisted each other even prior to the *African-American civil rights movement*. In 1899, for example, it became publicly known that the GUOOF District Grand Lodge in Springfield, Illinois, was struggling to raise funds for the purpose of building a home for widows and orphans. In response to this need, the IOOF Grand Lodge of Illinois donated to the GUOOF $100 to help build the home.[29] The Deputy Grand Master of the GUOOF, F.W. Rollins, in his thank you letter to IOOF members, addressed them as "brothers." In response, the Grand Secretary of the IOOF of Illinois, J.R. Miller, wrote: [30]

Odd Fellowship found in either one of the branches of our Order, teaches one and the same lesson, and it is not at all surprising or strange, that members of the IOOF should entertain a friendly regard and a Brotherly interest in the good work performed by the Grand United Order of Odd Fellows even though composed of men and women to a different race.

During the Installation of officers of the Key of the West Lodge No.1692 and Memphis Star Lodge No.1501 of the GUOOF in the State of Tennessee in the 1920s, thirteen representatives from five IOOF lodges were present on the stage as guests. Past Grand Master J.D. Danbury of the IOOF was introduced by Senior Past Grand Master D.W. Washington of the GUOOF and he remarked that the IOOF guests were well pleased with the ceremonies of the evening.

In 1989, Representative Dag Wallén of Sweden met a Past Grand Master of GUOOF in Ghana, Africa, who showed him their initiation rituals and secret work which was a little similar to the one used by the IOOF.[31] Beginning 1993, leaders of the IOOF from Europe, North America and Australia discussed about building better cooperation with other Odd Fellows organizations such as the Grand United Order of Odd Fellows.[32] Australians were the first to establish an *Odd Fellow Network* for better cooperation between the GUOOF, MUIOOF and GUOOF.

In 2008, representatives of the two organizations in Texas met to see greater cooperation, joint projects, and dual membership. In the United States, a number of people joined both the IOOF and the GUOOF. Informally, most of the members of the IOOF consider the members of the GUOOF as their "brothers." In 2018, Emanuel Page, Sr., Past Noble Father of Wayman Lodge No. 1339 of the GUOOF spoke infront of the leaders of the IOOF during the 192nd Annual Communication of the Sovereign Grand Lodge held in Baltimore, Maryland. In 2019, the IOOF Grand Lodge of Georgia even passed a bill promoting a positive fraternal relationship with the GUOOF.

Today, the Odd Fellows Network in Australia permits members and leaders of the various affiliated Orders of Odd Fellows (GUOOF, IOOF and IOOFMU) to collaborate and attend each other's conferences and meetings. Photo courtesy of Heather Bitter, 2018.

However, should an official amity between the GUOOF and the IOOF be established soon, this will only be similar to the "inter-fraternal visitation rights" developed between the IOOFMU and the IOOF. The main reason is not racial but structural. After how many decades, these three major Affiliated Orders of Odd Fellows have already developed diverging rituals, passwords, handshakes, customs, regalia, practices and organizational structure that it has become impossible to merge them into one single organization. Thus, a complete unification between the three major Odd Fellows' organizations will not be possible unless these groups will allow major revisions in their ritualistic works, unwritten work, and organizational structure to decrease substantial differences. The Odd Fellows lodges under the GUOOF of North America also remain male-only while the IOOF are becoming co-ed. This may also pose a question when it comes to establishing inter-fraternal relations. But what is certain and cannot be changed is the fact that both Orders are mutually harmonious and not in hostility against each other. Interestingly, some dual members of the IOOF and GUOOF have developed what they call the *Unified Initiatory Degree,* which is a combination of the IOOF and GUOOF initiation ceremony. This degree may be a key that will allow GUOOF and IOOF members to inter-visit each other's lodge meetings and initiations in the near future.

Growth and Decline of Fraternalism

Largest Fraternal Organization

After the American civil war, the Independent Order of Odd Fellows experienced a growth in their membership. An important addition was when the *Ancient Independent Order of Odd Fellows* in Australia affiliated with the Grand Lodge of the United States in 1869.[1] Further steps to open lodges in other countries were also taken and a lodge under the IOOF was established in Germany in 1870.[2] By the end of the 19th century, the IOOF had spread to most of the rest of the world. Lodges were established in the Americas, Australia, New Zealand, Asia, Africa and most of Europe.

From 1900 to 1910, the IOOF initiated an average number of 124,175 new members annually.[3] At the close of 1910, the IOOF had more than 1.5 million active members and 17,705 lodges in North America.[4] The peak of membership was in 1921 when the IOOF had more than 1.9 million active members, 16,986 lodges and a hefty $85 million in invested funds.[5] Combined with the two other major Affiliated Orders of Odd Fellows - IOOFMU and the GUOOF

Odd Fellowship was the largest fraternal organization during the *Golden Age of Fraternalism*. There were at least 40,000 members in every state or province in North America. In sum, there were about 4 million Odd Fellows and 1 million Rebekahs in more than 30,000 lodges worldwide. Photo from the collection of the author.

- there were more than 3.5 million Odd Fellows during that year.[6] This number even excluded the membership of smaller Orders of Odd Fellows. In addition to the numbers were the Rebekahs under the IOOF numbering more than 1 million women in 9,793 Rebekah Lodges and having more than $1.3 million in invested funds.[7] In 1929, Grand Sire Frank Martin of the Sovereign Grand boasted that "Odd Fellowship have more than two and one-quarter million members in the United States and more than three million members in the world".[8] The Odd Fellows eventually gained international popularity, so that many people were interested in obtaining a charter for an Odd Fellows Lodge in a location as far as Syria.[9]

Immigration to various parts of the world helped with membership growth of fraternal orders. More than 18 million people entered the United States between 1890 and 1920.[10] This encouraged the proliferation of hundreds of different fraternal organizations, benefit societies, college fraternities and sororities, and ethnic associations for almost every person or group.

1863	1872
The IOOF became a major trendsetter when it adopted a clear and guaranteed set of member financial benefits. This system became a model for various other fraternal organizations and the predecessor of the Social Security System.	The IOOF became the first fraternal organization to build Homes for orphans and elderly.

In 1896, there were nearly 70,000 lodges belonging to more than 150 organizations. Their memberships included some 810,000 Odd Fellows, 750,000 Freemasons, 475,000 Knights of Pythias, and thousands more belonging to other groups.[11] During the same year, African-American fraternal organizations such as the Prince Hall Freemasons had a membership of 224,000 and the Grand United Order of Odd Fellows had 130,350. [12] Overall, the membership of fraternal organizations in the United States during that year was around 6.4 million of a population of about 19 million.[13] This meant that at least one out of eight men at that time were members of a fraternal organization.[14] Many of these fraternities and benefit societies competed to attract prominent people by revising their rituals, improving their regalia, and employing an attractive benefit system.[15] Soon, nearly every prominent man was an Odd Fellow or a Freemason, or both[16] because it became common for people to hold membership in two or more organizations. Moreover, the fraternal organizations were widely involved in early-day philanthropic works and spent over

1915	1933
The Odd Fellows became the largest fraternal organization in the world from 1870-1920. In 1915, there were over 3.5 million Odd Fellows and 2 million Rebekahs around the globe. This excluded the members of smaller Orders of Odd Fellows.	During the Great Depression, Odd Fellow and US President Roosevelt introduced the New Deal to combat unemployment and poverty. Several of these programs were modeled after the system of financial benefits previously offered by Odd Fellows.

$649 million in relief assistance in 1897.[17] The three largest fraternal organizations of the era – Odd Fellows, Freemasons, and Knights of Pythias – spent an estimated $176 million per year in aid of members in need, excluding private monetary gifts of the members.[18] This phenomenal period of people rushing to join fraternal organizations between the years 1870 to 1920 is referred to as the "*Golden Age of Fraternalism.*"

Largest Provider of Sickness and Death Insurance

During the 19th century, life insurance was available only to the wealthy and was beyond the financial ability of the average working class. For these reasons, the Odd Fellows in the United States took on the responsibilities of visiting the sick, burying the dead, educating the orphans and caring for the widows and elderly as a way to support families in need. Aside from the social aspects of being a member, the main draw was the Odd Fellows' dedication to protect and care for their members and families at a time when many charitable and welfare services that people enjoy today were still absent.

Initially, the Odd Fellows provided funds for members as a matter of charity. Several *Odd Fellows' Relief Associations* were founded by members although as a separate entity from the lodge. In 1863, however, the IOOF "became a major trendsetter and was a predecessor of the Social Security System when the organization adopted a clear schedule of guaranteed benefits over the haphazard ways of granting financial assistance previously followed by most fraternal organizations".

The Odd Fellows also helped revise the language of fraternalism by using the terms "benefit" and "right" as compared to "charity" and "relief" to describe the aid given to its members. Hence, help from an Odd Fellows Lodge was not looked upon as a donation but a member's right, and was paid to every member who was sick, whether he was high or low, rich or poor.[19] Perhaps, these terms were preferred so that members who received financial aid would not feel ashamed or lose his self-esteem for accepting assistance from the lodge during a temporary crisis. Mutual-aid triumphed so that a member might be a donor one day and a recipient of help the next.[20]

Many Odd Fellows' Homes in North America, Europe, and Australia served as safe haven for the widows and orphans. Photo from the collection of the author.

During World War I and II, the IOOF raised large sums of money for the purchase of ambulances and airplanes used in medical missions at the war front. Photo courtesy Peter Sellars of the Grand Lodge of California, IOOF.

CLINTON LODGE

NO. 98, I. O. O. F.

LOCK HAVEN, PA., MAY 24, 1904.

To the N. G., V. G., Officers and Members of *Sec'y. Creek* .....

Lodge, No. *641* .. I. O. O. F.

DEAR SIRS AND BROTHERS:—

It is with deep regret that, for the first time in the history of this Lodge (which was instituted in 1844) we are compelled to appeal to our sister Lodges in this Jurisdiction to solicit aid in behalf of our worthy Brother, P. G. J. D. Miller, who as you can see in this picture, had both legs cut off on a railroad on March 31, 1903, on his way home from his work (he being an axe maker by trade) by avoiding one train of cars he stepped in front of another train and was in this way crippled for life.

Brother Miller is a poor man; he is 41 years of age; he has a wife and two children to support and he has no means of support except what aid he receives from this Lodge and his Brothers in the Fraternity, and this Lodge is not conditioned financially to make further donations.

Now Brothers, this is a very deserving case, and we hope it will receive a generous consideration at the hands of the Fraternity. Our aim is to start the Brother in a small business to make a living for himself. Therefore, Whereas, Clinton Lodge never refuses to assist Brothers in distress by appeal, we feel justified in making this our first appeal to our sister Lodges in time of need.

Send all contributions to GEORGE A. MILLER.

No. 518 E. Main St.,

LOCK HAVEN, PENNA.

We hereby submit the following as a true and correct report of this Lodge:

Number of members in good standing	- - - - - - -	55
Amount paid by the Lodge or its members to the petitioner	- -	$266.50
The fee for initiation	- - - - - - - - -	8.00
Weekly dues	- - - - - - - - - -	.10
Funeral assessments	- - - member 75 cents; Wife 35 cents	
Weekly benefits	- $3.50 first 15 weeks; 37 weeks $2.00, after $1.00	
Funeral benefits	- - - - - Member $50.00; Wife $25.00	
Invested funds	- - - - - - - - -	....
Cash in hands of officers	- - - - - - -	....

Resolved, That should the prayer of our petition be granted, we do hereby promise and agree to yield a strict compliance with the requirements of Sections 2 and 3 of Article XXXII of the By-Laws of the Grand Lodge.

Fraternally submitted,

S. G. DAVIS, Noble Grand,
GEORGE A. MILLER, Secretary.

I. O. O. F.

Office of the Grand Master of the
Grand Lodge of Pennsylvania.

Approved, Philadelphia, June 24, 1904.
GEORGE HAWKES, Chairman
AMOS H. HALL
CHARLES CHALFANT
JAMES H. AVERY
J. P. HALE JENKINS
Committee on the State of the Order.

SEAL OF GRAND LODGE

Approved, ROBERT GRAHAM,
Grand Master.

ATTEST:
JOSEPH H. MACKEY, Grand Secretary.

It has been a duty and tradition for Odd Fellows to help other members overcome struggles in life. From the collection of the author.

From 1863 to 1925, the IOOF was the largest provider of sickness insurance in the United States and Canada. Sick members could claim a regular stipend of around $3.00 to $6.00 per week to compensate for working days lost.[21] The lodges' shared resources helped members pay doctor's fees or buy medicine. Other than this, burial for a deceased member was usually covered by the lodge and the widowed families and orphans also received help. This ensured families against the disgrace of alms houses' and the embarrassment of a pauper's grave. From 1900 to 1910, the organization's financial strength greatly improved, so that IOOF was able to disburse an average amount of $4.4 million annually for the relief of distressed members, widowed families, orphans, burial for the dead, and other charities.[22]

Other branches such as the Encampments spent an average amount of $300,000 annually. The Rebekah Lodges spent an average of $77,000 a year for relief and charity.[23] At the end of 1910, the IOOF had already expended a grand total of more than $136 million for relief and charity and the organization's overall annual revenue was more than $275 million.[24] These were tremendous amounts during this era if calculated based on today's standards. In the IOOF, the poor were able to help the poor through mutual-aid. This implied a lesson that "the working classes were capable of creating effective, organized self-help efforts on a vast scale and distinguished fraternal organizations from some of the large, bureaucratically organized charities of the day, which practiced hierarchical relief wherein donors often came from a different economic class and social status than the recipients."[25]

Charity Works

The IOOF further proved its administrative abilities by establishing several significant major social welfare institutions such as orphanages, retirement homes, and medical clinics emphasizing preventive care and cemeteries. In 1872, the IOOF became the first fraternal organization to build a home dedicated to the care and education of orphans and the assistance of widows and the elderly when the Grand Lodge of Pennsylvania built the *Odd Fellows Home of Western Pennsylvania* in 1872.[26] Soon, almost every state in the United

States, Canada, and Australia had an Odd Fellows Home. These facilities were a fully functioning self-sustaining micro-community where widows, orphans and the elderly were cared and provided for. In 1909, the IOOF in Denmark also helped build a hospital for lepers in St. Croix, Virgin Islands.[27]

Yet the benevolent works of the IOOF were not limited to material and financial aid. Ethical or moral aid was often mentioned as the main objective of the fraternal organization. Through the teachings imparted during the ceremonies of initiation, members were taught to be compassionate to their fellowmen, be tolerant to other people's beliefs and to avoid excessive drinking or fight vices of every form.

Odd Fellows visited each other in times of sickness and distress. If a member needed a job, Odd Fellows would also help him find one. If they could not find one locally, they would pay his way to the next lodge and this would continue until he got a job. When a member dies, the officers of the lodge would seek permission from the family to have their own private moment with the deceased as they perform a funeral ceremony to honor their departed brother Odd Fellow or sister Rebekah. Odd Fellowship substantially grew in numbers because its members genuinely propagated a culture of caring and sharing.

Decline of Fraternalism

By the mid-late 20th century, membership in all fraternal organizations and service clubs began to decline. Commercial life insurance companies began to actively compete with the sick and death benefits offered by fraternal organizations.[28] President Franklin Roosevelt, who was an Odd Fellow member, later introduced the *New Deal* that provided federal programs and public work projects to mitigate the effects of the Great Depression.[29] Beginning 1934, Congress passed government measures that provided unemployment compensation, old-age and disability insurance, and aid to dependent children.[30] Later, the government focused on foster homes, which replaced the importance of the orphanages owned and managed by the Odd Fellows across North America.

The Great Parade

On September 29, 1920, the IOOF in Massachusetts organized one of the biggest parades ever held by the IOOF in history. Thirty-two divisions were lined up and the total number of people who participated in the parade was estimated at 40,000. The parade required hours to pass a given point. The streets along the line of march were thronged with thousands of people, many of them on reviewing stands erected for the purpose.

President Roosevelt and the New Deal

    Franklin Delano Roosevelt joined Park Lodge No.203 of the IOOF in New York on January 24, 1912. At the beginning of his term as U.S. President, he introduced the New Deal to combat mass unemployment. One of these programs, the Social Security System, was apparently modeled after the system of financial benefits previously offered by the Independent Order of Odd Fellows. On July 23, 1940, fifteen members of his lodge assembled at his home and presented to him his 25-year membership jewel. He remained an active member of the IOOF up until his death in 1945. Photo courtesy of The Sovereign Grand Lodge, IOOF.

    In time, the financial and charitable services offered by the Odd Fellows and other fraternal organizations were taken over by the government with the introduction of the *Social Security System* and *National Health Insurance*. The social safety net offered by these fraternal groups were no longer viewed as necessary to the point that many members ultimately gave up their membership.[31] As a result, nearly all fraternal organizations and friendly societies across the United States, United Kingdom, Australia, and New Zealand substantially lost their membership.[32] IOOF's sick and death benefit declined from 1929 to 1960.[33] By 1960, most IOOF Grand Lodges eventually abandoned the system of providing sick and death benefits and transitioned back into a social fraternity. But owing to the failure of many lodges to adapt to needed changes promptly, many became stagnant and eventually went out of existence.

In 1969, Past Sovereign Grand Master Donald Smith and Past Sovereign Grand Master Charles Worrell attended a *Brotherhood 2000 Conference* in New York City with many other fraternal organizations represented. Odd Fellowships' sister fraternities such as Freemasonry raised the concern of dropping membership[34] and all other organizations represented shared similar problems.[35] At the beginning of 1922, there were nearly 4 million Odd Fellows who belonged to the IOOF, GUOOF and IOOFMU.[36] Out of that number, almost 2 million were affiliated with the IOOF. But the total membership of all the three major *Affiliated Orders* of Odd Fellows decreased to 1 million members by 1983.[37] Membership in Freemasonry in the United States also went down from 4.1 million members in 1959 to 1.3 million in 2012.[38] The documentary film, *Inside the Freemasons (2017)*, mentioned that at least 100 Masonic lodges close every year. Rotary International was not exempted because "it had been losing about 112,000 members each year."[39] Lodges and clubs that failed to offer something exciting and new to the younger generations eventually surrendered their charters while some have become stagnant. Membership in some lodges literally skipped two generations and are currently suffering an aging membership.

Why are fraternal orders and service clubs in general suffering a decline in membership?

There is no single or simple reason for the decline; the causes are complex. In general, they were the outgrowth of changed conditions in the social and economic life.[40] A different time, a new age, a changed mode of living had the greatest influence on those who have dropped out.[41] Much of the assistance provided by fraternal organizations and service clubs has been absorbed by commercial insurance companies, hospitals, funeral homes and government agencies. Priorities have evolved. Both men and women now work

An abandoned Odd Fellows hall in Norcatur, Kansas, USA.

for a living. They have family commitments. They have other leisure activities. For their valuable time, people now have the option of joining a multitude of other groups, organizations, clubs and lodges. Yet many of these century-old organizations have hardly changed the way they do business and still continue to function virtually in the same way they did over 50 years ago.

Signs of Rebival

Recently, "the fancy trappings of dwindling fraternal organizations have caught the attention of Hollywood, musicians, artists and historians alike."[1] Fraternal regalia and antiques have been popping up all over the internet, television shows, and art exhibits. Movies and documentary exposés about so called "secret societies" caught the attention of some people, particularly the younger generations. The internet has become one of the best forms of advertising Odd Fellowship and communication for members. The popularity of social networking websites such as *Facebook* and *Instagram* and sharing services such as *Youtube* have made it a lot easier for younger generations to learn about these organizations. Lodges and Grand Lodges that are visible in their communities and combine the use of the most recent technologies are now getting the publicity they need with little or no cost at all.[2]

With the rise of Wi-Fi and mobile smart phones came the decline of in-person friendships and authentic human contact.[3] Many fell into the all-too familiar routine of work, school, home and the internet. People text and face-time one another but these only took away some of human's basic needs, some of which are purpose and legacy.[4] A number of younger generations are now reaching out for a better way of life. On the other side of the spectrum, the elderly are looking for a social outlet and some friends to spend time with. Some people have become interested in returning to basic beliefs of years ago such as

2016 International Odd Fellow Meeting held in Hildesheim, Germany.

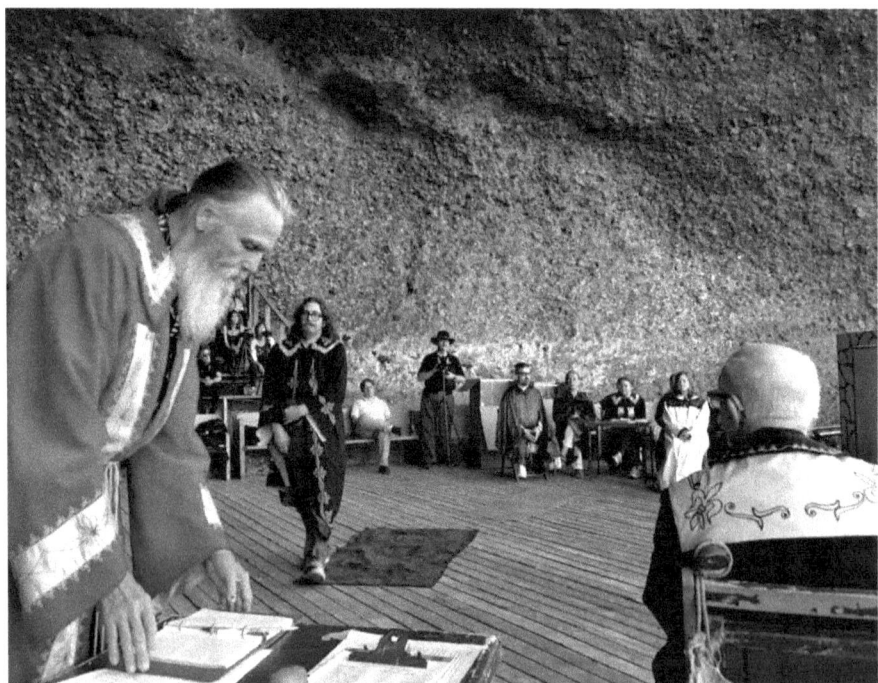

The Yreka Odd Fellows Lodge No. 19 in California annually hosts the "Cave Degree" since 1940. Customarily, the Initiatory Degree and the First Degree are conferred in the afternoon. After dinner, the participants proceed to the cave to receive the Second Degree. The next day, candidates receive the Third Degree. The 40-acre surrounding area of the cave was purchased by the IOOF in 1962. Photo courtesy of Peter Sellars, 2014.

"respect for our fellowmen, strong support to our communities, and sharing with others."[5] Some people are looking for a place where they can "better themselves through bettering our community."[6] In the Philippines, younger members view the Odd Fellows Lodge as a place "to improve character, make friends and help people." In Europe, younger members envision the Odd Fellows lodge as a place that is different from daily life. A place to rest, to think, to get energy, to obtain moral education, to learn to get to know fellow citizens and next-door neighbors.[7] As a result, there seems to be renewed interest from some men and women to join fraternal organizations like the Odd Fellows and rediscover new forms of community in the lodges.

Lodges that made extra effort to provide people the needs of modern times are now coming back to life in a dramatic way. A number of lodges are experiencing a resurgence of membership from different groups of young people - history buffs, tattoo artists, bikers, community activists, musicians, lawyers, businessmen, and the like. Although a large number of lodges are still struggling with membership at present, there are many success stories from different parts of the world about lodges that were revived and have grown their membership remarkably.

So, what are some of the secrets of success of these growing lodges?

1. Well-performed Rituals and Solemn Ceremonies

The long history of fraternal organizations such as the Odd Fellows, their rituals, symbols, regalia, and tradition of camaraderie are a preliminary attractive reason why some people inquire about and consider membership. For the past 50 years, the older members have been debating about how to modernize the organization. Some of the older generations were even ready to abolish the rituals and passwords and converted their lodges into some kind of service club. Younger members at present, however, see it differently. Many actually joined the Odd Fellows because it is different from service clubs and because of their interest in the traditional ritual ceremonies.[8] They see lodges as an avenue for "preserving long-lost traditions, fellowship, community service, and leadership."[9]

One reason Vic Anton Somoza of Watchdog Odd Fellows Lodge No.1 in Dumaguete, Philippines, joined is because of "the customs and rituals that have been followed through the years." Thomas Roam, a member who recently helped revive an Odd Fellows Lodge in his town, added that "people my age prefers the originality of the rituals and there is something about acting it out that is quite intriguing." He even suggested "memorization" to add drama to the ceremonies. Graham Fullerton, who recently joined at the age of seventeen, shared that he "enjoyed the chance to meet people who share my values, plus the initiation was kind of cool." In fact, many younger members throughout the world are even calling for an improved performance in the exemplification of the degrees of initiation.

The IOOF Grand Lodges in the continent of Europe have been worried about all the amendments to the Odd Fellows practices in North America, which have led to "a broader, more popular base, instead of going into the depth of improving the ritualistic work." The leaders of the IOOF in European countries expressed agreement that the rituals need to be revised and the words used need to be changed from time to time in order that the teachings of Odd Fellowship will remain attractive and effective to younger members. During the meetings of the IOOF International Advisory Board, the leaders agreed that they cannot allow Odd Fellowship to become a museum. On the contrary, the European IOOF leaders agreed that the lodge has to be a "constant ethical power station" and "provision should be made for modernizing such ceremonies."

The Sovereign Grand Lodge in North America, however, unsuccessfully revised the degrees of initiation by simplifying the degrees to the point of "dumbing it down" and allowing lodges to sloppily perform the initiations. On the other hand, the IOOF in European countries and in the Philippines have proven that it is possible to update the organization and meet the demands of modern people without totally abandoning some of the customs. Instead of simplifying the rituals, they moved towards further enriching the degrees so that its ethical lessons will be interesting to the younger generations. They removed terms and practices that may be considered as sectarian or politically incorrect in today's era. Many of their lodges also made sure that the degrees of initiation are performed in a dignified manner – their lodge rooms are clean, the members and candidates wear formal attire during ceremonies, and the charges in the rituals are mostly delivered by memory. The Danish version of the degrees of initiation has been positively accepted by members in their 20s, 30s, and 40's in the Philippines and is now used by the lodges in the country. A similar version of the Danish IOOF Ritual is being used by the IOOF in Norway, Sweden, Finland, and Iceland.

Nevertheless, no member is going to stay active because their lodge has a rich history, ancient rituals, secret grips, passwords, and signs, and because the members wear stylish regalia.[10] There must be more. Successful lodges are those that expand their lodge activities such as hosting social events for the members and their families and doing good works in the community.

2. Enjoyable and Fulfilling Social Events

Odd Fellowship originated in the pubs and taverns of England where members could experience an enjoyable social life with other members. Living in a concrete and asphalt jungles of metropolitan cities are many lonely people who do not have a feeling of belonging.[11] There are thousands of men and women hungry for sincere friendship.[12] That "old-fashioned and old-time connection is valuable today in our disconnected society."[13] People still seek a social network where they can have a good time and enjoy activities with others. Nobody wants to continue their membership in a lodge that is always serious and rigid. It had been observed by leaders of successful lodges that "a lodge cannot attract younger members if the only activity it can offer is a 30-minute formal meeting once or twice a month" and "an occasional potluck with little else going on."[14]

The lodges that are growing are those that do not just rely on the formality of opening and closing rituals. Clearly, monotony and boredom do not attract new members, and certainly do not retain them. Growing Odd Fellows' lodges today are those that allow their members to unwind and socialize at the lodge after a busy day at work. The early Odd Fellows lodges in the 1700s did offer food and liquor after meetings and this practice continued until alcoholic drinks were banned by the IOOF at the beginning of 1825 in compliance with the growing *Temperance Movement* that advocated against consumption of alcoholic beverages. This resulted in the passage of *Prohibition laws* in the United States that made the manufacture, sale or distribution of intoxicating liquors illegal. These laws were eventually repealed in all states from 1933 to 1966, bringing the *Prohibition era* to a close. Liquor is already legal in almost all countries today, but many lodges failed to update their old prohibition rules and still continue to ban alcoholic beverages within their buildings.

Possibly in the stress of degree work and community projects, many lodges have overlooked the fact that one of the principal purposes of Odd Fellowship is to develop true fraternity among its members.[15] Studies conducted by the Sovereign Grand Lodge in 1970 revealed that growing lodges are those that do not just hold ritualistic meetings or merely pass through a fixed agenda, but also bring its members together before or after the meetings so that they can "get acquainted and can be united in true friendship, and that they can leave from lodge meeting with a more fortified feeling."[16] Successful lodges are "those that provide an active social life within the lodge, because without a little fun, the lodge loses the friendship that Odd Fellows purports to espouse."[17] This means that there is a need to incorporate activities that would serve the common interests and hobbies of its members. Where do people of today usually hang-out with their friends during their free time? More successful and vibrant lodges today are those that have already allowed alcoholic beverages inside their lodge buildings. Some of these growing lodges actually have a bar as additional amenity for their buildings. Obviously, this encourages younger members to regularly attend lodge meetings and essentially stay at the lodge after the meeting to socialize with other members. From a psychological perspective, this also helps develop a stronger bond between members and can boost the morale of the lodge. But this does not mean that the Odd Fellows Lodge should be turned into a mere drinking club.

Scott Shaw, a Past Grand of Columbia Odd Fellows Lodge No.2 in British Columbia, Canada, sees Odd Fellowship as "a group of people coming together, working as a big family, supporting the local community, fund-raising together, and meeting each other's families." Thus, a dinner before or after a formal meeting is just not a selling point. The lodge must organize social events that bring members

The *Temperance Movement* (1784-1933) advocated against the consumption of alcohol and had a big influence on North American society, such that the manufacture, sale, or distribution of alcoholic beverages became illegal not just within the lodges but throughout the country. The prohibition became a nationwide constitutional ban in the United States from 1920 to 1933. After that, the manufacture of beer, wine, and distilled spirits became legal. Growing lodges today have updated their rules regarding consumption of alcoholic beverages and have incorporated in their buildings an industrial kitchen, a bar, and a reception area to allow their members to socialize before and after meetings. Photo courtesy of Scott Aitchison, 2019.

Lodges that are growing are those that also organize social and community events that cater to the hobbies and interests of their members whether it be about motorcycles, sports, wine-tasting, community outreach, volunteering and the like. These lodges grow because such activities outside the formal lodge structure further increases the bond of friendships between members and ultimately increases the morale of the lodge. Photo courtesty of Odd Fellows Riders Association, 2019 and Columbia Odd Fellows Lodge No.2, 2017.

together to enjoy each other's company and socially interact, whether it be biking, hiking trips, movie nights, game nights, wine tasting, beer brewing, dances, or concerts.

In Europe, younger members envision the Odd Fellows lodge as a place that is different from daily life. They want the lodge to be "a place to rest, to think, to get energy, to obtain ethical education, to learn to get to know fellow citizens and next-door neighbors." In response, most lodges in Switzerland and other parts of Europe hold lectures on ethical topics at least twice a month and this had been met positively.[18] Other lodges whose membership has tremendously increased developed their own "signature events" that their lodge organizes annually for their members and the whole community. Some examples of popular social and community events organized by Odd Fellows today are the "Odd Fest," "Oddtober Fest," "Oddventure," and "Odd Market." These are events that provide volunteer opportunities and showcase the talents of their members by providing music, arts, and other activities for the public to participate in. The funds raised will then be used to support local charities. When lodges have a full slate of such social activities, recruitment of new members is dramatically enhanced.[19]

3. Active Community Involvement and Volunteerism

One fraternal lesson from the history of Odd Fellowship is the necessity of community participation and involvement. Odd Fellowship rose to its "most glorious hour when members were active in the growth of communities and nations."[20] Citizens of early days recognized the value of Odd Fellowship, hence, they reciprocated by becoming members of "a Fraternity with the prime objective to serve."[21] Indeed, Odd Fellowship is one of the earliest forms of service organizations that provided its members opportunities to help each other and their fellowmen.

During the 19th century, the Odd Fellows and Rebekahs were a major presence in every town, providing essential medical aid, sick pay, and generally helping those who fell on hard times. IOOF in every state operated the first cemeteries, retirement homes, and orphanages. When these services were taken over by government programs and other agencies, many lodges eventually became stuck inside their lodge rooms and became virtually invisible in their towns. Today, there are people who are uncomfortable and uneasy over the economy, energy, morality, defense of their countries, the role of government in their lives, and myriad other problems. With several governments increasingly unable to provide adequate funding for health care, education, retirement, and unemployment and with the growing moral breakdown among citizens, the role of fraternal organizations such as the Odd Fellows is finding some relevance once again.

Growing lodges are those that become more involved with problems facing many communities today. *Davis Odd Fellows Lodge No.169* in Davis, California, has grown from less than 20 active members to over 300 members at present. Dave Rosenberg, a Past Grand of the Lodge, shared that their lodge "went in the direction of serving the community, reaching out into the community, being visible and doing good things, and having fun."[22] One of the reasons new members are attracted to join their lodge is because they actively do good works and are highly visible in their community. Graham, the youngest member of Davis Odd Fellows, emphasized that he "joined because of the opportunity to do something good in the community."[23] Oliver Peck, one of the former judges of the reality television show, *Ink Master*, is instrumental in rejuvenating the membership of *Waxahachie Odd Fellows Lodge No.80* in Texas. He opined that "most people just go to the bars and hang out or do whatever and nobody really has a sense of community anymore, and I think that's kind of what got me into the Odd Fellows."[24] He thinks of Odd Fellowship as "doing something social that didn't have to do with going to a bar, and doing something community-minded."[25]

However, community involvement must be more than just handing out a check to charities. Lodges of today must provide volunteer opportunities and community events that allow members to work together and be physically involved in their community. For growing lodges, increasing visibility and hosting an annual event open to everyone in the community has been a great way to attract new members.[26] These lodges also made their buildings available for the public for appropriate events.[27] For example, one lodge in North Dakota allowed their building to be a venue for hosting community plays.[28] Several lodges joined other civic organizations in decorating trees for the festival of trees program and participated in walk-athons. Some lodges create floats and rode in local parades. Others volunteered to clean streets and highways. Some served coffee and cookies at rest stops to keep drivers more alert.[29] Food drives have also proved very popular and one lodge filled shoe boxes with small gifts, including toys, candy, toiletries, and school supplies for *Operation Christmas Child* for needy children in Central America and South East Asia. Other lodges volunteered in local hospitals, the Red Cross, Salvation Army, schools, and nursing homes.[30] All these have been proven as a great way to expose the Odd Fellows to the community, to build a stronger bond among members, and to generate applications for membership.[31] Convincingly, a lodge grows when it identifies itself in some way with its community.

4. Strong and Quality Recruitment

Increase in membership will only happen when everyone involved is giving their all in the recruitment and reinstatement of members. The Sovereign Grand Lodge and the Grand Lodges can only do so much to increase the general membership. Efforts to attract new members must be sustained and has to happen at the "grassroots" level. That is, the individual lodge members must make the effort.[32] Complacency is a big issue. Lodges that became stagnant and still continue losing members are those that do not recruit but simply wait and hope someone will join.

This is a serious problem in both North America and Europe, where the general public barely know if a lodge exists in their area. It has become obvious that "long-time members' idea of secrecy about the lodge has come at the expense of the membership because many of their lodges almost secreted themselves to death."[33] These long-time members appear to send a message "that they don't wish to bring in younger members and are contented with the status quo of their lodge even when the aging of their membership is already significant." They just want to "keep it going in the same way as they have always known it probably until they pass away."

Lodges that are growing, on the other hand, are those who actively recruit every year. These lodges either send invitation letters to people or advertise in newspapers that they are looking for new members. Some do it by increasing their lodges' visibility and relevance in their community. Others organize "open houses" where prospective members are given tours inside Odd Fellows' buildings. Also, posting photos and videos about Odd Fellowship on social media websites like facebook.com has tremendously helped with recruitment. Still other lodges have grown simply because many of their current members asked their friends, families, and co-workers to join. Bottom line: members must get out of their lodge halls, let the public know about their existence, ask people to join, and create a new approach to meet and attract younger generations to join their lodges.

5. Mentoring and Educating New Members

When membership decline set in, many lodges became so desperate for new members that when they got an applicant, they immediately rushed him or her into initiation. Some lodges became so small that "it became difficult to form a team of adequate members to properly present the degrees of initiation."[34] Members and candidates alike did not understand some of the language of the degrees. Once the new member was initiated, the lodge never saw him or her again.

Growing lodges do not make joining too quick and easy for the prospective new members. They make them go through a "mentoring process" that takes about six months before conferring to them all the degrees of initiation.[35] During this period, the candidates are educated about the history, principles, purposes, and organizational structure of Odd Fellowship. In Davis Odd Fellows Lodge No.169, Dave Rosenberg shares that "the candidates are required to meet and interview a minimum of 13 of our members, and to attend a minimum of 8 of their social meetings, join and participate in the committees, plan events for the lodge and the community."[36] This gives them "a chance to meet the members and for the members to meet them and determine if Odd Fellowship is the right organization to join."[37] This process will also help prepare a new member to become a well-informed future leader of the lodge. A similar membership procedure had been proven successful in Europe. In 1999, the IOOF International Council (now known as International Advisory Board) emphasized that:[38]

To become an Odd Fellow is the result of a process. To appreciate its importance as an organization does not happen instantly. If the teachings about the history, purposes, teachings and the essence of Odd Fellowship shall have any significance and value, then the process cannot be overlooked. Without imparting to the new member these teachings and knowledge, you betray the new member, you betray the Order, of its important principles and goals.

When the time the traineeship is over, then each new member is well-equipped to go on: to spread friendship, love and truth in the surrounding community; to strengthen his or her trust of the Creator he or she believes in; to strengthen the love for thy neighbor, and to know that words are not enough. And because words are not enough, it is necessary to translate these principles into actions, each to the best of his or her ability, so that everyone of us may help participate in the uplifting of humankind. The purpose of odd Fellowship is found in the teachings of our rituals. The goal is to work for and to live with compassion, understanding and tolerance, based upon Friendship, Love and Truth.

6. Accepting New Ideas

Getting new members is not enough. If Odd Fellowship is to survive in the coming age, the organization must survive on the feet of the younger generations. Many stagnant and declining lodges frankly need new ideas, new approaches, and new visions. However, a lodge cannot get younger generations to stay active where majority of its members and officers are all in their 60s and 70s and have been the same officers for the past 10 years or so. At some point, long-time members have to allow a younger generation of leaders to develop and to grow. They cannot continue to dominate their Grand Lodge and lodge and impose the ways they are used to doing.

A big problem in several Grand Lodges and lodges is the presence of some long-time members who just cannot let go of the "control" they have exercised for many years.[39] This often results in a situation that is detrimental "to the organization and to the good fellowship among new and long-time members." [40] Situations could occur when a new member suggests a new idea for the lodge, but long-time members would vehemently reject this idea with statements such as "We can't do that," "It won't work," or "It's against the Code."[41] In many instances, this would make the young member feel that he doesn't have a voice in the lodge. As a result, he or she stops attending meetings because of frustration over being barred of participation in the decision-making.

Undoubtedly, a change of attitude on the part of the senior members is important if the organization is to overcome the great "generation gap." There is a need to allow younger generations to offer new ideas, take leadership roles, and make decisions for the organization if the old timers want them to stay active. This approach has been proven effective in lodges that continue to grow despite the challenging times. In one example, one lodge separated their younger group of members aged 18 to 45 and gave them a meeting room in the lodge hall, which they ran as their own lodge in implementing their own local programs. This way, they worked in their own age group and, after one year, they brought in three times the number of members that the older group secured.

Growing lodges are those who have an active training plan for the new members to assume leadership responsibilities. Lodges that are experiencing membership growth today are those who are able to develop new leaders every year. One way of knowing whether the lodge is producing new leaders is by finding out if younger and newer members are taking on leadership roles and positions.

Yet the organization cannot simply ask younger members to join and then turn them loose. The senior members must allow younger members to demonstrate strengths within the harness of what Odd Fellowship is all about for them in this day and age. Younger members, on the other hand, must also be willing to learn from the experience and wisdom of the senior members.

7. Embracing Diversity

It has been suggested that "lodges that are diverse - with men and women, coming from different ethnic origins, different ages, religion, and professions - are the lodges that will thrive in the future."[42] Bringing in members who are of the same age as existing members is not sustainable. Lodges that have become viable, vibrant, and active

Good leadership requires you to surround yourself with people of diverse perspectives who can disagree with you without fear of retaliation.

Doris Kearns Goodwin

are those that have members who encompass all generations (those who are in their 20s, 30s, 40s, 50s, 60s, 70s, and 80s).

The admission of women in the Odd Fellows Lodges has been proven effective for their growth and sustainability especially in areas where there are no Rebekah or Sister Lodges. *Dallas Odd Fellows Lodge No. 44* in Oak Cliff, Texas, is composed of both men and women, and is currently one of the fastest-growing lodges in the United States. Astonishingly, the lodge members' median age is 40 and there are more women members than men.[43] *Victoria Odd Fellows Lodge No. 1* in British Columbia has similarly grown by admitting women, and many of the new members are in their 20s and 30s.[44] Likewise, *Ocean View Odd Fellows Lodge No. 143* in Half Moon Bay, California has grown to more than 80 members and women comprise a substantial part of the membership.[45] One reason for the attraction is that some women want to do something together with their husbands. In other areas, the number of men or women is just not enough to organize two separate lodges for men and women. Single-sex lodges seem to work best only when the number of women and men members have substantially grown to at least 50 because it is only at this point when having separate branches for men and women may become practicable.

Embracing members from various ethnic and racial backgrounds also has helped sustain the charters of several lodges. One of the most diverse lodges in the United States, Y*erba Buena Odd Fellows Lodge*

No.15 in San Francisco, California, has proven that embracing people from different ethnic and social backgrounds helps in the growth of lodge membership. With globalization, those lodges whose members show racial prejudice will diminish and face negative public criticism. Indeed, many IOOF lodges in South Carolina and some parts in Latin America closed because some members simply refused to accept non-whites in their lodges. The problem can occur when the people who control the lodge still hold prejudicial attitudes towards people from other racial backgrounds.

8. Well-maintained Buildings and Technology

For many lodges, the Odd Fellows building is their most prized possession. Many Odd Fellows buildings are located in the center of town. It is fascinating that memberships have been revitalized in some lodges because of non-members' curiosity about historic Odd Fellows' Halls. In 2009, a group of people in Arbuckle, California, were able to successfully revive the *Spring Valley Odd Fellows Lodge No.316* because of their interest in the abandoned historic IOOF building in their area. However, many of these buildings are now in bad condition and need renovation. There are many lodges that do not even have a signboard telling the public that an Odd Fellows or Rebekah Lodge meets inside the building. There are lodges whose officers do not use e-mail or social media platforms and do not have Wi-Fi capability in their lodge halls.

Many buildings owned by the Odd Fellows in the United States and Canada are historic buildings and are attractive to historians and artists. Growing lodges of today are those who take great pride in their building's appearance and amenities. Their members have made sure that these are well-maintained and clean. They placed sign boards outside their buildings. Some made their buildings the hangout for their members by adding up-to-date technology – flat screen televisions, LCD projectors, Wi-Fi, PlayStation, etc. Pairing the rich history and antiquity with new technology undoubtedly aided several lodges to exponentially grow. However, some Odd Fellows buildings are located on the seedy side of town. The best option for some lodges in this situation is to sell their old building and relocate their lodge to a better area for it to attract more members. But they

The ornate meeting rooms, symbolism, and initiation ceremonies of Odd Fellowship has recently intrigued a number of younger generations to join. Photo by the author, 2019.

should use the proceeds of the sale of their old building to buy a new one. The mistake of many lodges in the past was selling their building and opting to lease a room from other similar organizations. After a few years, they eventually found themselves struggling to pay the rent and regretting why they did not use their lodge money to purchase a new one that is income-generating.

9. Effective Conflict Management

The biggest problem of most lodges is when internal issues or conflicts occur between members. Lodges that are declining are also those whose membership resort to back-biting and gossiping against each other. Infighting over lodge money or other petty disagreements is one of the major causes why many members quit. This usually happens when the leadership and membership fail to understand and internalize the true meaning of Odd Fellowship. Depending on how effective the conflict management is, misunderstandings can ruin the relationship between members and could lead to the closure of the lodge.

Successful lodges of today are those that have put in place an effective conflict resolution and risk management plan in place to resolve or prevent conflicts from happening. These are lodges that put greater importance on relationships over finances, position, and individual pride. These are the ones whose members do not necessarily agree all the time, but nevertheless have mutual-respect for each other. If effectively conveyed, the Odd Fellows motto - Friendship, Love, and Truth - and the teachings in the degrees of initiation will show the members how to capably deal with their differences.

The procedure for conflict resolution could vary per jurisdiction. But every lodge should first settle all controversies and conflicts internally or within the lodge. It is the duty of the officers to exert all possible efforts to settle the differences between its members before appealing to the Grand Lodge or The Sovereign Grand Lodge and before resorting to civil courts. To avoid injustice, the accused-member must always be given an opportunity to be heard and to present evidence in defense of the accusations against him or her. Due process may be achieved through the following steps:

- A written complaint with attached evidences shall be submitted to the Lodge Secretary who shall then forward it to the Noble Grand;

- The Noble Grand shall see if the issues can be settled amicably. He or she will exert his or her best efforts to personally meet the opposing parties and find ways to settle the matter peacefully through mediation or conference;

- If amicable settlement is impossible, the Noble Grand shall appoint an Investigation Committee composed of not less than three (3) impartial members in good standing (usually Past Grands). The Investigation Committee shall inform the accused of the charges in writing and shall give him or her an opportunity to answer and be heard.

- If the Investigation Committee finds that there is truth or probable cause about the charges, the Noble Grand shall present the case to the lodge during a regular or special meeting. Depending on the bylaws, the final decision to suspend or expel a member shall be by majority or 2/3 votes of the members in good standing. Usually, the penalty for first time offenders is only reprimand; suspension for second time offenders; and expulsion for third time or repeated offenders. But it is advised that expulsion shall only be resorted to when it involves grave offenses that causes irreparable harm to a member or serious disharmony in the lodge.

Grand Sire Gordon Bitter of the Grand Lodge of Australasia received a *Plaque of Appreciation* from the Grand Lodge of the Philippines of the Independent Order of Odd Fellows. Photo by the author, 2019.

- A member who is dissatisfied with the decision of the lodge may then appeal his or her case to the Grand Lodge following the procedure required thereof.

10. Positive Reward System

Growing lodges are those that show appreciation and recognition to their members. Every lodge should organize an awards ceremony once a year to recognize members who show exemplary service and involvement in the lodge and the community. These may be done by giving small certificates or pins to let the member know that his or her contributions are appreciated. From a psychological perspective, this will inspire members to do their best for the good of the organization and will increase the morale of the lodge. Below are some awards that can be bestowed to a member:

- **Veteran's Lapel Pin or Jewel**

The Veteran's lapel pin or jewel is awarded to members for a continuous membership in the Odd Fellows. A member with 5 years of continuous membership and onwards is entitled to a Veteran's button or jewel, with the number in the center set to the number of years of membership in the Order. The Veteran's button begins at 5 years and is available in 5-year increments. The available numbers for the Veteran's jewel are 25, 30, 35, 40, 45, 50, 55, 60, 65, 70 or 75.

- **Past Grand's Lapel Pin or Jewel**

      The Past Grand's lapel pin or jewel is awarded to an outgoing Noble Grand who has successfully served his or her term of office. This award is usually bestowed by the lodge upon being installed in the office of Immediate Past Grand during the Ceremony of Installation of Officers.

- **Merit Jewel**

      The Merit Jewel is a three-part jewel of gold metal. The jewel may be presented to an Odd Fellow in good standing for his lodge and community service worthy of special recognition. The lodge shall apply to Grand Lodge for permission to award this jewel, giving a detailed explanation of the services rendered. If the Merit Award Committee of the Grand Lodge approves, the lodge is notified to purchase the jewel.

- **Meritorious Service Jewel**

      The Meritorious Service Jewel may be awarded to an Odd Fellow for meritorious service performed on behalf of Odd Fellowship beyond the usual and customary duties of membership. The lodge shall apply to Grand Lodge or The Sovereign Grand Lodge for permission to award this jewel, giving a detailed explanation of the services rendered. If the Meritorious Service Award Committee of the Grand Lodge or The Sovereign Grand Lodge approves, the lodge is notified to purchase the jewel.

- **Other Awards and Certificates of Recognition**

      The Noble Grand or the Executive Committee of the lodge or Grand Lodge may also create and grant other awards and certificates in recognition for the admirable dedication and service of their members in good standing. *Example:* Odd Fellow of the Year Award, Community Service Award, etc.

Rituals, Secret Handshakes and Regalia

In order to fully understand the mission and vision of Odd Fellowship, it is a tradition that candidates undergo a formal and solemn ritual ceremony that involves a series of instructions divided into degrees. Traditionally, these degrees of initiation are presented largely by means of lectures, drama and symbols where every stage or degree concentrates on one of the principles of the organization.

Admittedly, the rituals are the most misunderstood aspect of every fraternal order. But, for Odd Fellows, each degree is a time for reflection for the candidates. The goal is to give new members an experience that is unique from everyday life while imparting wise lessons and noble principles that are applicable to daily life. These rituals are also "a means by which members could define one another as brothers and sisters."[1] It is common belief that the bond between people is stronger when they share common knowledge and similar experiences.

The dramatic ceremonies of the degrees of initiation are attractive and impressive to younger generations if performed from memory or at least with solemnity and especially with costumes. Photo by the author, 2019.

When a member visits an Odd Fellows Lodge in a different city or country, he or she will feel "at home" because the ceremonies are performed almost in the same way. Through these rituals, members are welded together and will feel a sense of belonging in their pursuit of the Odd Fellows' high ideals, ethics and teachings. But it is the lessons taught by the degrees, not the degrees themselves, which are fundamental.[2] The degrees are complementary to and not the primary purpose of the organization's existence.[3] Having shared customs and core values is very important in every organization. San Francisco Metaphysical lecturer Dadisi Sanyika observed:

> Where there is no formal initiation process, an unconscious rite of passage will occur. This unconscious initiation will often be anti-social rather than a systematic transmission of values and knowledge. Initiation into urban street gangs is a case in point, where the aspects of initiation appear in a process that does not renew the community or its values.

There is no hazing or horseplay in the initiation rituals of Odd Fellowship. There is nothing sinister that happens inside the lodge rooms. Although a certain level of secrecy or privacy prevails around its ceremonies, the Odd Fellows is in no sense an occult or secret society. The Independent Order of Odd Fellows has a very public agenda to promote and does not claim any secret knowledge to conceal from the public. In fact, some of its degrees and symbols are largely drawn from the Old Testament. For the most part, the initiation rituals only serve as a method of teaching the candidate the ethical lessons and core principles shared among members and, at the same time, provide a sense of mystery and fascination to both members and candidates. In the past, the degrees also provided entertainment at a time when television and other modern leisure activities did not exist as yet. If done properly, witnessing an initiation ritual is like watching a theatrical play and also gives a sense of decorum during meetings.

Handshakes, Passwords and Symbols

There are confidential or private hand signs, grips, and passwords for each degree known as *The Unwritten Work* (TUW).

Evolution of the IOOF Rituals

The rituals of initiation in Odd Fellowship have evolved through time. Older versions were often revised by newer groups. And because of the numerous *Affiliated Orders* of Odd Fellows that previously existed, there occur several variations of the Odd Fellows' rituals today. Evidence suggests that the succession chronologically began with the *Ancient Order of Odd Fellows*, which changed to the *Improved Order of Odd Fellows*, the *Patriotic Order of Odd Fellows*, the *Union or United Order of Odd Fellows*, and the *Manchester Unity Independent Order of Odd Fellows* from which the *Independent Order of Odd Fellows* seceded.[1]

It had been asserted that the earliest ritualistic ceremonies of the Odd Fellows consisted only of an *initiation* or *making* and a form of *opening and closing* the lodge.[2] Just like other fraternal organizations, the additional degrees and dramatic work in Odd Fellowship were an evolution of later years because of the demand for additional attractions in the ceremonies.[3] The oldest surviving initiation rituals and degrees belonged to the *Order of Patriotic Odd Fellows* as revised and agreed by their Grand Lodge in London on March 12, 1797. It contained an *Opening and Closing Service*, an *Initiation* and four degrees, namely: *White or Degree of Covenant*, *Royal Blue Degree*, and *Pink or Merit Degree*, and *Royal Arch of Titus or Fidelity Degree*.[4] These degrees were conferred one after the other, one degree only every three or four months. Although the lessons of the Odd Fellowship emphasized tolerance and understanding, the legend and basis behind these ancient degrees showed the Judeo-Christian roots of the early members of Odd Fellowship. Undeniably, England was a predominantly Christian state and majority of its population remain to be Christians. It is but natural for the rituals of Odd Fellows to be highly influenced by Judeo-Christian traditions.

When the *Ancient Order of Odd Fellows* and the *Patriotic Order of Odd Fellows* merged into the *Grand United Order of Odd Fellows* (GUOOF) in 1798,[23] evidence suggests that most of the political and religious terms were removed. The late-18th to mid-19th century was actually the beginning of the de-Christianization and de-politicization of the rituals. Most fraternal orders such as Freemasonry and Odd Fellowship revised their rituals to become religiously neutral as possible and members were forbidden to discuss politics and religion within their meetings. This is to promote the harmony and welfare of its members despite their differences in creed and politics.

In 1814, the Independent Order of Oddfellows Manchester Unity started a major revision of the ancient rituals. The first printed ritual of the Manchester Unity IOOF divided the degrees into the *Initiation* or *Making*; *First Degree* or *White*; *Second Degree* or *Royal Blue*, *Scarlet Degree* or *Priestly Order*.[5] There was also a lecture book that consisted of *Lectures to Prove a Secretary*, *Lectures to Prove a Vice Grand*, and *Lecture to Prove a Past Grand*.[6] Further revisions were made since 1816.

For a time, the Independent Order of Odd Fellows in the United States adopted similar rituals with those of the Manchester Unity IOOF. In 1820, the Grand Lodge of the United States added the degrees of *Covenant* and *Remembrance* written by John Pawson Entwisle.[7] However, evidence shows that these degrees bore some similarity with those used by the Order of Patriotic Odd Fellows. Somehow, this suggests that the *Covenant* and *Remembrance* degrees were but a revision or re-introduction of what were abandoned from Ancient Ritual. These two degrees were adopted by both the IOOFMU and IOOF in 1826. By 1835, the ritualistic work had been divided into the *Initiatory Degree*, *First Degree*, *Degree of the Covenant*, *Second Degree or Royal Blue*, *Degree of Remembrance*, *Scarlet Degree or Priestly Order*.[8] The same lecture book also contained merit degrees for the Secretary, Vice Grand, and Noble Grand.

In 1834, the IOOFMU revised the lecture book and dropped the *degrees of the Covenant and Remembrance*. This, along with other substantial revisions, led to the separation of the IOOFMU and the IOOF. Afterwards, the IOOF further revised the ritualistic works into the *Initiatory Degree* and five degrees, namely: *White or First Degree*, *Pink or Second Degree (Covenant)*,

Blue or Third Degree, Green or Fourth Degree (Remembrance), and *Scarlet or Fifth Degree*.[9] This system of degrees continued without material change until 1880 when the number of degrees was reduced into three. The Initiatory Degree was expanded. The teachings of the White or First Degree and the Pink or Second Degree were combined into the *Degree of Friendship* or *First Degree*.[10] The teachings of the former Blue or Third Degree and Green or Fourth Degree became the basis of the *Degree of Love* or *Second Degree*.[11] The Scarlet or Fifth Degree became the nucleus for the *Degree of Truth* or *Third Degree*. A number of amendments followed but these only involved minor alterations. In 2018, the Sovereign Grand Lodge approved an alternative version of the Initiatory Degree but this is not widely used in the United States nor is this adopted by lodges in other countries.

Historically, the Odd Fellows provided material and financial aid for their members in times of sickness, economic distress, or for finding employment when out of work. Because of this benefit, there were many instances when some people would pretend to be members to defraud or obtain funds from the lodge. So, how can the Odd Fellows verify membership and protect their funds from impostors? How can a person prove that he is a member eligible to avail himself of the fraternal benefits?

As there were no telephones at that time and the mode of communication was still very slow, secret hand signs, grips, passwords and symbols were created mainly to verify membership and protect the funds of the organization from impostors.[33] These tools are really unimportant to the outside world since they served simply the purpose of mutual recognition between members. The logic behind this is almost the same why banks and people today use secret PINs and passwords to protect their money from theft and other fraudulent activities.

Until today, the Independent Order of Odd Fellows has preserved these hand signs, grips, passwords, and symbols mainly to honor a tradition. For many members, these still remain as a faster way of identifying each other even without the assistance of modern

During the 1700s to 1900s, secret hand grips, hand signs and symbols were a very important way of verifying membership and communicating ideas at a time when communication was very slow and illiteracy was widespread. These allowed people from various social classes to understand each other whether or not they could read or write, or what language they speak. This practice is still being used by Odd Fellows today as a mode of identifying members and to preserve the Order's heritage. Shown is an obsolete hand sign formerly used by Odd Fellows before the revision in 1879.

Courtesy of The Sovereign Grand Lodge IOOF.

technology, although some think they are nonsense. Moreover, these signs and symbols stand as reminders for some of the basic ethical principles and teachings of the fraternity. Some of the moral lessons of the IOOF are actually incorporated as symbolic meanings of the unwritten work. These signs, grips, passwords, and symbols are designed to speak one universal language to the initiated of every nationality across the world. The passwords are not translated into any other language, nor spoken other than as they are written. This is for every member to learn to give them "one universal sound as nearly as possible, so that the sound of the password will be familiar to the ear as the signs are to the eye, or the grip to the touch of the hand, to the end that an Odd Fellow of any country may be known and recognized in any part of the inhabited globe as a brother or sister."[4]

Regalia

Fraternal orders, like the Odd Fellows and Freemasons, drew on a common folk tradition of civic and guild dress and custom.[5] Like other ancient fraternities, the early members of the Independent Order of Odd Fellows wore collars and aprons represented by different colors for each degree. The IOOF abandoned the use of aprons when

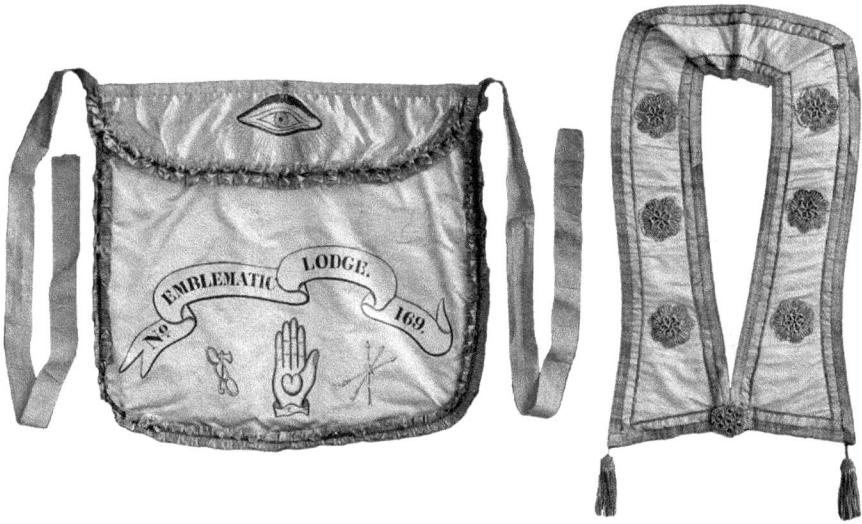

Early 1800s Past Grand collar and hand-painted apron showing some of the early symbols of Odd Fellowship: heart-and-hand, all-seeing-eye, three links chain, axe, and arrows.

it revised its rituals in 1880 but still continue to use either collar, rope or chain regalia. The principal reason for the removal was to relieve the membership from the burden of having to buy too many regalia. Other affiliated Orders, such as the Manchester Unity (IOOFMU) and Grand United Order of Odd Fellows (GUOOF) still use aprons as part of their ritualistic customs.

The wearing of regalia is historic and symbolic. Like a uniform, the regalia indicates the rank of the wearer in the organization. The regalia also represents equality. It enforces that all brothers and sisters are one and the same. The markings of color represent the degree or duties which the wearer has received but this does not imply that those with more degrees are more valuable or more important than others. The differences in color simply means that the bearer has attained higher duties and moral vows as an Odd Fellow - each color is a reminder to translate into deeds and actions the teachings they have learned.

How many degrees are there in Odd Fellowship?

It will depend which Odd Fellows organization you will join.

Different Versions of the Odd Fellows' regalia through the years

From upper left: A sash and apron of the IOOF Manchester Unity Friendly Society. Next is a collar and apron used by IOOF in North America during the early 1800s. The apron was removed in the IOOF starting in 1881. The third photo is an early 1900s Past Grand collar regalia of the IOOF. ***From lower left:*** Rope-type regalia with officer's jewel commonly used by the IOOF lodges in the Netherlands, Belgium, Cuba and some lodges in the United States. The second photo shows the modern chain-type regalia with officer's jewel, which is commonly used in the United States and Canada. The last is the more ornate velvet-type regalia with officer's jewel. Photos by the author, 2019.

The rituals between the GUOOF, IOOFMU and IOOF vary. As it stands, the IOOF rituals consist of the *Initiatory Degree* and three (3) degrees: *Degree of Friendship or First Degree, Degree of Love or Second Degree,* and *Degree of Truth or Third Degree*

What is the working degree in the Odd Fellows Lodge?

All Odd Fellows Lodges open and hold their meetings in the Initiatory Degree except when conferring a particular degree. This is to allow a new member to participate in the meetings. The Lodge will open in a higher degree when advancing its members to a higher degree.

Is memorization required while conducting the ritual?

Traditionally, the officers and members conducting the ritual are required to put in memory the charges in the rituals. In the past, the degrees were not actually put into print so every member must memorize the whole ritual. Memorization is still being done in several lodges. Of course, a theatrical play is more impressive when the actors are not reading their lines from a script. However, this custom had been already relaxed in other lodges especially those located in the United States and Canada. A number of lodges now allow the reading of the ritual book while performing the degrees.

Is there a dress code in the Odd Fellows?

It depends on the lodge and Grand Lodge. Traditionally, members and candidates were expected to wear formal or business attire during lodge meetings and especially when conferring the degrees. Dress code was a *symbol of equality* in the past, so that everyone inside the lodge would look the same regardless of their social and economic status. This remains to be the tradition in Europe where members and candidates are required to wear suit and tie. In the Philippines, members and candidates are also required to wear their traditional formal attire especially when conferring the degrees.

But the dress code has been relaxed in other countries especially in the United States and Canada. In many rural places, members are

The cultural shift of the 21st century has led toward casualness in the way people dress during lodge meetings. Photo by Scott Wayne McDaniel of Dallas Odd Fellows Lodge No.44, 2017.

agricultural workers, barbers, mechanics and farmers and they travel for how many miles after work to attend their lodge. Many of these lodges have allowed casual clothes – jeans, shorts, and denim shirts. Many cultures are also becoming more casual or informal. In fact, many business corporations now encourage their employees to wear their most comfortable casual attire at work. This cultural change had an impact on the requirement of dress code inside the Lodge. But most IOOF jurisdictions still strictly require a business attire during Grand Lodge sessions.

Do Odd Fellows use a goat in their initiations?

No. The Odd Fellows never used a goat in their initiations and still do not use any animal whatsoever in the rituals. The lodge goat was started by people who wanted to discredit the solemn ceremonies of fraternal orders. It was started as a rumor to destroy the image of fraternal orders. The lodge goat eventually became a popular "joke or prank" for candidates and among members. This joke was usually done outside of the lodge room during social gatherings and before the solemn initiation ceremony is held. But the rules of the Odd Fellows strictly prohibit the use of animals in the ceremonies of Odd Fellowship.

The "Lodge Goat" eventually became a fad within fraternal orders. It became a popular prank for several years that many members used the goat in pins, banners and all sorts of lodge paraphernalia and merchandise.

Initiatory Degree

The Initiatory degree is an introduction to the Odd Fellows Lodge. The candidate is led into the Lodge room in darkness and deprived of liberty as a representation of human being's lesser state of consciousness or limited wisdom. These symbolic limitations are later removed to symbolize awakening or rebirth.

The very first lesson this degree teaches to the candidate is the comparison of the Lodge room with the outside world. In that comparison, it is shown that while competition, struggle and division exist in the outside world, there are none inside the Odd Fellows because "friendship and love mildly assert their dominion while faith and charity combine to bless the mind with peace and mellow the heart with sympathy."[1] This sends a message that the Lodge room is designed to provide its members harmony and peace of mind. Subsequently, the candidate will witness a representation of mortality and further reminded of the temporary nature of life on earth. The quality of human life is fitly represented by four seasons of the year: *Spring*, represents the stage of childhood and youth when innocence and beauty are so manifest; *Summer*, represents maturity or adulthood when full stature is attained and the muscles of the physical are developed; *Autumn* represents age and its infirmities when the face becomes pale, sallow and the brow becomes wrinkled; *Winter* represents death as the final destination of all humankind.[2] The latter stages are symbolically represented by the coffin, fading leaf, dead rose and old man, which begs the question "how will I live my life?" The candidate is then introduced to the very foundation of Odd Fellowship – *universal fraternity* in the family of humankind. Odd Fellowship do not believe in the divisions and classifications of society. The rich and poor, high and low, learned and unlearned, come together as brothers and sisters to work for the common good.

It is a common characteristic of many ancient rites that they begin in sorrow and gloom, but end up in life and joy. The symbolic purpose is to remind candidates of their weakness, their ignorance, their sinfulness of character and the shortness and uncertainty of life. Being reminded of death as unstoppable, the candidate is encouraged to live a virtuous life. What a virtuous life means to an Odd Fellow is taught in the succeeding degrees.

Why are there coffins and skeletons inside abandoned Odd Fellows Lodges?

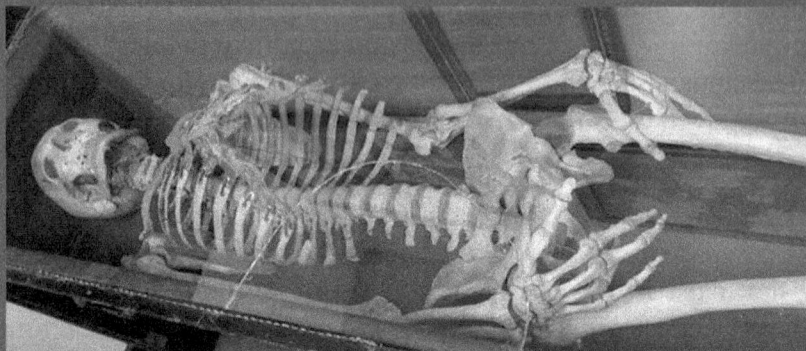

"George", who was an Odd Fellow in the 1800s, donated his remains for lodge ceremonies. Photo from Odd Fellows Home in Liberty, Missouri.

Some people buying, renting, repairing or renovating old Odd Fellows' buildings have opened floorboards, attics or drawers and found inside a coffin and a full-body skeleton. These incidents have caused alarm and worry from people and have been published in a number of newspapers and online blogs. But there is really nothing creepy about it and such is not used to scare people.

Customarily, the Odd Fellows use a life-sized coffin and skeleton as a prop in acting out a drama in the Initiatory Degree. For this reason, lodges usually keep a fake coffin and skeleton or one made of papier-mâché. In the old days, the skeleton is usually bought from a supplier. In rare cases, some deceased members actually donated their skeletons to the lodge. This prop merely represents the mortality of humankind. The goal is to make the initiate aware of his or her own mortality in hope that he or she will be encouraged to live a virtuous life. What a virtuous life means for Odd Fellows are then taught in the next degrees.

Some lodges no longer use full-body skeletons. Instead, they use a fake skull, or a plastic gravestone, or an urn to remind the initiates of their temporary nature here on earth.

Regalia and Symbolic Color of the Initiatory Degree

The regalia of the Initiatory Degree is a *white collar* with *white lining*. White is symbolic color for the Initiatory Degree because it represents purity and innocence. Symbolically, it stands for everything that is good and right. White also represents a successful beginning and the cleansing of the mind and body. The Initiatory Degree is the leaving of the old and the beginning of a new life for the initiate.

Symbols of the Initiatory Degree

The symbols of the Initiatory Degree are the following: All-seeing Eye, Three Links Chain, Skull and Crossbones, and Scythe.

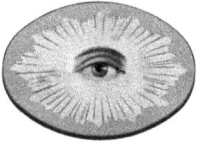

The *All-Seeing Eye* represents the eternal presence of the eye of the Supreme Being upon all of us, day and night. A liar and pretentious individual may fool other human beings but the Supreme Being can penetrate and see through every dishonesty and exaggeration. This symbol also represents trust – an Odd Fellow is obliged to keep private any confidential matter that a brother and sister or the Lodge confides to him or her. Destroy the element of trust and the very foundation of every fraternity is broken into pieces. A genuine Odd Fellow remains honest and faithful to his or her obligations even when others are not looking.

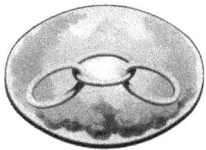

The *Three Links Chain* represents the principles of Friendship, Love and Truth. The first link is Friendship, the second link is Love and the third link is truth. This is emblematical of the chain that binds us together in an enduring union and establishes the principles every Odd Fellow is ought to live in accordance with.

The *Skull and Crossbones* remind us of our mortality and the duty we have to a departed brother or sister. All that lives will eventually die.

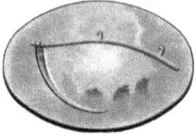

The *Scythe* reminds us of death and the fact that it can arrive without warning. As the grass falls before the mower's scythe, so we shall fall before the touch of time. It is a reminder of the fact that there is always an end to everything and this ending will unexpectedly happen any hour, any day and anywhere. This admonishes an Odd Fellow to live his or her life responsibly.

The Unwritten Work

Traditionally, the candidate in this degree will be taught the following: (1) Entersigns, (2) Password of the Degree, (3) Countersign and Answer, (4) Grip of the Initiatory Degree, (5) Link, (6) Sign of Recognition and its Answer, (7) Odd Fellows' grip, (8) Sign of Distress, (9) Voting Sign, (10) Interfraternal Sign and (11) Honors of the Order. These must be learned during the degree itself and must not be communicated to anyone unauthorized to receive them. However, a number in the list are no longer taught in most jurisdictions especially in the United States and Canada.

Degree of Friendship or First Degree

This degree reenacts an ancient story to exemplify the lesson of true friendship. Two different individuals are shown: One is a shepherd and the son of a comparatively poor and insignificant person while the other is a prince and the son of a King. Though different in their positions and backgrounds, the royal prince looked at the shepherd as his equal.[1] As their acquaintance developed, they pledged themselves into a covenant of friendship.

As the story unfolds, the candidate will further witness two sides of human nature: *hate and jealousy* on one hand while *love and protection* on the other. When the King became jealous of the triumphs of the shepherd, he wanted to kill him but the royal prince pleaded for the life of his friend. When the King was hunting for the life of the shepherd, the royal prince warned his friend of the approaching danger. The royal prince protected the shepherd even though he knew that, in doing so, he would sacrifice his wealth, power and status as successor of the king. In the end, he even gave the throne in favor of his shepherd friend whom he believed was more worthy to become the leader of the kingdom. And when the shepherd became King,

The goal of the Degree of Friendship is to promote sincere and unselfish friendships among its members. Photo by the author, 2019.

he made the royal prince a member of his household and gave him royal inheritance.[2] The Prince never betrayed the shepherd even though he knew all his power and wealth would be given to the latter. The Shepherd likewise never hurt nor betrayed the Prince but even welcomed him in his kingdom despite the fact that the latter was the son of the King who tried to kill the shepherd.

This degree teaches that true friendship will not be divided by wealth, power and ambitions. True friends will help, protect, and rejoice in each other's accomplishments and will not be divided by jealous competitions and selfish desires. True friends will not abandon their friendship in exchange of fame, wealth, titles and honors. Jealousy or envy is a malicious foe of virtue. This degree admonishes Odd Fellows to help and protect each other through good and bad times. This degree furthermore teaches that the good should unite together to fight against the evil.

Regalia and Symbolic Color of the Degree of Friendship

The regalia of the Degree of Friendship is a *white* collar with *pink* lining. Pink is the symbolic color for friendship because it is associated with the feelings of nurturing, tenderness and care. As a mixture of red and white, pink takes all the passion and energy of red and tempers it with the purity of white, leaving a color of tenderness and affection. The color also symbolizes gentleness and carefulness in handling any situation or thing. A true friend is gentle and caring to his or her friends.

Symbols of the Degree of Friendship

The symbols of the degree of friendship are the following: Bow and Arrows, Quiver and Bundle of Sticks.

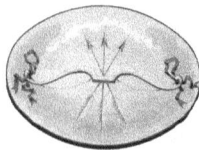

The *Bow and Arrows* remind us of the friendship between the prince and the shepherd. This was used by the prince to warn the shepherd of an approaching danger. Normally, the bow and arrows are weapons used to repulse enemy attacks. For Odd Fellows, this weapon is not used as an instrument of destruction or injury. Instead, this is used as protection from danger and to maintain peace. This is also emblematic of mutual-assistance. A bow is useless without an arrow and an arrow does not have its power without the bow. In a true friendship, one friend helps another or sometimes he or she is the one receiving help. This also reminds us that we should always be ready to do battle in the cause of truth and justice.

The *Quiver* is the receptacle from which the prince drew his arrows. Without the quiver, the arrows would become bent and useless. Without compassion for each other, the friendship that we want to teach is incomplete. This reminds us to put forth every effort to protect and help a brother or sister when in danger, and to watch over his or her interests when in distress.

The *Bundle of Sticks* symbolizes the strength of unity as compared with the weakness of one who is alone. While one single stick is easily broken, a bundle of sticks cannot be easily broken. Separated, we can easily be broken and destroyed by the accumulated tide of worldly selfishness; but united as brothers and sisters, we can face all opposition and win over the greatest difficulties. United in the bonds of fraternity, we are also able to better organize and execute our benevolent purposes and accomplish the goals that Odd Fellowship proposes to accomplish.

The Unwritten Work

Traditionally, the candidate in this degree will be taught the following: (1) Alarm, (2) Password of the Degree, (3) Sign of the Degree and its Answer, (4) Grip of the First Degree, (5) Memento and (6) Token. These must be learned during the degree itself and must not be communicated to anyone unauthorized to receive them. However, the First Degree handgrip is no longer taught in almost all jurisdictions located in North America and Europe.

Odd Fellowship aims to teach and promote worldwide friendships beyond nationality, ethnicity, gender, religion, political inclination or socio-economic status in life. Photos from Lagos Lodge No.2 (Nigeria), Sant'Ambrogio Lodge No.2 (Italy), and Hijos del Mar Lodge No.11 (Cuba).

Degree of Love or Second Degree

This degree is likewise based on an ancient story, depicting the lesson of brotherly or sisterly love which transcends race, religion or nationality. In this story, two travelers from two opposing religions and cultures are portrayed.

The candidate will witness one traveler who fell among thieves and was wounded. He has been robbed and left dying by the roadside. By chance, a priest came that way but passed by on the other side when he saw the wounded person. Likewise, a Levite just looked at the wounded and passed on the other side. Subsequently, a second traveler from an opposing tribe and creed saw him. The second traveler knew that the wounded person belonged to a tribe and creed that was hostile to his. He was an enemy of his people. But instead of walking away and leaving him behind, he set aside his own prejudices and differences to help the wounded. He wrapped the wounded person with his garment, brought him to a place of safety and paid for all the expenses needed for his recovery. This is genuine kindness.

As an Odd Fellow, one is expected to make the same commitment not to look at people with prejudiced eyes. The principles

One of the goals of Odd Fellowship is to promote the ethic of reciprocity based on a famous maxim found in almost all world religions and cultures known as the Golden Rule: "Do unto others what you want others to do unto you." Photo from public domain.

The Warden and the Broad Axe

Customarily, Odd Fellows' lodges collect donations for the needy and distressed members using the Warden's axe, which usually have the heart-and-hand symbol engraved or painted on it.

The taking of a collection for any member "in distress" is a custom that originated from the guilds. On the continent, an artisan would work as an apprentice for a term of at least seven years and was not permitted to work in one place for more than two years. So, he would go "tramping" from one town to another with his goods on his back and a stick in hand. Sometimes, the poor artisan does not have enough funds to pay his expenses. Thus, members who are traveling from place to place in England frequently receive temporary assistance from lodges.

When the Noble Grand asked the question, "Is there any tramp in waiting?" If answered in the affirmative, the Warden quickly made the rounds with his broad axe to receive contributions to help a traveling member. The Warden walks around the lodge room holding the axe flat and those that wish to offer up some pocket change or a couple bucks then place the money on the blade.

of this degree carry assistance to the needy and distressed of every caste and environment.[1] Every person is a brother or sister. Love is the principle which unites the different factions and classes of people in one or more great parties and organizations. This is the central link in the chain of Odd Fellowship because it is the link of toleration, understanding and charity.[2] This is based on the Golden Rule: "*Do unto others as you would have them do unto you.*" The person who serves others, serves himself or herself best. The degree further teaches the candidate that fraternity, unless linked with acts of kindness, is but an empty name.

Regalia and Symbolic Color of the Degree of Love

The regalia is a *white* collar with *royal blue* lining. Royal blue is the symbolic color for brotherly or sisterly love because it is the color of both the sky and the oceans whose heights and depths know no limits. It is also the color of empathy and dependability. This color further represents equality, since its hue suggests a shade midway between white and black. Blue also symbolically represents the kindhearted, the helper, the rescuer, the friend in need. Odd Fellows are expected to provide such kindness without distinctions.

Symbols of the Degree of Love

The symbols of the degree of love are the following: Axe, Heart and Hand, Globe, Ark and Serpent.

The *Axe* is the emblem of progress. In the hand of the pioneer, the axe is used to cut the trees of the forest and make way for progress. This represents the advancement and spread of civilization, with which all Odd Fellows must work hand-in-hand. This is also emblematic of open-mindedness and a reminder of the progressive nature of Odd Fellowship. Odd Fellowship has evolved and must continue to evolve and adapt to the current needs of society.

The *Heart and Hand* symbolizes the sincerity and fidelity that we owe to each other as brothers and sisters. It refers to the help which an Odd Fellow should give to those in need, which must come from the heart. The hand of a true Odd Fellow should always be open to the needs of others. The heart should always go with the hand.

The *Globe* reminds members that we are citizens of the world and suggests that we should reach out our helping hands throughout the world whenever and wherever possible. It not only teaches us that we are to move forward in our work until no more misfortunes and sorrows to relieve and no more tears to dry; but also, that from whatever nation our brothers and sisters may come, they are not to be sent empty away.

The *Ark of the Covenant* represents the receptacle of the stone tablets on which were inscribed the Ten Commandants. This emblem admonishes us to be good and upright citizens by obeying good and wholesome laws.

The *Serpent* is a symbol of wisdom and placed among our symbols to indicate the necessity of a wise caution, which will protect our mysteries from improper disclosure and guide us in the proper regulation of life and conduct. This symbol also teaches us that without wisdom to control our words and actions, life will have no clear direction and drifts about without reaching its goals.

The Unwritten Work

Traditionally, the candidate in this degree will be taught the following: (1) Alarm, (2) Password of the Degree, (3) Sign of the Degree and its Answer, (4) Grip of the Second Degree and (5) Token. These must be learned during the degree itself and must not be communicated to anyone unauthorized to receive them. However, the Second Degree handgrip is no longer taught in almost all jurisdictions located in North America and Europe.

Degree of Truth or Third Degree

There are various versions of the Degree of Truth within the Independent Order of Odd Fellows. The Odd Fellows in Sweden, Denmark, Norway and the Philippines use a slightly distinctive version from that used in the United States and Canada.

But generally, this degree completes the three links chain of Odd Fellowship - Friendship, Love and Truth. This sums up all the lessons of the former degrees and teaches the deeper meanings of the symbols and emblems of Odd Fellowship. The candidate is reminded of the many truths they can apply in their daily lives. And that Odd Fellows must be committed to those truths. By knowing this, the member is expected to speak the truth and apply honesty in all his or her dealings with his or her church, community, lodge and family. The people of truth are the best and strongest people.[1] They will never defraud the IOOF or any organization but will prevent the unlawful use of its funds and property and, at every occasion, promote its welfare. They will never deceive, gossip and slander other people. Their speech and actions are always just – they win involuntary respect - they bless and purify all around them.[2] Therefore, this degree admonishes every member to practice truth in all actions and not just through words.

Regalia and Symbolic Color of the Degree of Truth

The regalia is a *white* collar with *scarlet* or *red* lining. Scarlet is the symbolic color for truth because it is the color of strength and action. Strength to stand for the truth not just through words but also through actions. Scarlet also symbolizes human sin, the blood of sacrifice, and have been used to warn and signal caution and danger – a watchful reminder to always think before we speak; to always think first before we act. In this degree, the purity of truth is taught and impressed by the color of white, while the grandeur of truth as an imperial virtue is taught and impressed by the color of scarlet.

Symbols of the Degree of Truth

The symbols of the degree of love are the following: Scales and Sword, Book of Sacred Law or Holy Bible, Hour Glass and Coffin.

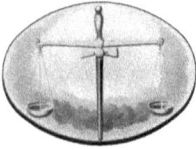

The *Scales and Sword* is an emblem of Justice, which judges with candor and rewards with impartia- lity. This emphasizes the importance that we place on justice, which must prevail for all without distinctions between rich and poor, high and low, or learned and unlearned. This is also an emblem of equality. Whatever distinctions there may be in society outside the fraternity of Odd Fellows, there are no distinctions in it.[3] All meet on a common level, and are brothers and sisters united for the promotion of friendship, love and truth.[4]

The *Book of Sacred Law* or *Holy Bible* is an exhaustless fountain of truth, the storehouse from which all our principles are derived. It is also an emblem of faith. To be faithful is a duty of every true Odd Fellow. The book of our faith will provide us the rules for the proper conduct of our life.

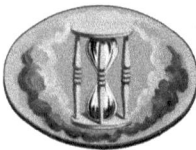

The *Hour Glass* is an emblem of time. And so, as the sands in the hour-glass quickly run down, the sands of life's are soon gone.[5] This reminds us of the passing of time, and the shortness of human life. All of us have been guilty of wasting time, wasting opportunities and wasting days. As the sands begin to fall more rapidly, we begin to recognize that we are running out of time. With this idea in mind, we are admonished to improve ourselves every day and make the best out of our life.

The *Coffin* is the symbol of our final destination, another reminder of the mortality of our physical body and the certainty of death. Death is the destination we all share. No one can escape it. How great or small, high or low, we will all meet on this common level – all must submit to the dominion of death. The honors, pleasures and riches we have secured and the fame we may have won for ourselves will all terminate in death.[6] If we have done good, we will perish without regrets. This also reminds all us of our duty to give every brother and sister a proper burial.

The Unwritten Work

Traditionally, the candidate in this degree will be taught the following: (1) Alarm, (2) Password of the Degree, (3) Sign of the Degree and its Answer and (4) Grip of the Third Degree. These must be learned during the degree itself and must not be communicated to anyone unauthorized to receive them. However, most jurisdictions already teach the Third Degree handgrip during the Initiatory Degree because it is the generally-used Odd Fellows' Grip inside and outside the lodge room.

Funeral Ceremony or Last Degree

The funeral ceremony, sometimes referred to as the *last degree*, is performed by the members of the lodge to honor every departed member. The ceremony begins with a speech delivered by the Noble Grand and a prayer by the Chaplain. The Noble Grand then advances to the coffin and cast into it, with the right hand, the *sprig of evergreen*. The other members shall then advance to the coffin and also cast into it the sprigs of evergreen. This ceremony is in line with the duty and one of the missions of Odd Fellowship, "To bury the dead".

Heart-in-Hand and Three Links Chain

The *heart-in-hand* is symbolic of charity, which is given from the heart. This is the oldest known symbol used by the early Odd Fellows. In fact, this is the central symbol used in the ancient rituals and official seals or emblems of older Orders of Odd Fellows. This remains to be true with the Grand United Order of Oddfellows (GUOOF) and the Independent Order of Oddfellows Manchester Unity (IOOFMU).

For the Independent Order of Odd Fellows (IOOF), the *three links chain* represents its motto: "Friendship, Love and Truth." This symbol was actually not the main symbol of the early Odd Fellows nor was this used in the ancient rituals and ceremonies. There is a hint that this was used by the *Ancient and Honorable Order of Bucks* and was passed-on when it ceased operations and its remaining lodges merged with the Odd Fellows. Other accounts suggest that the three links symbol was used as a "*recognition badge*" on or before the 1790's when all fraternal orders and friendly societies were banned in the United Kingdom as a result of the *French Revolution of 1789*. It is suggested that this badge was secretly used by Odd Fellows in order to recognize each other in public. At that time, only Odd Fellows had knowledge that the one who wears the three links chain was a member of the fraternity in order to avoid persecution or arrest. Others propose that this symbol was only introduced by the early leaders of the Independent Order of Odd Fellows in the United States. But all these assertions cannot be proven because many of the early records were destroyed and only a few survived.

It is suggested that the three links chain symbol is modeled after the ancient "Borromean Rings" (Valknut), which consists of three circles interlocking each other. The interpretation is that, if one were to cut or take away one ring, the other two would fall apart. As such, the three rings were used since the ancient times to symbolize "strength in unity." Christians also used a similar symbol to portray or represent the unity and characteristics of the Holy Trinity, also known as Trinity Rings.

Lodge, its Officers and their Functions

The organizational structure of the Independent Order of Odd Fellows developed gradually. At first, lodges were self-instituted and members managed their own affairs without control and supervision from any higher organization or national governing body. But as the numbers increased, the lodges united themselves to form a Grand Lodge for better administration. And after Grand Lodges were established across North America and across the world, the IOOF formed the Sovereign Grand Lodge. Being *progressive* in character, the IOOF have been transformed and restructured from time to time.

Odd Fellows Lodge

The local unit of the Odd Fellows is called a *Lodge*. The term lodge refers to both the place where the members hold their meetings and the members themselves as a basic unit or branch of the Odd Fellows. A lodge may be organized upon receipt by the Grand Lodge or Sovereign Grand Lodge of a signed petition for a charter by a minimum of five (5) or more Third Degree members or a minimum of fifteen (15) applicants qualified to become a member in a community within a defined jurisdiction. Five (5) Third Degree members in good standing, of which two-fifths (2/5) may be associate members, shall be required to keep the Lodge charter active.[1]

Lodge rooms around the world follow a very similar arrangement with only a slight difference - some lodges place an altar in the middle while others don't. Photo by the author, 2019.

The Odd Fellows is not like a company that is run from the top to down. A lodge is operationally and structurally similar to a franchise. Each Lodge is granted a charter or dispensation by a Grand Lodge or The Sovereign Grand Lodge to authorize it to use the rituals, symbols, teachings and trademarks of the IOOF. But the said Lodge possesses the right to organize its own local projects and enact any law not contravening the customs and usages of the organization, not altering the work of the IOOF or any of the several degrees, not in conflicting with the laws of the land, and do all such other acts as to promote the interest of the Order, or that appertain thereto by ancient usage or custom.[2] Each lodge is entitled to have their own ideas, projects and can independently manage its finances. And as long as they stick to the general rules, they are entitled to do things their way. Each lodge may also be registered as a separate corporate entity with its own Trustees who are responsible for holding the finances and property of that particular Lodge. Generally, a Lodge shall have the following purposes:[3]

- To have general supervision over Odd Fellowship in its area.

- To make recommendations to the Grand Lodge for legislation and such other matters that will improve the Order.

- To provide fraternal support and assistance to its members.

- To promote Odd Fellowship in the community.

- To be an active participant in the community and offer support and assistance where needed in the community.

Regular Meeting and Special Meeting

The regular meetings of a Lodge shall be held weekly, bi-weekly or semi-monthly depending on the their By-laws.[4] Usually, regular meetings are held at least once (1) a month following the opening and closing ceremonies as specified in its rituals. But one meeting may be conducted as a social/informal type meeting if the Grand Body so provides.[5] A Grand Lodge may grant a dispensation to a Lodge enabling the Lodge to dispense with meetings for a period not to exceed two (2) months in a calendar year.[6] But a Lodge shall not move from the place of meeting without approval of the Grand Lodge.[7] The IOOF rituals suggest the following Order of Business during a regular meeting but this may be changed to suit the convenience of the lodge:[8]

- Roll call of Officers.

- Introduction of visiting brothers and sisters.

- Reading of records of the last session.

- Members reported sick or in distress

- Report of visiting committee.

- Bill read and referred.

- Communications read and disposed of.

- Reading of applications for membership.

- Reports of interviewing committees.

- Balloting on applications for membership.

- Applications and balloting for degrees.

- Report of committee on finance.

- Initiation of conferring of degrees.

- Report of committees.

- Unfinished business.

- New business.

- Receipts and disbursements.

- Good of the Order.

- Closing the Lodge.

The Noble Grand may call for a Special Meeting of the Lodge at any time, or when petitioned by at least seven (7) members of the lodge.[9] Notice of such special meeting must be given at least thirty (30) days; stating the time, place and purpose of the meeting, and no business shall be transacted except as specified in the notice.[10]

Quorum

Quorum for Lodge meetings shall be a minimum five (5) members in good standing in the Lodge that is meeting, including one who shall be qualified to preside.[11] When the Noble Grand is absent, the Vice Grand shall preside. If there is no Vice Grand, the Immediate Past Grand shall be authorized to preside. Should the Lodge during a meeting, be left without a quorum; it shall not transact business and shall close without ceremony. All members in good standing have the right to submit legislation, make motions, debate and vote.[12]

Lodge Officers

Each lodge is governed by a set of officers. The titles of the officers of a lodge slightly vary among the various Odd Fellows organizations. But usually, the presiding officer is called a *Noble Grand* or *Most Noble Grand*. In the Independent Order of Odd Fellows (IOOF), there are more or less sixteen (16) officers of a Lodge depending on the country or jurisdiction. Usually, five officers are elected by the members, namely: Noble Grand, Vice Grand, Recording Secretary, Financial Secretary, and Treasurer. The elected Noble Grand appoints nine additional officers: Right Supporter of the Noble Grand, Left Supporter of the Noble Grand, Warden, Conductor, Chaplain, Right Scene Supporter, Left Scene Supporter, Musician, Color Bearer, Inside Guardian, and Outside Guardian. The Vice Grand appoints two additional officers: Right Supporter of the Vice Grand and Left Supporter of the Vice Grand.

Only a Degree of Truth or Third Degree member in good standing is eligible to become an officer of a Lodge.[13] To be eligible to the office of Noble Grand, one must have served in the office of Vice Grand.[14] To be eligible to the office of Vice Grand, a member must have served a term in each of two (2) different stations or offices or two (2) terms in one (1) station or office of an Odd Fellows Lodge.[15] But if there are no qualified members to hold either office, the Lodge may elect any Third Degree member to either office.[16] A member cannot also hold the two offices of Secretary and Treasurer at the same time in any Odd Fellows Lodge. All officers are expected to commit to memory the several charges in the opening and closing ceremonies of their respective offices and pass examination on this qualification before installation.[17] A dispensation must be obtained from the Grand Master or Grand Sire before installation.[18] Finally, each officer usually wears a set of regalia along with jewels to denote their office and rank.

The Lodge Gavel

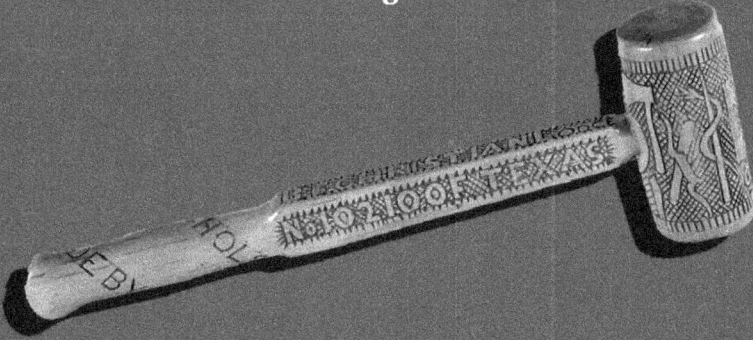

This instrument has two uses: one, as the voice of the Lodge in the hands of its officers; second, as a symbol or emblem of authority.[1] Custom requires it to be used in commanding attention or silence, or requiring members to stand or be seated. One rap by the presiding officer is to call attention or order in the Lodge or ask members to be seated.[2] Three raps call up the lodge or ask members to stand.[3] The instrument is used only to promote order and attention. A frequent or continual rapping is not advised because it only increases noise and confusion.

The rap or raps of the gavel shall only be given by Noble Grand or the Right Supporter of the Noble Grand. The raps are never to be repeated by the Vice Grand, except in cases where the written work calls on him or her to specially to do so. But the Vice Grand may use the gavel only when the Noble Grand is so engaged that he or she cannot attend to it. The Past Grand is not an executive officer, and is therefore not entitled to use a gavel in his or her chair. The Past Grand is to command order only by his or her example.[4]

Term of Office

The term of office of Lodge officers is usually annual or one (1) year but lodges that hold meetings weekly may have six (6) month terms.[19] In the absence of regular officers, the presiding officer of a Lodge may appoint pro-term officers.

LODGE OFFICERS, REGALIA AND THEIR FUNCTIONS

Noble Grand

The regalia of the Noble Grand is a *scarlet collar or chain* trimmed with *white or silver* lace. The jewel of office is *crossed gavels* of white or silver metal. Station is at the upper end of the room, in the principal chair, usually placed on an elevated platform about three steps. The general duties of the Noble Grand are the following:[20]

- The Noble Grand alone may call the Lodge together and open and preside over its session, and when present no one else may preside except during degree work. If absent, the Vice Grand will preside, and if both are absent a Past Grand will preside.

- The Noble Grand will construe and interpret the Laws of the Order, subject to appeal to the Lodge or to higher authority.

- The Noble Grand will see that the Laws of the Order are observed and enforced and will admit no member of another lodge who is not qualified and not in possession of the proper password.

- The Noble Grand will appoint the majority of all committees not otherwise provided for.

- The Noble Grand shall preside over the casting vote on all matters or questions before the Lodge. Traditionally, the Noble Grand does not vote except to break a tie or when electing new set of officers.

- The Noble Grand shall inspect and announce the result of all votes by the Lodge, have charge of the charter, which must always be in the Lodge while in session, draw upon the Treasurer for all sums that have been voted by the Lodge, and none other.

- The Noble Grand will sign all necessary warrants, certificates and other documents.

- The Noble Grand will also perform such other duties as usually pertain to the office.

Committees

The Noble Grand shall appoint the following committees:[1]

Finance: The Committee on Finance shall consist of three (3) members to be appointed on the night of installation. They shall audit and inspect the accounts, books, securities, funds, and other property in the hands of the Treasurer, and the books and reports of the Secretaries, and of other officers and committees charged with the receipt and expenditure of money. For this purpose, they shall fix a time and place to meet the Secretaries and Treasurer, after the last regular meeting in each semi-annual term, and shall report in writing at the first regular meeting in the next term upon duplicate blanks as approved by the Grand Lodge and furnished by the Grand Lodge, one copy of which shall be mailed to the Grand Secretary of the Grand Lodge and the other retained by the lodge. They shall also examine all other financial matters referred to them, and report thereon to the lodge a soon as practicable. Neither the Treasurer, the Secretary, the Financial Secretary, nor any member of the Trustees shall be a member of the Finance Committee.

Instruction: The Committee on Instruction shall consist of a minimum of three (3) members who are charged with scheduling training for members of the Lodge to include, but not limited, schools of instruction, mentoring of new members, coordinating efforts with the Grand Lodge Membership Committee. This Committee shall submit an annual report to the Lodge, and made a part of the representative's report to the Grand Lodge.

Membership: The Committee on Membership shall consist of at least three (3) members to be appointed on the night of installation. It shall be the duty of this committee, in conjunction with the Noble Grand, to promote plans for securing new members for the lodge and to work with the Financial Secretary / Secretary in promoting among the members the habit and practice of paying their dues promptly in advance.

Visiting: The Committee on Visiting shall consist of at least three (3) members, one of whom shall be the Noble Grand. They shall keep themselves informed at all times as to the condition of a member who has been reported ill; they shall report to the Lodge as to what benefits the member is entitled; and they shall provide for any care required and the laws of the Order permit. If a member of another lodge be sick and applies to this lodge for relief, the case shall be referred to the Visiting Committee as if a member of this lodge; and, if entitled to receive benefits from own lodge, this lodge shall advance the sum thus due and forward an account of the same to the member's lodge without delay. The lodge may add to the number of this committee and prescribe more specific details of their duties; provided, that in cities or towns having more than two lodges, the Visiting Committees of the different lodges may, if they see fit, appoint one of their number to act with a like number from the other Lodge in the town or city as a special Visiting Committee, whose duty shall be to take care of traveling or sojourning Members who may be sick or disabled in the town or city where such lodges exist.

Youth Activities: The Committee on Youth Activities shall consist of three (3) members to be appointed on the night of installation. They shall promote under the direction of the Noble Grand all youth activities, make annual report to the lodge of all youth activities, not limited to, sponsorship of athletic teams, scholarships, institution of Junior Odd Fellows Lodges, United Youth Groups, etc., including lodge participation in the Pilgrimage for Youth Program.

Other Committees as Authorized: The Noble Grand may appoint such other committees deemed necessary for the operation of the Lodge.

Vice Grand

The regalia of the Vice Grand is a *blue collar or chain* trimmed with *white or silver* lace. The jewel of office is an *hour glass* of white or silver metal. Station is at the end of the room nearest the entrance. The general duties of the Vice Grand are the following:[21]

- The Vice Grand shall assist the Noble Grand in presiding in the Lodge.

- In the absence of the Noble Grand, the Vice Grand shall preside, discharging all the duties of Noble Grand, and perform all other duties required by the charges and usage of the Order. In the absence of the Vice Grand, a Past Grand or Past Vice Grand will occupy the chair, if one is present otherwise a Third Degree member may occupy it.

- The Vice Grand shall appoint the Left and Right Supporters to the Vice Grand.

- The Vice Grand shall have special charge of the inner door.

- The Vice Grand will perform the duties herein pertaining to the office or as may be delegated. In the absence of the Noble Grand from the lodge room or anteroom, the Vice Grand is the proper and legal officer to take the station. That is not only the right but also the duty of the Vice Grand.

Immediate Past Grand

The regalia is a *scarlet collar or chain* trimmed with *white or silver* lace. Collars usually have *three five-pointed stars* on each side. The jewel of office is a *five-pointed star with a heart and hand* in the center made of white or silver metal. Station is midway at one side of the room, on the right of the Noble Grand. The general duties of the Immediate Past Grand are the following:[22]

- After his or her term as Noble Grand ends, he or she will serve as Immediate Past Grand and his or her duties are to deliver the charge to the candidate at initiation and, in many lodges, officiate as outside Conductor and assists in examining and introducing visitors.

- The Immediate Past Grand may also act as Noble Grand or Vice Grand when legally called thereto.

- The rank of **Past Grand** makes him or her eligible to receive the *Grand Lodge Degree* and hold office in the Grand Lodge.

Secretary

The regalia is a *scarlet collar or chain* trimmed with *white or silver* lace. The jewel of office is *crossed quills* of white or silver metal. Station is on the right of the Noble Grand but not on the same level. The general duties of the Secretary are the following:[23]

- The Secretary shall keep an accurate account of the proceedings of the lodge, write all communications; fill up all certificates and cards granted by the lodge, issue all summonses or notices required, and attest to all moneys ordered paid at regular or special meetings.

- The Secretary shall read to the lodge all communications addressed to the lodge.

- The Secretary has full charge of the Rituals and will safeguard the same and insure that they are kept in the hall, except, when permitting a member to take a Ritual out of the hall to learn a charge, providing the Secretary obtains a receipt therefore and same is entered in the Minutes.

- The Secretary shall assist the Financial Secretary in making out the Semi-annual and Annual Reports to the Grand Lodge, by seeing that the reports are completed and properly signed, sealed, attested to and mailed, with remittance due the Grand Lodge, to the Grand Secretary. But the Secretary shall perform the duties of Financial Secretary, if none were chosen.

- The Secretary shall also keep a list of all warrants drawn on the Treasurer, recording the date, amount, and the name of the person in whose favor drawn, and if the warrant be payable from any special fund, that fact shall appear both on the warrant and on the list.

- The Secretary shall also keep a register of membership, enrolling the names of members of the lodge, with the date of proposal, election, initiation (or signing of the member's register upon admission by Card or Dismissal Certificate), resignation, withdrawal by card, death, suspension, reinstatement, or expulsion also recording and conferring of degrees and attainment of official rank.

- The Secretary will prepare the lodge reports for submission to the Grand Lodge and read them to the lodge, and bring the books up to date before the end of each term so the Committee on Finance may examine them.

- When a member moves away, the Secretary will notify the nearest lodge thereof so that it may contact the member.

- When a member who belongs to an encampment takes a withdrawal card, or is expelled, suspended or reinstated from an Odd Fellows Lodge, the Secretary will promptly notify the Scribe of the member's encampment thereof.

- At the end of the term, the Secretary will promptly deliver to the elected successor all books, papers and properties belonging to the office.

- The Secretary will perform such other duties as usually pertain to the office or as may be delegated.

- The Secretary may also receive such compensation as the lodge may have fixed prior to election.

Financial Secretary

The regalia is a *scarlet collar or chain* trimmed with *white or silver* lace. The jewel of office is *crossed quills and a book* of white or silver metal. Station is on the left of the Noble Grand but not on the same level. The Financial Secretary always sits beside or near the Treasurer. The general duties of the Financial Secretary are the following:[24]

- The Financial Secretary shall notify all members who are at any time in arrears for an amount equal to eleven months' dues, delivering the notice in person, if practicable. If not, then mailing it to the member's last known address, and at the expiration of the next succeeding month, if said member's account is not settled, in whole or in part, sufficient to reduce the arrears to less than one full year's dues, shall present the name of such member to the lodge.

- o Notices of arrearage and liability to being dropped shall be given by the Financial Secretary and a record thereof shall be made in the minutes.

- o Dropping for non-payment of dues is illegal, if the member was not notified of arrearage and a proper record of the notice made in the minutes of the lodge. A member may not be dropped for non-payment of dues until a period of one year has lapsed.

- o It is unlawful for a Financial Secretary to give any receipt except for dues, assessments, or fines except the official certificates, and it is unlawful for any lodge to permit the same to occur.

- The Financial Secretary shall pay over to the Treasurer immediately all monies received, and at the same time shall inform the Treasurer how much of the money paid belongs to any special fund of the lodge.

- Prior to the last meeting in March, June, September and December, respectively, the Financial Secretary shall notify all members who are in arrears for one or more quarter's dues.

- The Financial Secretary shall at the close of each term, make to the lodge a detailed report of the business of the office, and have the books written up for the Finance Committee, with whom the Financial Secretary shall meet prior to the first meeting of the next succeeding term, to exhibit the books and papers and to aid them in the examination thereof, and at the first regular meeting of the new term shall present a report to the lodge, with a statement of the balance of account of all members, subject to suspension for arrearage.

- The Financial Secretary shall make out the Semi-annual and Annual Reports to the Grand Lodge, and shall deliver them to the Secretary for record and for forwarding to the Grand Lodge receiving such compensation as the lodge may have fixed prior to election.

- At the end of the term, promptly deliver to the elected successor all books, papers and properties belonging to the office.

- This position is *optional*. If there is no financial secretary, then the duties shall be assigned to the secretary.

Treasurer

The regalia is a *scarlet collar or chain* trimmed with *white or silver* lace. The jewel of office is *crossed keys* of white or silver metal. Station is on the left of the Noble Grand but not on the same level. The Treasurer always sits beside or near the Financial Secretary. The general duties of the Treasurer are the following:[25]

- The Treasurer shall be custodian of the funds, notes and securities of the lodge and pay all orders drawn by the Noble Grand and attested by the Secretary, and none other keep a full account of all moneys expended, and give the lodge, at the first meeting in each month, a statement of its funds. The Treasurer, and not the Trustees, is the proper custodian of the funds, and all notes, bonds belonging to the lodge except official bonds.

- The Treasurer shall keep a separate account of any special fund instituted by the lodge, and report to the Financial Secretary, at or before the last meeting in each term, any money received by the Treasurer as interest or dividends on any notes, securities or stocks held.

- At the close of the term, the Treasurer shall make for the lodge a full report of the receipts and disbursements, and have the books written up for the Finance Committee, whom shall meet prior to the first meeting in the next succeeding term, to exhibit the books, papers, securities, bonds, funds and other property in the possession of the Treasurer and at the first regular meeting of the next term shall present a report to the lodge.

- The Treasurer shall pay over and deliver up, when legally called upon, all moneys, bonds, books, papers, and other property in possession or under the control of the Treasurer, belonging to the Lodge, to the elected successor in office, or to such person as the lodge may appoint to receive same.

- In some jurisdictions, the Treasurer is required to give a joint and several bonds to the Trustees of the lodge, with two sureties to be approved by the lodge, with such penalties and conditions as from time to time may be prescribed by the lodge. Such bond must have been submitted to and approved by a majority of the Trustees before being presented to the lodge.

Warden

The regalia is a *black collar, sash, or chain* trimmed with *white or silver* lace. The jewel of office is *crossed axes* of white or silver metal. Station is in front of the Noble Grand at the right side but not on the same level. The general duties of the Warden are the following:[26]

- The Warden has charge of the regalia and lodge room property, and will place the regalia in the lodge room before opening and remove it on closing, reporting any damage to the Noble Grand.

- The Warden will prepare the ballot box, and will canvass votes on motions when required to do so, act as messenger and will perform such other duties as usually pertain to the office or as may be delegated.

- Traditionally, the Warden holds a broad axe while on duty, which he or she uses while walking around the lodge room to collect donations from the members.

- The Warden presents the flag if there is no Color Bearer.

- The Warden is usually appointed by the Noble Grand but, in some lodges in Europe, the Warden is an elective officer.

Conductor

The regalia is a *black collar, sash, or chain* trimmed with *white or silver* lace. The jewel of office is *crossed wands* of white or silver metal. Station is in front of the Noble Grand at the left side but not on the same

level. The general duties of the Conductor are the following:

- The Conductor shall receive the candidates for initiation when they enter the lodge room and perform all duties assigned to him or her in conferring the degrees of initiation and otherwise, and assist the Warden while in the lodge.

- The Conductor is usually appointed by the Noble Grand but, in some lodges in Europe, the Conductor is an elective office.

- The office of Conductor is very important in conferring the degrees so it should be expected that he is a competent reader.

Chaplain

The regalia is a *white sash or chain* trimmed with *white or silver* lace. The jewel of office is an open *Book of Sacred Law, Holy Bible, Qur'an, or Holy Book* of white or silver metal. The station is in the middle of one side of the room, opposite the station of the immediate Past Grand, and usually at the left side from the Noble Grand's station. The general duties of the Chaplain are the following:[27]

- The Chaplain shall lead in the opening and closing prayer in the lodge and perform all functions assigned to him or her during initiations.

- The Chaplain is an *optional* position. Some lodges, especially those whose members represent numerous creeds, do not have a chaplain.

Right Supporter of the Noble Grand

The regalia is a *scarlet sash, collar or chain* trimmed *white or silver* lace. The jewel of office is a *gavel* of white or silver metal. The station is at the right side of the Noble Grand. The general duties of the Right Supporter of the Noble Grand are to support the Noble Grand in keeping order in the lodge room, commands, open and close the lodge in due form, see to it

that the signs are given correctly, and occupy the chair of the Noble Grand when vacated temporarily during lodge hours.[28]

Left Supporter of the Noble Grand

The regalia is *scarlet sash, collar or chain* trimmed with *white or silver* lace. The jewel of office is a *gavel* of white or silver metal. Station is at the left side of the Noble Grand. The general duty of the Left Supporter of the Noble Grand is to see that all members who enter the lodge room are in proper regalia and give the signs correctly and to officiate for the Right Supporter when absent.

Right Supporter of the Vice Grand

The regalia is a *blue sash, collar or chain* trimmed with *white or silver* lace. The jewel of office is a stylized *hour glass* of white or silver metal. Station is at the right side of the Vice Grand's chair. The general duties of the Right Supporter of the Vice Grand are to observe that members give the signs correctly and report to the Vice Grand members who do not conduct themselves according to the regulations of the Order.[29] During the temporary absence of the Vice Grand, the Right Supporter to the Vice Grand will occupy the chair.[30]

Left Supporter of the Vice Grand

The regalia is *blue sash, collar or chain* trimmed *white or silver* lace. The jewel of office is a stylized *hour glass* of white or silver metal. Station is at the left side of the Vice Grand's chair. The general duty of the Right Supporter of the Vice Grand is to assist the Right Supporter and officiate for that officer when absent.[31]

Right Scene Supporter

The regalia is a *white sash, collar or chain* trimmed *white or silver* lace. The jewel of office is a *burning torch* of white or silver metal. The station is in front of the Vice Grand at the right side but not on the same level. The general duty of the Right Scene Supporter is to assist during initiation, bear the wands of office during processions or funerals, and perform roles specified in the charge book.[32]

Left Scene Supporter

The regalia is a *white sash, collar or chain* trimmed *white or silver* lace. The jewel of office is a *burning torch* of white or silver metal. The station is in front of the Vice Grand at the left side but not on the same level. The general duty of the Left Scene Supporter is to assist during initiation and perform roles specified in the charge book.[33]

Inside Guardian

The regalia is a *scarlet sash, collar or chain* trimmed *white or silver* lace. The jewel of office is a pair of *crossed swords* of white or silver metal. The station is beside the inner door of the lodge room. Traditionally, guardians carry a sword while on duty. The general duties of the Inside Guardian are to guard the inner door; receive the password for the degree that the lodge is open, and sees to it that all members who enter the lodge room are in proper regalia. The Inside Guardian also officiates for the Outside Guardian when the latter is absent. Traditionally, the Inside Guardian carries a sword or spear while on duty.

Outside Guardian

The regalia is a *scarlet sash, collar, or chain* trimmed *white or silver* lace. The jewel of office is a pair of *crossed swords* of white or silver metal. The station is beside the outer door of the lodge room or ante-room. The general duties of the Outside Guardian are to see that anyone who tries to enter the lodge room is qualified, asks members to give the password before they can enter, and prevents any interference during ritualistic ceremonies. Traditionally, the Outside Guardian carries a sword or spear while on duty.

Musician

The regalia is a *white sash, collar, or chain* trimmed *white or silver* lace. The jewel of office is a *harp* of white or silver metal. The station is usually on the right side of the Noble Grand's station but not on the same level. In most lodges, the musician sits by a piano or organ. The general duty of the Musician is to play required music or accompaniment during meetings and ceremonies. This position is *optional* and does not exist in all Odd Fellows lodges of the IOOF.

Color Bearer

The regalia is a *scarlet sash, collar, or chain* trimmed *white or silver* lace. The jewel of office is the *flag of the country* of white or silver metal. The station is in front of the Noble Grand at the right side beside the Warden. The general duty of the Color bearer is to present and retire the flag of the country and see that it is properly cared for. This position is *optional* and does not exist in all Odd Fellows lodges of the IOOF.

Jewels of Office of Lodge Officers

Past Grand

Noble Grand

Vice Grand

Secretary

Financial
Secretary

Treasurer

Warden

Conductor

Chaplain

Musician

Right
Supporter
of the Noble
Grand

Left
Supporter
of the Noble
Grand

Right
Supporter
of the Vice
Grand

Left
Supporter
of the Vice
Grand

Right Scene
Supporter

Left Scene
Supporter

Inside
Guardian

Inside
Guardian

Color
Bearer

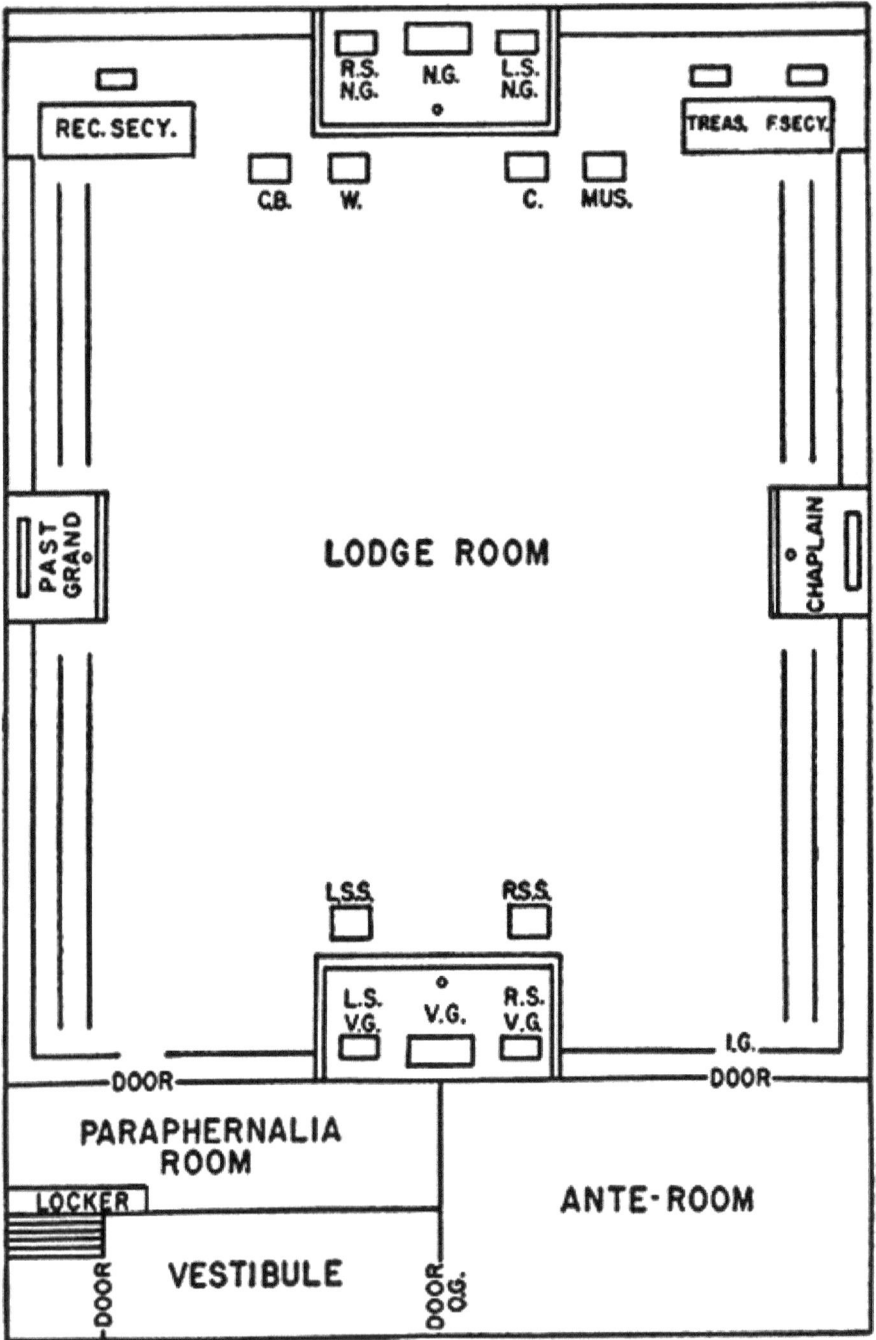

Odd Fellows' meeting rooms around the world follow similar arrangements and each officer sits at a definite location within the room. Illustration courtesy of The Sovereign Grand Lodge, IOOF.

Regular lodge meetings usually involve proper decorum, wearing of regalia, following an order of business and parliamentary procedures.

Representatives to the Grand Lodge

Each active Lodge shall be entitled to representation in the Grand Lodge. Each active Lodge shall be entitled to a Representative for its Charter and the first fifty (50) members; those Lodges with more than fifty (50) members shall be entitled to an additional Representative for each fifty (50) members. Each Lodge will elect Representative(s) and Alternate Representative(s) as set forth in the Grand Lodge Constitution or By-laws from among the Past Grands.[34] It shall be the duty of the Representatives to attend sessions of the Grand Lodge, represent the Lodge and report all legislation and other matters that occurred at the session pertaining to the Lodge.[35] In some jurisdictions, the Immediate Past Grand customarily becomes the Representative to the Grand Lodge.

Trustees

Depending on the by-laws, a Lodge may have at least three (3) or more Trustees who are elected at the same time as the officers of the lodge. They usually serve three (3) terms or more. They function as official agents of the lodge, and handle property and investments subject to approval of the Lodge. Trustees are not officers in the same sense as the elective or appointive officers so they may also hold any other office in the lodge unless prohibited by their by-laws.

Voting

The method of voting inside the Lodge is by the voting sign, written ballot, the ballot box, and acclamation.[36] Every qualified member present is required to vote on all questions unless excused by the lodge. An illegal vote shall not invalidate the ballot unless it changes the result. In that event, a new ballot shall be taken. However, a member shall not be eligible to vote on any matter relating to the fiscal affairs of the lodge in which the member has personal interest. Customarily, the Noble Grand or presiding officer is not allowed to vote except to break a tie or to elect new set of officers.

Elections

Elections shall take place on the first regular meeting of the last month of the lodge term.[37] In most jurisdictions, the elections are usually held in the month of November or December. Nominations shall be made as set forth in the lodge By-laws. All elections shall be by written ballot, unless there be but one nominee, in which event the Noble Grand shall declare the nominee elected.

The nominees shall each name one teller at elections, who with the Warden shall canvass the votes cast, and the Warden shall declare the result to the Noble Grand, by whom it shall be announced to the Lodge.[38] A majority of the votes cast shall be necessary for election. Should no candidate receive a majority on the first ballot, the candidate having the least number of votes shall be dropped at the next ballot, and so on until a candidate receives a majority of the votes cast.

Impeachment

An officer, member or Representative may be impeached and removed from office, suspended or expelled from membership in the Lodge.[39] A motion to impeach requires a majority vote for passage. Charges with specifications may be filed with the Secretary at any time but no action to impeach shall be taken until the accused has received three (3) days prior written notice. A member under impeachment shall be afforded the opportunity to be heard and present evidence. A two-thirds (2/3) vote of the members present is required for conviction and punishment.

Revenues and Funds

The revenues of a Lodge shall come from annual dues, assessments adopted in regular meetings, profit from the sale of supplies, investment income, devises and bequest and income from any lawful source. It is very important for the Lodge to collect sufficient dues to pay the expenses and fraternal obligations.[40] Without enough funding, the Lodge will have difficulty functioning and organizing projects for its members and the community.

Like a franchise, a Lodge enjoys financial autonomy and have control of its financial affairs and its funds as long as it acts in accordance with the Constitution and the Laws of the IOOF.[41] It may use its income for any purpose which is for the Good of the Order and which will exemplify the broad spirit of Odd Fellowship, unless expressly restricted by the laws or mandate of the Grand Lodge or The Sovereign Grand Lodge.[42]

But all funds of the Lodge, from whatever source derived, are trust funds and are to be accounted for and used in accordance with the Laws of the IOOF.[43] All moneys shall be deposited in the name of the Lodge in an approved bank or trust company. All investments shall be in the name of the Lodge and in such securities as would be approved for investment of trust funds. The Grand Lodge has a reversionary interest in all funds and investments and any division among members or any improper distribution is illegal and void.[44]

A Lodge may also create special funds by voluntary contributions or the holding of entertainment or bazaars where no part of the expense is chargeable to the regular funds of the Lodge and to use such funds for any purpose authorized by the Code of General Laws.[45] But no funds of the Lodge shall be invested or used in the purchase, construction or alteration of a building unless the plans, specifications and full particulars of financing are submitted to and receive the approval of the Grand Lodge.[46] The Lodge shall not also incur any debt or obligation nor enter into any contract for such purpose without the prior approval of the said Grand Lodge.[47]

Dues and Assessments

The amount of annual dues payable by contributing members shall be determined by the By-laws of the Lodge.[48] The dues charged must be sufficient to meet the expenses and obligations of the Lodge. Dues are payable in advance, but at the option of a member may be paid quarterly in advance. But if the expenses and current liabilities for any year is in excess of the income and current assets, on hand, to an extent that it might tend to impair the financial standing of the lodge, an assessment shall be levied by the Lodge on all contributing members to meet the deficiency.[49] All members must pay their dues and assessments to be considered in good standing. Failure to do so within a period of one (1) year shall result to suspension of his or her membership.

Expenses and Compensation of Officers and Committees

Elective officers, appointed officers and committees, may

receive such allowances for expenses if appropriated. Reimbursement for expenses shall be on signed vouchers accompanied by receipts whenever possible.[50] Appropriation or reimbursement is usually made by majority vote of all members in good standing.

Officers and employees of the lodge may also be allowed expenses for their services as provided in the budget of the lodge.[51] But allowances cannot be retroactive and must be fixed before the officer is elected or appointed.[52]

Returns and Records

At the end of each year, a Lodge is required to submit to the Grand Secretary, using the form provided the following:[53]

- Full report of the names of those initiated, reinstated, admitted by card, rejected, withdrawn, suspended or expelled, and the cause therefore, and deceased.

- Names of the Past Grands, the whole number in each class of membership and an alphabetical list of the members.

- Number of brothers and widowed families relieved, and brothers buried; the amount of money applied to each of these purposes, and the amount paid for the relief of orphans.

- Complete statement of all investments, funds and liabilities of the Lodge and the result of the election of officers.

- If a Lodge owns and/or operates a cemetery, senior or youth facility, park or camp, it shall also submit to the Grand Secretary an annual report as prescribed by the Grand Lodge.[54]

The reports shall be accompanied by whatever amount may be due to the Grand Lodge. If a lodge fails to make its returns and report for one (1) year, it shall be deprived of its rights and privileges and its charter may, by direction of the Grand Master or Grand Sire, be declared forfeited.[55]

It is also important for the Lodge to keep a permanent record in book form of all persons admitted to membership, setting forth all information regarding admittance to the Lodge, honors obtained in the Order and the termination of membership.[56] A Lodge shall also keep a record of its members who are members of a Rebekah Lodge, an Encampment, a Canton, or an associate member of another Odd Fellows Lodge. Upon withdrawal, suspension, expulsion or reinstatement of a member notice of that fact shall be given at once to the Rebekah Lodge, Encampment, Canton, or other Lodge to which the member may belong.

In addition, a Lodge shall keep sufficient financial records to show at any time the accounts of its members, its receipts and disbursements, all investments of its funds and other effects.[57] The records and accounts shall be audited by qualified members within thirty (30) days after the end of the term. The records shall conform to all requirements prescribed by the Grand Lodge and government agencies.

But the Lodge shall not sell or distribute for any purpose outside the fraternity, any of the member rosters, mailing lists, including personal information held by the Lodge to any person or persons, institutions, or agencies for sales promotions, or for other purposes within or without the Lodge, without the expressed permission of the member.[58] Any distribution must have the expressed permission of the voting members of the Lodge present and voting at any regular or called special meeting.[59]

Lodge Assets

Although the lodge enjoys some level of automony, it is required that the Grand Lodge must grant prior approval before the Lodge can dispose or sell any of its property and assets. In the event the Lodge ceases to exist, all property and assets revert to the Grand Lodge.[60]

Grand Lodge, its Officers and their Functions

Local lodges can form a state, provincial, national or territorial organization called a *Grand Lodge*. This governing body can be organized upon the petition of five (5) or more chartered lodges having an aggregate of at least seven (7) or more Past Grands. Five (5) Chartered Lodges, not including the Grand Jurisdictional Lodge, must be maintained in good standing with an aggregate of seven (7) Past Grands to keep a Grand Lodge charter active.[1]

Each Grand Lodge has exclusive jurisdiction over all local lodges in their State, Province, nation or territory. Each may also adopt legislation concerning minimum fees, dues and assessments necessary to meet fraternal obligations within their jurisdiction. But the design and government of a Grand Lodge is *democratic* not autocratic.[2] The Grand Master or Grand Sire and other Grand officers are not treated like monarchs or kings. The Grand Master or Grand Sire do not have the authority to interfere with the affairs of a Lodge or its Presiding Officer so long as it is in good standing and complying with the laws of the Order.[3] Customarily, the Grand Master or Grand Sire is not even allowed to vote during the sessions except to break a tie or to vote for new set of officers. As a state, provincial or territorial body, a Grand Lodge is *popular* and *purely representative*. The decisions of the elective officers are not absolute and may be overturned by majority or 2/3 votes of the representatives. Any bills and resolutions need the required votes of the representatives of the lodges and other branches within its jurisdictions.[4] Ideally, a Grand Lodge shall have

Sessions of the Odd Fellows' Grand Lodge of Denmark. Photo courtesy of Morten Buan of the Grand Lodge of Norway, 2017.

the following general functions:

- To act as a central office of records of all members, lodges and recognized branches in the State, Province, nation or territory.

- To grant charters and dispensations to lodges and other recognized branches within its jurisdiction; of suspending or taking away the same for proper cause.

- To act as a source of unity between and among members, lodges and other recognized branches towards attaining the general purposes of Odd Fellowship.

- To act as an agency of service and inspiration that will assist members, lodges and recognized branches in maintaining growth and development, training and education of its leaders and members, and in promoting and protecting the principles and traditions of Odd Fellowship:

  o To protect the use of rituals, ceremonies, ethical lessons, object clause, logo, signs and symbols and assure that they remain effective in improving members' morals.

  o To help generate funding and coordinate the activities, projects and programs in the State, Province, nation or territory .

  o To promote positive exchange of information and ideas among and between members and develop recommendations to all members for the good of the Order.

  o To provide counsel and support to members, lodges and all recognized branches; receive, determine and hear appeals; redress grievances and complaints arising in the several lodges and recognized branches.

- To act as an agency of promotion that will monitor publicity, initiate research studies and review and adopt such action for the purposes of promoting advancement and expansion of the Odd Fellows in the State, Province, nation or territory, and maintaining goodwill and understanding between the IOOF and the general public.

- To have general supervision over the Lodges and other recognized branches in the State, Province, nation or territory, including properties and assets such as:
  - Lodge Halls
  - Orphanages and Homes
  - Camps
  - Cemeteries
  - Building Associations
- To make recommendations to The Sovereign Grand Lodge for legislation and such other matters that will improve the Order.

Regular Session and Special Session

The sessions of the Grand Lodge must be opened and closed in the *Grand Lodge Degree* according to the Grand Lodge Ritual.[5] But the business of the Grand Lodge shall be conducted in the Third Degree.[6] The business sessions of the Grand Lodge shall be conducted in the following manner:[7]

- The Grand Master or Grand Sire shall call the members to order, ascertain by roll call that a quorum is present, direct the Deputy Grand Master to proclaim the Grand Lodge duly opened, require all members to be in proper regalia, and ascertain from the Grand Secretary if all reports have been printed and distributed.

- The Grand Master shall cause the previous session's journal to be read, or may declare them approved as printed except for corrections that may be brought to the attention of the Grand Lodge.

- The Grand Master shall preserve order and decorum.

Regular sessions of the Grand Lodge shall be held at predetermined places on a date as specified in the By-laws of the Grand Lodge. When the first IOOF Grand Lodge was established, the regular sessions were held biennially or once every two (2) years.

Today, most Grand Lodges in the United States and Canada hold their sessions annually or once (1) a year. In other countries, the regular sessions are still held once every two (2) years or once every four (4) years. The leaders in other countries believe that the gap between regular sessions will allow the Grand Lodge officers enough time to implement their desired programs and needed changes.

The Grand Master may call Special Sessions of the Grand Lodge at any time, or when petitioned by at least seven (7) Past Grands representing at least three (3) lodges; or majority of lodges as detailed in the By-laws.[8] Depending on the laws of the jurisdiction, notice of such meeting must be given at least thirty (30) days prior; stating the time; place and purpose of the meeting, and no business shall be transacted except as specified in the notice.[9]

In the event of an emergency when it is not financially feasible to hold a special session, the Representatives of all active lodges within its jurisdiction may be polled by mail as to their vote upon the proposition or propositions, not exceeding two (2) in number, with the pros and cons to be disclosed in full.

Quorum

Quorum for Grand Lodge sessions shall be a minimum of at least seven (7) Past Grands who are in good standing from not less than three (3) or a majority of the lodges in good standing.[10] But the by-laws of the Grand Lodge may state a larger number.[11]

Grand Lodge Officers

The officers and members of the Grand Lodge must all be Past Grands in good standing in their Lodge and have received the *Grand Lodge Degree*.[12] Usually, the elective officers of the Grand Lodge are as follows: Grand Master or Grand Sire, Deputy Grand Master or Deputy Grand Sire, Grand Warden, Grand Secretary, and Grand Treasurer. The appointive officers are usually the following: Grand Marshal, Grand Conductor, Grand Chaplain, Grand Musician, Grand Guardian and Grand Herald. The Grand Lodge may also provide for additional elected or appointed officers: Grand Instructor, Director of Publicity,

Grand Color Bearers, etc.

Term of Office

The term of office of Grand Lodge officers depends on the jurisdiction but the minimum is not less than one (1) year. When the first Grand Lodge was formed in the United States, the term of officers was biennial or two (2) years. Most Grand Lodges in the United States and Canada now have a term of annual or one (1) year. In other countries in Europe, Australia and the Philippines, the term of the Grand Lodge officers is between two (2) years to four (4) years.

GRAND LODGE OFFICERS, REGALIA AND THEIR FUNCTIONS

Grand Master or Grand Sire

The regalia is a *scarlet collar or chain*, but color and design may vary depending on the country. The jewel of office is usually the *Sun with the Scales of Justice* made of white or silver metal. The general duties of the Grand Master or Grand Sire are the following:

1. When in session, the Grand Master or Grand Sire shall:[13]

- Preside at all meetings of the Grand Lodge, preserve order and enforce the laws or cause the same to be done during a temporary absence.

- Cast a vote only when the Grand Lodge is equally divided, except on a ballot for officers, or on a secret ballot.

- Fill vacancies in office for the remainder of the term.

2. When not in session, the Grand Master or Grand Sire shall:[14]

- Have supervision over the affairs of the Odd Fellows Lodges, Grand Junior Lodges, Junior Lodges, United Youth Groups and Rebekah Assembly within the jurisdiction. Where there is no

Rebekah Assembly, the Rebekah Lodges, Theta Rho Assembly and Theta Rho Girls' Clubs shall fall under the Grand Lodge.

- Require all members to conform to the laws and customs of the Order but may not suspend them.

- Make any recommendations considered necessary for amendment of the By-laws.

- Execute all legal documents which shall be attested and acknowledged as required.

- Select and communicate the Term Password, for those units under the direct supervision of the Grand Lodge.

- Issue proclamations and directives requesting observances by appropriate ceremonies of the Anniversary of the Order, Wildey's Birthday, and such other anniversaries and events as deemed necessary.

- Visit lodges within the jurisdiction and shall instruct and assist them in all matters for the welfare and business of the Order.

- Instruct, with approval of the Board/Executive Committee, the Committee on Investigation of Grievances to make a thorough investigation when of the opinion that the laws and customs of the Order have been violated and no proper action is being taken.

- Remove from office any officer of a Lodge who is found to be physically or mentally incapable or is willfully failing to perform the prescribed duties, but only after due notice and hearing and concurrence of the Board/Executive Committee.

- May fill vacancies in office until adjournment of the next session, with approval of the Board/Executive Committee.

- The Grand Master may, with the approval of the Board, suspend a member or members for up to ninety (90) days while an investigation is conducted to determine if the member or members should be charged with violating the laws and/or customs of the Order.

Committees

The Grand Master or Grand Site may appoint the following standing and special committees.[1] Only Past Grands in good standing who received the Grand Lodge Degree and belonging to the jurisdiction of said Grand Lodge shall serve on committees, except on Joint Committees – with the Rebekah Assembly or other Grand Bodies.[2]

1. Standing Committees

Appeals and Petitions: If authorized by the Grand Master, it meets prior to the Annual Session. The Committee shall consider no appeal unless the record has been filed with the Grand Secretary in the manner and for the length of time prescribed by law, or unless directed to do so by the Grand Lodge. All appeals and petitions of petitioners shall be referred to it.

By-laws: Shall receive from the Grand Secretary on a rotating basis amendments to and revised by-laws. This committee shall review all by-laws and amendments thereto of all Lodges under the jurisdiction of the Grand Lodge.

Every six (6) years, the committee shall complete a review of all Lodges, doing one-sixth (1/6) of these each year. The Grand Secretary shall notify each Lodge to be examined that year to send three (3) copies of its laws for review. If a Lodge fails to comply, the Grand Secretary shall notify it that its Representative(s) shall be deprived of voice, vote, mileage and per diem.

The committee shall not only see that the Lodge laws comply with the laws of The Sovereign Grand Lodge and the Grand Lodge, but it shall also point out to the Lodge any failure to take advantage of its rights and privileges available to the Lodge.

Credentials: Shall pass upon the qualifications of Representatives and Members (Past Grands to receive the Grand Lodge Degree).

Distribution of Officers' Reports: Shall recommend reference to appropriate committees of the several parts and recommendations of officers' reports.

Drawing of Seats: Shall arrange the meeting place and see that it is properly set up before each daily session in accordance with plans provided by the Grand Master or Executive Committee.

Finance: Prepares and submits for consideration a proposed budget, setting out expected revenues and expenditures for the next fiscal year. After approval no appropriation shall be exceeded. This budget shall be presented, at the session. If the proposed budget results in a deficit, it shall only be adopted by roll-call vote with two-thirds (2/3) of the voting members present voting in favor. All matters pertaining to finance and appropriations of money shall be referred to it. The Committee on Finance shall also secure the CPA for the audit of the Grand Secretary and Grand Treasurer, and any additional books of entities of the Grand Lodge.

Judiciary: If authorized by the Grand Master, it meets prior to the annual session. This committee shall review the decisions of the Grand Master and report thereon to the Grand Lodge. Interpretations of the Laws of the Order on other matters shall be reported on at any time during the session. This committee shall serve as a Trial Committee when so directed by the By-laws of the Grand Lodge.

Legislation: Examine all legislation proposed and make recommendations with reference thereto, as well as such matters as may be referred to it.

Mileage and Per Diem: If required, makes corrections on the table of mileage and per diem prepared by the committee and the Grand Secretary.

Miscellaneous Business: Shall be referred matters not herein specified for reference to any other committee.

Odd Fellows Property: Shall be referred matters pertaining to the Homes, Camps, Cemeteries and Odd Fellow owned/sponsored Property of the Order.

Rebekah Matters: Shall be referred matters relating to the Rebekah Degree, and other activities of the Rebekah Branch of the Order. When requested to do so, this committee shall consider recommendations from the Rebekah Assembly and shall prepare the necessary Committee Bills or Resolutions for submission to the Grand Lodge.

Relief: Shall be referred matters pertaining to relief and relief projects, or otherwise involving the interests of the Order.

State of the Order: Shall be referred all matters and questions in relation to the general welfare and activities of the Order.

Instruction: Shall be responsible to provide instruction in the unwritten work, rituals, laws, customs and history of the Order. Its services shall be available to all lodges, District Deputies, Degree Captains and Staffs. The committee may conduct such schools of instruction as appropriations permit.

Courtesies Extended: Shall ensure that appropriate courtesies are extended.

2. Special Committees

Communications: Shall follow the guidelines as set by The Sovereign Grand Lodge and the Grand Lodge.

- Jurisdictional Newspaper, etc.

- Jurisdictional Web Sites, etc.

Executive Committee/Board: The Board/Executive Committee meets between sessions to manage the affairs of the jurisdiction; and promulgates plans and programs and works with the officers of all bodies under the immediate supervision of the Grand Lodge for the development and expansion of the Order. It shall direct and promote the operations and general welfare, consistent with the laws, customs and usages of the Order. The Executive Committee/Board shall submit a Master Report of their minutes to the Grand Lodge so the Representatives may ratify or change their actions.

Grand Lodge/Rebekah Assembly Joint Youth Committee: This shall consist of a minimum of six (6) members. The Grand Master-elect shall appoint a replacement for a three-year (3) term. The President-elect of the Rebekah Assembly shall recommend a member sister for a three-year (3) term. The replacements are to be appointed thirty (30) days before the annual session and confirmed the first day of the annual session. All terms of members are for three (3) years. The committee shall:

- Meet to select a chairman from among its membership.

- Be reimbursed for expenses as budgeted by the Grand Lodge.

- Promote all youth branches and activities.

- Make necessary reports to the Executive Committees/ Board of the Grand Lodge and Rebekah Assembly and an Annual Report to the Grand Lodge and Rebekah Assembly. Its actions, when the Grand Lodge is not in session, shall be subject to review and approval of the Grand Lodge Board/ Executive Committee.

Pilgrimage for Youth Committee: Each Jurisdiction may have this Committee consisting of no fewer than three (3) members appointed by the Grand Master, with one member designated as the Jurisdictional Chairman. Shall adopt rules and regulations governing Grand Lodge participation in the Pilgrimage for Youth Program subject to approval of the Grand Master and the Executive Committee and shall submit an annual budget for expenses of the Program.

Investigation of Grievances: At least one (1) member shall be a Past Grand Master. Whenever any situation arises that may be detrimental to the welfare of the Order, the Grand Master shall take necessary action as authorized by the laws of the Order. Members shall be reimbursed as authorized by the Grand Master within the Budget.

Membership: Committee shall consist of a minimum of three (3) members, and a General Chairman. The Grand Master-elect shall make appointments thirty (30) days prior to session. All appointments to be confirmed by the Grand Lodge. The General Chairman shall direct the affairs of the Committee, which will include the plans and procedures for the promotion of membership and may include such programs as Training Conferences, Degree Rallies and other related activities. Each Lodge shall appoint a membership chairperson (and co-chairperson or committee) as the program may deem from year to year.

Memorials: Shall be referred all matters of commemorating the memory of deceased members of the Grand Body who died in good standing to be referred to this committee for their action and report, and it shall be their duty to secure any available statistics in regard to death and report on same.

Joint Planning Board: The Grand Lodge may participate in the/a Joint Planning Board.

Other Committees as Authorized: The Grand Master may appoint such other committees deemed necessary for the operation of the Lodge.

3. Duties and Responsibilities of committees:

Only Grand Lodge Members may serve on standing committees. No person shall, simultaneously, serve as chairperson of more than one (1) standing committee.

Committees are to perform the duties prescribed by law, special assignments by the Grand Master or the Grand Lodge and other duties pertaining to such committees as have been customarily performed in the past.

A committee chairperson is not an officer of the Grand Lodge, but may upon occasion become its agent.

Any committee may request from the Grand Master, the appointment of a Past Grand Master to act in an advisory capacity.

- The Grand Master shall have power to appoint District Deputy Grand Masters and Special Deputies.

- May grant dispensations and charters as authorized by the constitution and laws of the Grand Lodge, which do not violate the laws of The Sovereign Grand Lodge. The Grand Master, or one designated by the Grand Master in writing, shall institute a Lodge or other unit when the charter/warrant/dispensation is issued.

- The Grand Master, with written consent of a majority of the Representatives, in the event of war, grave emergency, or other like cause omit the holding of a regular session or may change the regular time and place.

- Perform other duties as required of the Grand Lodge.

3. Powers and Limitations:[15]

- The Grand Master shall not hold any elective office in any Odd Fellows lodge, Rebekah lodge, Degree lodge or Rebekah Assembly within the jurisdiction.

- The Grand Master shall cast a vote only when the Grand Lodge is equally divided, except on a ballot for officers or on a secret ballot.

- The decisions shall be rendered in writing by the Grand Master only when requested in writing by a Lodge.

- All decisions of the Grand Master are binding until the Grand Lodge meets. Decisions shall be reviewed by the Committee on Judiciary, their report being acted upon by the voting members of the Grand Lodge. Unless reversed, they become law after being presented in Bill form and adopted by the voting members.

- The Grand master may not delegate the vested powers except as provided in the Code of General Laws.

- The Grand Master has no authority to interfere with the affairs of a Lodge or its Presiding Officer so long as it is in good standing and complying with the laws of the Order.

Deputy Grand Master or Deputy Grand Sire

The regalia is a *scarlet collar or chain*, but color and design may vary depending on the country. The jewel of office is a *Half Moon* made of white or silver metal. The general duties of the Deputy Grand Master or Deputy Grand Sire are the following:[16]

- To open and close the meetings of the Grand Lodge and preside in the absence of the Grand Master or Grand Sire.

- To perform all duties assigned by the Grand Lodge, perform the duties and make visitations as may be directed by the Grand Master or Grand Sire or the Executive Committee.

- To act for the Grand Master in case of the latter's continuing disability to such an extent of being physically or mentally unable to perform the duties as determined by the Executive Committee.

Grand Warden

The regalia is a *scarlet collar or chain,* but color and design may vary depending on the country. His or her jewel of office is a pair of *crossed gavels* made of white or silver metal. The general duties of the Deputy Grand Warden are the following:[17]

- To have charge of the doors and through the Grand Marshal

and Grand Conductor examine and ascertain that all members and visitors are qualified to sit in the session prior to opening. The Grand Lodge shall be the sole judge of qualifications and validity of credentials of Representatives.

- To have charge of the diagrams and unwritten work of the Order during the session of the Grand Lodge. To confer the Grand Lodge Degree upon all Past Grands presenting proper credentials.

- To make visitations and perform such duties as the Grand Master, the Grand Lodge, or the Executive Committee may direct.

- To study the programs and projects of all lodges and report and make recommendations concerning them to the Executive Committee.

Grand Secretary

The regalia is a *scarlet collar or chain*, but color and design may vary depending on the country. The jewel of office is a pair of *crossed quills* made of white or silver metal. The general duties of the Grand Secretary are the following:[18]

1. When in session, the Grand Secretary shall:[19]

- Attend all sessions of the Grand Lodge, keep a record of all proceedings and handle correspondence and business pertaining to the office or as may be delegated.

- At the opening of each session report to the Grand Master in writing the names of Lodges that are delinquent in reporting, paying dues and fees, or that are indebted for supplies as of sixty (60) days before the session. This report shall be delivered to the Committee on Credentials immediately upon its appointment.

- Make a detailed financial report of all accounts.

- Provide for use of committees and Representatives an adequate supply of Codes of General Law, Journals of Proceedings, Robert's Rules of Order, and necessary forms and stationery.

- Appoint such Assistants as required.

- Keep a record of the proceedings of each session.

- In compiling the Journal, to number every bill, resolution, petition and document. At the end of each item, indicate by number the committee report and disposition.

- Edit and print the reports of officers of the Grand Lodge for use by the Committee on Distribution of Officers' Reports; this to include minutes of the Board.

- Cause to be printed in the Journal, all legislation including those Bills laid over for the next session.

2. When not in session, the Grand Secretary shall:[20]

- Execute a bond in the sum of an amount designated by the Grand Lodge with corporate surety, to be approved by the Grand Master, to account for all funds and property that come into possession of the Grand Secretary's office. The bond shall remain in the custody of the Grand Master.

- Employ assistants and others to serve and to be compensated from funds appropriated.

- Have custody of the Seal of the Grand Lodge, attesting necessary documents.

- Prepare, for use of the Committee on Mileage and Per Diem, a table of mileage of the officers of the Grand Lodge, Past Grand Masters, and a numerical list by Lodge of Representatives expected to attend the session, with any other information deemed necessary for examination and correction by the Committee; where Mileage and/or Per Diem are paid.

- Close the books of the Grand Lodge at the end of the fiscal year, and make proper report thereon.

- Keep all accounts in accordance with approved accounting methods, keeping a separate account for each appropriation.

Payments shall not exceed specific appropriations and no transfers from one appropriation account to another may be made without specific approval of the Grand Lodge. Appropriations shall be made for the fiscal year. All books and accounts shall be promptly posted. Sell copies of the Journal of Proceedings, Code of General Laws and Supplements thereto, and other supplies for cash, on consignment, or for credit not exceeding sixty (60) days, as deemed for the best interest of the Order.

- Transmit to the Grand Treasurer all moneys collected for various funds and obtain receipts.

- Prepare a complete Journal of Proceedings of each session containing statistical and other information directed by the Grand Lodge, properly indexed, to be printed and bound; and distributed as designated in the By-laws.

- Keep a library of the proceedings of the Grand Lodge. To archive all paraphernalia that may come into possession of the Grand Lodge.

- To transmit all appeal papers to the Chairman of the Committee on Appeals and Petitions so as to arrive prior to the annual session. Attest proclamations of the Grand Master and distribute same to each Lodge.

- Prepare forms for annual reports of the Lodges containing information required by The Sovereign Grand Lodge. Reports shall be due on the date stated in the By-laws, such that the membership is based on a twelve (12) month period, along with such other information as may be necessary for tax purposes that may be required.

- Require payment of all fees and dues together with the reports. Failure to comply by *March 1st* shall give the Grand Secretary sufficient reason to take the following actions:
  - Notify the Lodge of its Representative(s) loss of accreditation;
  - Require monetary penalties of ten percent (10%) as of date stated in the by- laws, based on dues payable

and an additional one and one-half percent (1 1/2%) interest per month thereafter until paid. If all dues and penalties are not received, the Representatives may be seated with only the right of debate and to make motions but not permitted to vote. If mileage and per diem are paid, the Lodge shall be billed for mileage and per diem, unless good cause for such failure can be shown to the satisfaction of the Grand Lodge.

- Keep an adequate supply of jewels and items of supply for sale.

- Keep accounts between the Grand Lodge and all components under its jurisdiction and that all accounts to the Grand Lodge which becomes delinquent sixty (60) days shall bear a penalty of one and one-half percent (1 1/2 %) per month which shall be collected on the gross amount of the invoice.

- Notify all members to attend special sessions of the Grand Lodge. Make a full report of the proceedings of the Board/ Executive Committee to the Grand Lodge at its annual session.

- Receive from the Secretaries, in triplicate, amendments to their respective by-laws together with three (3) certified copies of their current laws. Amendments shall be forwarded to the Committee on By-laws, or appropriate member for review and reporting on at the Grand Lodge Session. The files shall be forwarded within thirty (30) days of receipt.

Grand Treasurer

The regalia is a *scarlet collar or chain,* but color and design may vary depending on the country. The jewel of office is a pair of *crossed keys* made of white or silver metal. The general duties of the Grand Treasurer are the following:[21]

- To attend all sessions of the Grand Lodge and perform the duties of the office and those assigned.

- To keep all monies, securities, and evidence of indebtedness of the Grand Lodge, pay all orders drawn by the Grand Secretary, and submit an annual statement of all accounts prior to the annual session.

- To receive all monies collected by the Grand Secretary, giving receipt therefore, and deposit same in depositories selected in the name of the Grand Lodge.

- To sign all checks drawn by the Grand Secretary or by authorized use of a facsimile signature. The Grand Secretary or other designated signer shall countersign checks.

- To disburse funds collected for General Relief, keeping a proper record thereof.

- Some jurisdictions require the Grand Treasurer to furnish bond in the amount and under the terms and conditions required of the Grand Secretary.

Grand Marshal

The regalia is a *scarlet collar or chain,* but color and design may vary depending on the country. The jewel of office is a *baton* of white or silver metal. The general duties of the Grand Marshal are to assist the Deputy Grand Master in supporting the Grand Master and to supervise the arrangements of all processions ordered or permitted by the Grand Lodge.

Grand Conductor

The regalia is a *scarlet collar or chain,* but color and design may vary depending on the country. The jewel of office is a *sword* of white or silver metal. The general duties of the Grand Conductor are to examine the certificates for admission, and, if correct, to introduce the bearers to the Grand Lodge; and to assist the Grand Marshal in his or her duties.

Grand Guardian

The regalia is *scarlet collar or chain,* but color and design may vary depending on the country. The jewel of office is *crossed swords* of white or silver metal. The general duties of the Grand Guardian are to guard the inner door during Grand Lodge sessions; see to it that anyone who tries to attend the Grand Lodge sessions is qualified; and ask from members the term password before they can enter.

Grand Herald or Grand Messenger

The regalia is *scarlet collar or chain*, but color and design may vary depending on the country. The jewel of office is a *trumpet* of white or silver metal. The general duties of the Grand Herald or Grand Messenger are to announce the Grand Master during ceremonials and to precede and usher the Grand Lodge officers in its processions. The Grand Herald or Grand Messenger is the messenger of the Grand Lodge and is equivalent to the outside guardian in the lodge.

Grand Chaplain

The regalia is *scarlet collar or chain*, but color and design may vary depending on the country. The jewel of office is an open *Holy Bible, Holy Book* or *Book of Sacred Law* of white or silver metal. The general duties of the Grand Chaplain are to open and close the Grand Lodge with a prayer and to officiate at public ceremonials and funerals which are under special charge of the Grand Lodge. In some Grand Lodges, the Grand Chaplain is an *optional* office.

Grand Musician

The regalia is *scarlet collar or chain*, but color and design may vary depending on the country. The jewel of office is a *harp* of white or silver metal. The general duty of the Grand Musician is to play required music or accompaniment during grand lodge sessions and ceremonies. In some Grand Lodges, the Grand Musician is *optional*.

Grand Color Bearer

The regalia is *scarlet collar or chain*, but color and design may vary depending on the country. The jewel of office is a *flag of the nation in which the* Grand Lodge *is located* made of white or silver metal. The general duty of the Grand Color Bearer is to present and retire the flag of the country, state, province, or territory during Grand Lodge sessions and see that it is properly cared for. In some Grand Lodges, the Grand Color Bearer is *optional*.

Representative and Alternate Representative

A Grand Lodge is composed of Grand Representatives or Alternate Grand Representatives who are Past Grands in good standing and voted by each lodge.[22] Each active Lodge shall be entitled to a Representative for its Charter and the first fifty (50) members; those Lodges with more than fifty (50) members shall be entitled to an additional Representative for each fifty (50) members.[23] An alternate Representative shall be elected at the same time as the Representative to serve in the event that the elected Representative cannot attend the upcoming session.[24] The Duties of a Representative are the following:[25]

- To attend sessions of the Grand Lodge, represent the Lodge and report all legislation and other matters that occurred at the session pertaining to the Lodge.

Jewels of Office of Grand Lodge Officers

Grand Master /
Grand Sire

Deputy Grand Master
/ Deputy Grand Sire

Grand Warden

Grand Secretary

Grand Treasurer

Grand Chaplain

Grand Marshal

Grand Herald

Grand Musician

Grand Color Bearer

Grand Conductor

Grand Guardian

Past Grand Master

After serving his or her term, the Grand Master or Grand Sire will receive the rank and title of a Past Grand Master or Past Grand Sire and will hold such designation for a lifetime. The regalia is a scarlet chain or collar trimmed with white or silver lace or fringe, but color and design may vary depending on the country. Those who have attained the Royal Purple Degree in the Encampment may have trimmings of yellow. The jewel of office is the Sun with Heart and Hand of white metal.

- To vote on every roll-call vote. If any member shall be temporarily absent from the hall, the other Representative from the Lodge shall be allowed to cast the vote of such temporarily absent member, in which event the Grand Secretary shall place the word "absent" opposite the name of the absent Representative and thereafter such vote cannot be changed.

- To vote on all matters except on personal qualifications to be seated.

- To serve on all committees to which appointed unless excused by the Grand Lodge.

Each Representative and alternate Representative must be a Past Grand, a member in good standing of an Odd Fellows Lodge in good standing; provided that residence is within its own or an adjoining jurisdiction; and further providing that the one elected may qualify after election by obtaining the Grand Lodge Degree at a Regular or Special Session of the Grand Lodge.[26] The Lodge shall furnish the Representative with a certificate of election with a duplicate under seal to the Grand Secretary.[27] One (1) elected, as a Representative shall not be recognized as such, nor entitled to its rights and privileges until the credentials have been received and approved. A Representative cannot be seated in the Grand Lodge unless the Lodge are in good standing.[28] A Representative shall represent only one (1) Lodge. There shall be no proxy representation, nor vote by proxy; one (1) person –

one (1) vote.[29]

The terms of Representatives commence at the beginning of the Grand Lodge Session for which elected.[30] Depending on the jurisdiction, a Representative may be elected to any number of terms.[31] However, some jurisdictions impose limited terms to provide other Past Grands an opportunity to represent their lodge. But a Representative may hold any other office in the Lodge.[32]

The officers of the Independent Grand Lodges in Europe do not use the scarlet or red collar regalia like those used by Grand Lodges directly under the Sovereign Grand Lodge. To be a Grand Lodge officer in Europe, one must not only be a Past Grand in the Lodge but also a Royal Purple Degree member in the Encampment. Thus, their Grand Lodge officers wear a purple or violet collar regalia with scarlet or red upper rim decorated with three white stars on each side. But each IOOF Grand Lodge in Europe has a unique regalia for their Grand Sire. Photo courtesy of The Sovereign Grand Lodge, IOOF.

District Deputy Grand Masters or District Deputy Grand Sires

The Grand Master shall appoint a District Deputy Grand Master for each District.[33] Such District Deputy shall be a Past Grand in good standing. The term of a District Deputy Grand Master shall commence at the end of the annual session and end at the next annual session.[34]

The District Deputy shall be the special agent and representative of the Grand Master, shall supervise the affairs of the Order in said district, and perform other duties as the Grand Master may direct.[35] The District Deputy may also receive reimbursement for expenses from appropriated funds when approved by the Grand Master. At the expiration of the term shall be entitled to the rank of Past District Deputy Grand Master and may acquire an appropriate jewel.

Special Representatives

The Grand Master may commission a Special Deputy over any lodge under the supervision of the Grand Lodge to perform all the duties specifically designated in the commission.[36] Upon completion of the duty, the Deputy shall report in writing the action taken with recommendations. A Special Deputy to take control and supervision over the affairs of any component body under the supervision of the Grand Lodge which is acting in violation of law, failing to meet its responsibilities, or unlawfully dissipating its assets. The officers of the component involved may continue to perform their duties under the supervision of the Deputy and to the extent allowed. When the situation has been alleviated the Deputy shall be relieved and commission terminated.

A Special Deputy may also be appointed to take charge of the property, funds, and affairs of a component under the supervision of the Grand Lodge whose charter has been arrested, suspended, or forfeited. If the charter of a Lodge is arrested, suspended, or forfeited, it shall come under the immediate supervision of the Grand Lodge and remain until the charter is restored.

Directors

A Grand Lodge may elect additional directors; up to three (3) (to be known as Term Directors) to the Board so as to create continuity on the Board/Executive Committee. The Term Directors shall serve not more than three (3) terms consecutively. The Term Directors shall not be considered elective officers in regards to officers receiving Honors of the Order or Honors of Degrees and shall not wear any jewel or special regalia designating same.

A Grand Lodge also have the authority to elect members to any corporate boards or committees with the responsibilities to operate homes, camps, retirement centers, etc., trust accounts. The qualifications for office are the following:[37]

- A Past Grand in good standing in an Odd Fellows Lodge and a member of a Rebekah Lodge, and in possession of the Grand Lodge Degree is eligible to hold any office.

- An officer must maintain membership in the jurisdiction to hold office.

Voting and Motions

The Grand Master shall permit a member to speak but once until every member who chooses has spoken.[38] No member shall speak more than twice on a question without unanimous consent of the members present.

Voting for officers shall be by ballot. All other voting shall be by the voting sign, except that one-fifth (1/5) of the Representatives present may demand a roll call vote. Except as otherwise provided, a majority of a quorum shall prevail.

Nominations and Elections

The Grand Master shall call for nominations under the regular order of business as adopted by the Grand Lodge. Nominations shall be made by members of the Grand Lodge, as specified by the jurisdictional By-laws with exception being that a member may ask for the Noble Grand of the nominee's Lodge, a nominee's family member or close friend – who may be a member of the Order, but not yet a member of the Grand Lodge to address the Grand Lodge and make a nomination.

Elections shall follow in the general course of business. All elections shall be by written ballot, unless there be but one nominee, in which event the Grand Master shall declare the nominee elected. A majority of the votes cast shall be necessary for election. Should no candidate receive a majority on the first ballot, the candidate having the least number of votes shall be dropped at the next ballot, and so on until a candidate receives a majority of the votes cast.

The nominees and the Grand Master shall each name one teller at elections, who shall canvass the votes cast. The Teller appointed by the Grand Master shall declare the result to the Grand Master, by whom it shall be announced to the Grand Lodge. Counting of the Ballots shall be by custom of the Grand Lodge as stated in the by-laws or order of business.

Impeachment

An officer, member or Representative may be impeached and removed from office, suspended or expelled from membership in the Grand Lodge.[39] A motion to impeach requires a majority vote for passage. Charges with specifications may be filed with the Grand Secretary at any time but no action to impeach shall be taken until the accused has received three (3) days prior written notice.[40] A member under impeachment shall be afforded the opportunity to be heard and present evidence.[41] A two-thirds (2/3) vote of the Representatives present is required for conviction and punishment.

Vacancy

A Grand Lodge shall prescribe methods and procedures for impeachment or removal of officers after notice and hearing for nonfeasance, misfeasance, malfeasance, misconduct or other cause.[42] A Grand Lodge shall enact legislation for filling vacancies caused by suspension, expulsion, removal, impeachment, death, or if the officer's lodge does not remain in good standing.[43] In case of vacancy, the Sovereign Grand Lodge requires that the said offices are filled in the following manner:[44]

Grand Master: In case of death, resignation, or impeachment of the Grand Master, or should the office be vacated by continued physical or mental incapacity of extreme nature, then the office with the approval of the Executive Committee shall be filled by the Deputy Grand Master, who may, having served a majority of and to the end of the term, be ranked as a Past Grand Master, or has the option to stand for election for a regular term as Grand Master.[45]

Deputy Grand Master: In case of death, resignation, or impeachment of the Deputy Grand Master, or should the office be vacated by reason of continued physical or mental incapacity of extreme nature, then the office with approval of the Executive Committee shall be filled by the Grand Warden, and the Grand Warden, who may, having served a majority of and to the end of the term, be ranked as a Past Deputy Grand Master, or has the option to stand for election for a regular term as Deputy Grand Master.[46]

Grand Warden: In case of death, resignation, or impeachment of the Grand Warden, or should the office be vacated by reason of continued physical or mental incapacity of extreme nature, then the office with approval of the Executive Committee shall be filled by appointment, the appointee who may, having served a majority of and to the end of the term, be ranked as Past Grand Warden or has the option to stand for election for a regular term as Grand Warden.

Grand Secretary: In case of death, resignation, or impeachment of the Grand Secretary, or should the office be vacated by reason of continued physical or mental incapacity of extreme nature, then the office with approval of the Executive Committee shall be filled by appointment, the member shall be entitled to rank as a Past Grand Secretary, or has the option to stand for election as Grand Secretary at the close of the term for which appointed.

Grand Treasurer: In case of death, resignation, or impeachment of the Grand Treasurer, or should the office be vacated by reason of continued physical or mental incapacity of extreme nature, then the office with approval of the Executive Committee shall be filled by appointment, the member shall be entitled to rank as a Past Grand Treasurer at the close of the term. Has the option to stand for election as Grand Treasurer at the close of the term for which appointed.[47]

Grand Representative: In case of death, resignation, or impeachment of the Grand Representative, or should the office be vacated by reason of continued physical or mental incapacity of extreme nature, then the office shall be filled by the Alternate Grand Representative.[48] The Alternate Grand Representative shall be entitled to rank as a Past Grand Representative at the close of the term.

Term Director: In case of death, resignation, or impeachment of a Term Director, or should the position be vacated by reason of continued physical or mental incapacity of extreme nature, then the position shall be filled by the Board.[49]

Should the term be for more than one (1) year, the appointment shall be to the next session of the Grand Lodge.[50] If there be additional time in the term, there shall be an election to fulfill the remainder of the term.

Visiting the Grand Lodge Sessions

A Third Degree member in good standing in an Odd Fellows

Lodge that is in good standing may visit Sessions of the Grand Lodge upon being vouched for by a Representative of the lodge or by presenting an Official Certificate to the Grand Guardian showing dues paid up-to-date.[51]

A Third Degree Member of an active Lodge will have a voice when recognized by the presiding officer but is not entitled to present Bills, make Motions nor be entitled to vote during the Sessions of the Grand Lodge.[52]

Revenues and Funds

Revenue of the Grand Lodge shall be from charter fees, per capita dues, assessments adopted in regular session, profit from the sale of supplies, investment income, rent, devises and bequest and income from any lawful source.[53] The Grand Lodge shall also collect sufficient per capita dues to supplement the funds required to pay the expenses and fraternal obligations.[54]

Excess funds of the Grand Lodge shall be invested by the Grand Treasurer and the Finance Committee or such other committee appointed to confer with the Grand Treasurer. This officer and Committee shall also determine the amount that constitutes excess funds.

The Board/Executive Committee may borrow funds, not exceeding the amount previously approved by the Grand Lodge, as may be necessary to meet expenses and appropriations, and to pledge the credit of the Grand Lodge.[55] The chairman of the Committee on Finance shall also attest evidence of the indebtedness.[56] Real or personal property may be mortgaged or pledged if necessary.[57] Funds derived therefrom shall be delivered to the Grand Treasurer.[58] Funds to be borrowed if in excess of the approved amount must be authorized by special resolution adopted at a session of the Grand Lodge.[59] A complete list of all securities shall be currently maintained by the Grand Treasurer and delivered to the Grand Master. Securities shall be kept in safe deposit boxes. Access shall be limited to any two (2) of the Board/Executive Committee.[60]

The Grand Lodge may also authorize the raising of funds for particular purposes, by contributions or other legal money-raising activities. But no lodge, officer, or member may petition funds outside the jurisdiction without written approval of the Sovereign Grand Master.[61]

Bills, Resolutions, and Reports

When a committee reports favorably upon a bill the vote shall be upon passage of the bill. Amendments shall be voted upon first, and then the bill or bill as amended.[62] Majority reports will normally be considered first, unless there is a motion to adopt the minority report.[63] Motions to table, lay-over, indefinitely postpone, or subsidiary motions are always in order.[64]

When a Committee submits an adverse Report on a subject (Bill, Resolution or Report) referred to it, the subject shall be placed before the Grand Lodge as a committee of the whole. A proponent of the subject shall have five (5) minutes to speak to the subject.[65] A vote shall then be taken to place the subject upon passage. If the vote is favorable, then the subject shall be open to debate. After debate the vote shall be upon the subject.

A bill, resolution, or other proposition that is to be referred to a standing committee shall be submitted in triplicate, on standard letter or legal-size paper, either printed or typewritten. Resolutions involving appropriation of funds must be referred to the Committee on Finance. The proponent of a bill, resolution, or report is privileged to speak for three (3) minutes in explanation thereof, prior to final action. The adoption of an officer's report containing recommendations or proposed expenditures must be implemented by a resolution approved by the Grand Lodge, following a committee report.

Expenses and Compensation of Officers and Representatives

Elective officers, Appointed Officers, Special Representatives of the Grand Master, Immediate Past Grand Master while on the Board/ Executive Committee, and Committees may receive such allowances for expenses from appropriated funds on vouchers accompanied by receipts whenever possible, when performing official duties during recess of the Grand Lodge.[66] Salaried officers shall receive such salaries as may be appropriated. Representatives and Past Grand Masters may receive such mileage and per diem as may be computed and appropriated.[67] But all salaries, expense allowances, mileage, and per diem shall be paid from funds appropriated. Mileage shall be computed in accordance with any Certified Mileage Guide.

Reports of Elective and Appointive Officers

At least one (1) month prior to the annual session of the Grand Lodge, all elective and appointive officers shall submit to the Grand Secretary the following:[68]

- Report of their activities during the preceding year.

- Minutes of the Board shall be a matter of record in the advance reports. The reports shall be printed for distribution at the annual session and inclusion in the Journal of Proceedings.

- The Grand Master may submit a supplemental report to be printed in the Daily Journal.

Issuance, Suspension, and Revocation of Charters

Petitions for charter shall be on forms supplied by the Grand Secretary.[69] The petition for the charter shall be sent to the Grand Secretary who shall make a copy for the permanent file and then forward the petition to the Grand Master.[70] If satisfied, the Grand Master may issue the charter or reserve action and present it to the Grand Lodge in regular session.[71] The application shall be accompanied by a fee as determined by the Grand Lodge, which shall be refunded if the petition is not granted. In practice, the Grand Master may issue Dispensations/Warrants in the recess of the Grand Lodge, resolving at the Grand Lodge session to issue the Charter.[72] The Grand Master, or one designated by the Grand Master in writing, shall institute a Lodge or other unit when the charter/warrant/dispensation is issued.[73]

Surrendered, arrested, or forfeited charters may also be restored by the Grand Master or the Grand Lodge.[74] Assets of Lodges whose charters are surrendered or revoked vest in the Grand Lodge, which has discretion to return them if the charter is restored, and must return them if an appeal is sustained.[75]

Laws of the Grand Lodge

Laws of the Grand Lodge shall be passed by Bills. Bills proposed by one (1) or more members shall begin with a title followed by the enacting clause, "Be it enacted by the Grand Lodge", and contain only one (1) subject. The Bill shall reference the chapter number, Article and/or Section of the chapter and if applicable, the subsection(s) and/or paragraph(s) and page number (i.e., II-25 of the By-laws to be enacted, amended or repealed). Striking through that portion to be deleted and underlining the portion being added.[76]

Bills must be submitted in triplicate, typewritten or printed, in the form stated in the By-laws and mailed to the Grand Secretary a minimum of forty-five (45) days prior to the session.[77] Bills must be referred to the Committee on Legislation and any additional Committee(s) as essential before action can be taken.[78] The Grand Secretary shall reproduce the bills after review by the Committee on Legislation and send copies to each Representative, Representative-elect, Past Grand Master, Grand Lodge Officer, and to the Secretarial Officer of each Lodge, at least thirty (30) days prior to the annual session. Bills may be amended but no amendment shall be considered which changes the original purpose of the Bill. Bills held over from the previous annual session may be acted upon on the reading of the Committee(s) Report.[79] But a member may introduce a bill at the session if two-thirds (2/3) of the voting members agree.[80]

A hearing on the Bill may be held. The Chairperson of the Committee on Legislation shall announce the time and place of the meeting of the committee each day.[81] Any member in good standing may appear before the committee and be heard for or against a Bill.[82]

The vote shall then be taken and the number for and against entered upon the Journal.[83] No Bill shall become law unless two-thirds (2/3) present and voting shall vote in its favor.[84] On demand of one-fifth (1/5) of the Representatives present, a roll call vote shall be had with the yeses and noes recorded.[85] For Grand Lodges in the United

States and Canada, Bills become effective upon ratification by The Sovereign Grand Lodge.[86]

Information

The local lodges and other branches under its jurisdiction shall annually furnish to their Grand Lodge, who will in turn annually furnish the same to The Sovereign Grand Lodge, the following:[87]

- The most current mailing address for the Unit.

- The physical location of their meeting facilities.

- The Meeting dates and times as reflected in their by-laws.

- The current mailing address of each member whether regular, associate or non-contributing. Said address to reflect status of membership.

The Grand Lodge shall not sell or distribute for any purpose outside the fraternity, any of the member rosters, mailing lists, including personal information held by the Grand Lodge or its local lodges, to any person or persons, institutions or agencies for sales promotions, or for other purposes within or without the Grand Lodge, without the expressed permission of the member.[88] Further any distribution must have the expressed permission of the voting members of the Grand Lodge present and voting at any regular annual or called special session.[89]

Each unit of the IOOF shall also furnish to their Grand Body a complete legal description of all real property owned, including property owned by a hall association and any other property that may be owned outright or in cooperation with others, which includes cemeteries.[90] This information shall be furnished by the Grand Lodge to The Sovereign Grand Lodge upon request.[91]

Every Grand Lodge in the United States and Canada shall furnish to The Sovereign Grand Lodge a complete legal description of all real property owned including Homes, Camps, Cemeteries or other property that may be owned outright or in cooperation with others.[92]

INDEPENDENT GRAND LODGES

Other countries outside North America where there are IOOF lodges may form *Independent Grand Lodges*. Generally, these Grand Lodges possess final and supervisory powers over the lodges within their jurisdiction and adhere only to the founding principles and ancient customs of the IOOF. These jurisdictions include the Grand Lodge of Australasia, Denmark, Finland, Germany, Iceland, Cuba, The Netherlands and Belgium, Norway, Philippines, Poland, Sweden, and Switzerland. The Sovereign Grand Master usually appoints a D*istrict Deputy Sovereign Grand Master* to serve as liaison officer between an Independent Grand Lodge and the Sovereign Grand Lodge. Typically, the District Deputy Sovereign Grand Master is the same as the Grand Master or Grand Sire of the Grand Lodge. These Independent Grand Lodges have a seat in the International Advisory Board.

Grand Lodge of Europe

There had been discussions of establishing a governing body for the IOOF in the continent of Europe since the 1890s. Grand Sires of European jurisdictions had been holding a Conference of the European Grand Sires for many years. This eventually led to the establishment of the *Federation of Independent European Jurisdictions of the Odd Fellow Order IOOF* in 1989. During the same year, the leaders of the Rebekahs in Europe also established the *European Rebekah Leaders Association* (ERLA). In 2003, the Executive Committees of both the Federation and ERLA realized that the time has come to assemble both male and female leaders in one Grand body.

This eventually culminated in the *Grand Lodge of Europe* in 2006. This Grand Lodge is empowered to direct, supervise, and control all matters pertaining to the Independent Order of Odd Fellows within and throughout Europe except the United Kingdom of Great Britain, Northern Ireland and the Republic of Ireland, which are under the jurisdiction of the Manchester Unity Independent Order of Odd Fellows. The criteria for membership and election to an office in the Grand Lodge of Europe are: 1) be a Grand Lodge Officer or Past Grand Lodge Officer in a European Jurisdiction; 2) have received the *Degree of Wisdom*. The officers of the Grand Lodge of Europe are: the European

The Grand Sire and Deputy Grand Sire of the Grand Lodge of Australasia together with the delegates of the 2019 Sessions of the Grand Lodge of the Philippines held in Manila, Philippines. Photo courtesy of Joel Mari Espiritu of Manila Lodge No.8, 2019.

Grand Sire, one male Deputy European Grand Sire, one female Deputy European Grand Sire, European Grand Secretary, Deputy European Grand Secretary, European Grand Treasurer, European Grand Marshal and European Grand Chaplain.

Grand Lodge of Latin America

In 1948, the Grand Lodge of Latin America was empowered to direct, supervise, and control all matters pertaining to the Independent Order of Odd Fellows within and throughout Argentina, Brazil, Bolivia, Chile, Columbia, Costa Rica, Cuba, Dominican Republic, Ecuador, El Salvador, Guatemala, Honduras, Belize, Mexico, Nicaragua, Panama – except the Canal Zone which shall remain under the jurisdiction of The Sovereign Grand Lodge, Paraguay, Peru, Uruguay, and Venezuela.

Grand Lodge of Asia Pacific

In 2018, the Grand Lodge of Australasia and the Grand Lodge of the Philippines constituted themselves into the Grand Lodge of Asia Pacific to direct, supervise, and control all matters pertaining to the Independent Order of Odd Fellows within and throughout Australia, New Zealand, Asia and the Pacific.

Sovereign Grand Lodge

The highest governing body of the Independent Order of Odd Fellows is the *Sovereign Grand Lodge,* which consists of Grand Lodges, Grand Encampments and Grand Bodies all over the United States and Canada. The Sovereign Grand Lodge is considered to be the source of all true and legitimate Odd Fellowship and possesses final and supervisory power over the IOOF. The Sovereign Grand Lodge has exclusive power:[1]

- To establish, regulate and control Rituals, ceremonies, lectures and the Unwritten Work of the IOOF.

- To prescribe forms for all cards, certificates, ceremonies, jewels and regalia and to serve as sole source of supply thereof.
  To prescribe minimum qualifications for membership in the Order.

- To organize component units under the direct supervision of The Sovereign Grand Lodge where no Grand Body exists.

- To grant charters to Grand Bodies. Only one Grand Body of each component may be established in any state, province, region or territory.

- To enact and construe its laws and actions, which shall be final.

- To authorize Grand Bodies to enact laws consistent with the Code of General Laws for promoting Odd Fellowship in the jurisdictions governed by them.

- To prohibit all members and components from resorting to civil courts prior to exhausting the tribunals of the Order, concerning the construction of the laws of the Order, matters pertaining to its affairs or directives or orders.

However, the Independent Grand Lodges chartered by The Sovereign Grand Lodge, which generally follow the founding principles and ancient customs of the IOOF shall be the guiding force of Odd Fellowship within the regions in which they operate and shall individually possess final and supervisory powers over the IOOF within those regions.[2]

International Headquarters

The International Headquarters of the Sovereign Grand Lodge of the Independent Order of Odd Fellows and the International Association of Rebekah Assemblies is located at 422 Trade Street in Winston-Salem, North Carolina, USA. It is a 21,835.00 square feet 4-storey building consisting of the Odd Fellows international office, Rebekah international office, Thomas Wildey Museum, Schuyler Colfax Museum, a lodge room, supplies room, a storage area and attic.

Composition of the Sovereign Grand Lodge

The working members of The Sovereign Grand Lodge are the Grand Representatives from dues paying Grand Bodies.[3] The elected, appointed, past presiding officers, Special and District Deputy Sovereign Grand Masters and Representatives from Independent Grand Lodges are non-voting members, having the right only to make motions and debate questions.[4]

Grand Lodges directly under the Sovereign Grand Lodge are represented by one (1) to three (3) votes during Sovereign Grand Lodge sessions.[5] Each Grand Lodge with a combined membership of 1,000 or more members, based on regular and non-contributing members from Odd Fellows Lodges, Junior Lodges, Rebekah Lodges and Theta Rho Girls' Clubs; each Grand Encampment with a combined membership of 1,000 or more members, based on regular and non-contributing members from Encampments and Ladies Encampment Auxiliaries; is entitled to *two (2) Grand Representatives* or *two (2) votes.*[6] Grand Lodges or Grand Encampments with less than 1,000 members are entitled to *one (1) Grand Representative* or *one (1) vote.*[7] The General Military Council is entitled to *one (1) Grand Representative* or *one (1) vote.*[8] The International Association of Rebekah Assemblies is entitled to *one (1) Grand Representative* or *one (1) vote.*[9]

In some respects, the Sovereign Grand Lodge resembles the United States Senate in that the classification of its members secures its perpetuity. It is also similar to the United States House of Representatives in that the number of representatives is dependent on the respective constituencies. Representatives of the Independent Grand Lodges, on the other hand, are *non-voting members* having the right only to make motions and debate questions. In its current

The headquarters of The Sovereign Grand Lodge, Independent Order of Odd Fellows in Winston-Salem, North Carolina. Photo by the author, 2012.

186th Annual Communication of The Sovereign Grand Lodge held in Cincinnati, Ohio. Photo by David Burns and author, 2012.

setting, no Grand Representative outside the jurisdiction of the United States and Canada can become an elective officer of the Sovereign Grand Lodge. So, the Sovereign Grand Lodge is really the governing body for the IOOF in the United States and Canada. But it is not an international governing body in the real sense.

Annual Sessions and Special Sessions

The annual sessions of the Sovereign Grand Lodge shall be held at predetermined places on the third Monday of August or as otherwise provided in the Code of General Laws.[10]

The Sovereign Grand Lodge may also meet specifically on the call of the Sovereign Grand Master or upon the request of a majority of Grand Representatives, of which the Sovereign Grand Master shall cause sixty (60) days' notice to be given to the Officers of The Sovereign Grand Lodge and to the Grand Representatives, communicating to them the purpose for which the special meeting is called, and in no case shall any other business be transacted at a called meeting unless by unanimous consent and adopted on roll call; provided, said meeting may be called on shorter notice, a majority of the Grand Representatives of record agreeing thereto.

Quorum

The quorum of the Sovereign Grand Lodge shall consist of a majority of the elected Grand Representatives from the active Grand Lodges in the United States and Canada.

Sovereign Grand Lodge Officers

The elective officers of the Sovereign Grand Lodge are as follows:[11] Sovereign Grand Master, Deputy Sovereign Grand Master, Sovereign Grand Warden, Sovereign Grand Secretary, and Sovereign Grand Treasurer chosen among the Grand Representatives of each Grand Lodge directly under the Sovereign Grand Lodge. There are also appointed officers namely:[12] Sovereign Grand Marshal, Sovereign Grand Conductor, Sovereign Grand Chaplain, Sovereign Grand Musician, Sovereign Grand Guardian, and Sovereign Grand Messenger.

Their functions are almost synonymous with that of the Grand Lodge but their roles are on the international level.

Qualifications of Office

A member nominated for an elected Officer's position must meet the same qualifications of a Grand Representative. Candidates for the office of Sovereign Grand Warden, Deputy Sovereign Grand Master, or Sovereign Grand Master of The Sovereign Grand Lodge shall not have previously held the presiding officer position in any of the other three (3) International Grand Bodies.[13]

Grand Representative and Alternate Representative

Each Grand Lodge Grand Representative and alternate must be a member in good standing in the Grand Lodge and a Past Grand of an active Lodge. Each Grand Encampment Grand Representative and alternate must be a member in good standing in the Grand Encampment and Past Chief Patriarch of an active Encampment. The Grand Representative must also be a member in good standing of an active Odd Fellows Lodge, Encampment, Rebekah Lodge, and a Canton all in good standing; provided that residence is maintained in the Jurisdiction or adjoining Jurisdiction; and further providing that the one elected may qualify after election. The Grand Body shall furnish the Grand Representative with a certificate of election with a duplicate under seal to the Sovereign Grand Secretary. A Grand Body must properly certify its Grand Representative to the Sovereign Grand Secretary. An elected Grand Representative shall not be recognized as such, nor entitled to its rights and privileges until the credentials have been received and approved and the Grand Representative shall have been obligated. The duties of a Grand Representative are the following:[14]

- To attend sessions of The Sovereign Grand Lodge, represent the Grand Body and report all legislation, Ritualistic Work and other matters that occurred at the session pertaining to the Grand Body.

- To vote on every roll-call vote. If any member shall

be temporarily absent from the hall, the other Grand Representative from the Jurisdiction shall be allowed to cast the vote of such temporarily absent member, in which event the Sovereign Grand Secretary shall place the word "absent" opposite the name of the absent Grand Representative and thereafter such vote cannot be changed.

- To vote on all matters except on personal qualifications to be seated.

- To serve on all committees to which appointed unless excused by The Sovereign Grand Lodge.

A Grand Representative may be elected to any number of terms. An associate member may serve as Grand Representative unless prevented by the laws of the jurisdiction. A Grand Representative cannot be seated unless the Grand Representative and the Grand Body are in good standing. A Grand Representative may also hold any other office of the Grand Body represented. But a Grand Representative shall represent only one (1) Grand Body.

Each Independent Grand Jurisdiction is authorized to elect one (1) Grand Representative. Said Grand Representative shall have the right to debate and make motions on all matters coming before The Sovereign Grand Lodge. Each Independent Grand Jurisdiction's Representative shall serve at no cost to The Sovereign Grand Lodge. All Independent Grand Jurisdictions will also need to certify their respective Grand Representative.

Impeachment

An officer, member or Grand Representative may be impeached and removed from office, suspended or expelled from membership in The Sovereign Grand Lodge.[15] A motion to impeach requires a majority vote for passage.[16] Charges with specifications may be filed with the Sovereign Grand Secretary at any time but no action to impeach shall be taken until the accused has received three days prior written notice.[17] A member under impeachment shall be afforded the opportunity to be heard and present evidence. A two-thirds vote of the Grand Representatives present is required for conviction and punishment.[18]

District Deputy Sovereign Grand Masters

District Deputy Sovereign Grand Masters, having jurisdiction of lodges in areas outside the North American Continent of 100 or more dues paying members, may serve as or select a Grand Representative with powers, duties and responsibilities of the Grand Representatives as set out in the Code of General Laws. No expense is to be incurred by The Sovereign Grand Lodge in implementing this Section except those already set forth in the Code of General Laws.

Visiting The Sovereign Grand Lodge Sessions

A Third Degree member in good standing may visit Sessions as long as he or she presents an Official Certificate showing dues paid in advance and a letter, written on the member's Lodge letterhead, stating that the member has attained the Third Degree.[19] The letter must be signed by the Noble Grand, attested by the Secretary and bear the Seal of the Lodge.[20] It must also be signed by the Grand Secretary of the Jurisdiction and bear the Seal of the Grand Lodge, thus attesting that said Lodge is in good standing.[21]

On presentation of this letter and Official Certificate to the Sovereign Grand Guardian, the member shall be issued a colored guest card, which must be signed and then presented to the Sovereign Grand Guardian each time the member enters the Sessions.[22] As there are no signs used in The Sovereign Grand Lodge, the said member will not have to give the sign of the Third Degree.[23] The member will have no voice or vote during the Sessions of The Sovereign Grand Lodge.[24]

Official Language

The official language of The Sovereign Grand Lodge is the English language.[25] All communications with The Sovereign Grand Lodge and all business carried on in The Sovereign Grand Lodge will be in the English language. This is in no way to limit or prohibit Grand Lodges or Local Lodges from using another language more appropriate to their needs.

In 2018, Emanuel Page, Sr., Past Noble Father of Wayman Lodge No. 1339 of the Grand United Order of Odd Fellows spoke during the 192nd Annual Communication of The Sovereign Grand Lodge held in Baltimore, Maryland. Photo by Peter Sellars, 2018.

Revenues and Funds

The revenues of shall of The Sovereign Grand Lodge shall be from charter fees, dues, assessments adopted in regular session, profit from the sale of supplies, investment income, donations, devises and bequests and income from any lawful source.[26]

No funds of The Sovereign Grand Lodge shall be disbursed in excess of the amount budgeted unless such disbursement is approved by The Sovereign Grand Lodge in session.[27] But excess funds of The Sovereign Grand Lodge shall be invested by the Sovereign Grand Treasurer and the Sub-Committee on Finance in safe and marketable securities.[28] This officer and sub-committee shall also determine the amount that constitutes excess funds.[29] A complete list of all securities shall be currently maintained by the Sovereign Grand Treasurer and chairman of the Sub Committee on Finance and delivered to the Sovereign Grand Master.[30] Securities shall be kept in safe deposit boxes. Access shall be limited to any two (2) of the following, acting jointly, to wit: Sovereign Grand Master, Sovereign Grand Secretary, Sovereign Grand Treasurer, and Assistant Sovereign Grand Secretary.[31]

The Sovereign Grand Master and the Sovereign Grand Secretary, or in the absence or inaccessibility of the Sovereign Grand Master or the Sovereign Grand Secretary, then the Deputy Sovereign Grand Master and/or the Assistant Sovereign Grand Secretary may borrow funds, to meet the immediate needs not exceeding $25,000.00, as may be necessary to cover expenses and appropriations, and to pledge the credit of The Sovereign Grand Lodge.[32] Evidence of the indebtedness shall also be attested by the chairman of the Sub Committee on Finance.[33] Real or personal property may be mortgaged or pledged if necessary. Funds derived there from shall be deposited by the Sovereign Grand Secretary keeping the Sovereign Grand Treasurer informed.[34] Funds to be borrowed if in excess of $25,000.00 must be authorized by special resolution adopted at a session of The Sovereign Grand Lodge.[35]

Laws To Be Liberally Construed

The rules and regulations set forth in the Constitution and Code of General Laws of the Sovereign Grand Lodge shall be liberally construed. The chief concern shall be following the spirit of the law and the good of Odd Fellowship rather than harshly enforcing rules to the letter of the law.[36]

International Advisory Board

Before World War II, communication between the Sovereign Grand Lodge and Grand Lodges outside North America was challenging. The distance and difficulties during the war years made close relationships difficult and even severed relationships between the Sovereign Grand Lodge and several Grand Lodges in other countries. In 1946, a legislation was passed to form the International Council. The aim of the council was to strengthen the ties between the Sovereign Grand Lodge and all Grand Lodges of the IOOF; to protect the usage, customs, and ancient teachings of the organization; exchange ideas, discuss concerns, and make endorsements to all affiliated bodies of Odd Fellows around the world. This body was renamed the *IOOF International Advisory Board* in 2012.

The Board meets a day prior to the Sovereign Grand Lodge Sessions and consist of four (4) members of the Sovereign Grand Lodge, three (3) members of the International Association of Rebekah Assemblies, one (1) from the General Military Council, three (3) from the Grand Lodge of Europe, three (3) from the Grand Lodge of Australasia, and two (2) from the *Manchester Unity Independent Order of Oddfellows Friendly Society* in the United Kingdom.[37] The Board will be able to create recommendations to the Sovereign Grand Lodge but without legislative authority.[38]

Benefits of Membership and Philanthropy

The benefits of membership in the Odd Fellows are a two-way process. A lodge must provide fulfilling activities and programs. But you, as a member, can only feel and appreciate your membership by attending and sharing your time, resources and talents in the activities and projects of the lodge, and by being a true friend to all brothers and sisters.

Ideally, Odd Fellowship is about getting more out of life! Working together with others, you may develop your character and live a more purposeful and fulfilling life based on your experiences and relationships with others. Depending on your level of participation in your lodge, membership may give a fulfilling life experience. Through your reflections of the rituals and active participation in the Lodge (local), Grand Lodge (national level) and Sovereign Grand Lodge (international level) within the organization, you may:

- Broaden your mind and improve yourself into a better person.
- Share your talents and resources for the common good.
- Participate in community projects and activities.
- Help others and receive help from others.
- Foster life-lasting friendships.
- Develop tolerance of other people's opinions, beliefs and culture
- Gain the ability to effectively work with others.
- Learn how to handle challenging responsibilities and situations.
- Improve your leadership and inter-personal skills.
- Give and receive recognition and awards.
- And an inner satisfaction that no money can buy.

SO, WHAT CAN ODD FELLOWS OFFER?

1. Opportunity to Improve and Elevate Character

Odd Fellowship is not just a fraternity, it is a school of ethics. The Degrees of Initiation teaches a member practical morality based on humanitarian principles with the aim of improving character and increasing one's capability to do good. Through thought exchanges and self-reflection in the degrees, you are expected to try to find your own way to the truth and you are encouraged to practice these lessons in daily life. As a member, you should strive to align your behavior and actions with the organization's principles and benevolent purposes so that our world becomes more peaceful and humane. Thus, Odd Fellowship is more than just a social club; Odd Fellowship is a way of life!

2. International Social Network

Ideally, Odd Fellowship aims provide genuine and life-lasting friendships. By friendship, we mean mutual-assistance, kindness, warmth, benevolence, toleration, forgiveness and understanding. This requires respect and sincerity in dealing with each other noting that we are composed of people from different backgrounds, nationalities, ethnicities, cultures, creeds, political inclinations, attitudes and walks of life. Odd Fellowship is also an international "social network" composed of approximately 600,000 people located in more than 30 countries.

3. Collaboration in Community Service Activities and Philanthropic Projects

Alone you can do so little but together with others, you can do more. The Odd Fellows is not a charity foundation per se because our lodges do not habitually rely on external donations and government grants. But an Odd Fellows Lodge is a fraternal organization with humanitarian purposes. Members contribute their personal time, talents and resources not just for their own welfare but also to

Unselfish, honest, caring, sincere and enduring friendships

In theory, the goal of Odd Fellowship is to build an unselfish, honest, caring, sincere and enduring bonds of friendship between people from various nationalities, races, religions, professions and social backgrounds guided by the principles of genuine Friendship, Love and Truth.

volunteer and support various charitable, social and community projects in a local, national and international level.

Locally, every Odd Fellows Lodge finds time to organize community projects, fund-raising activities; or combine personal contributions among themselves to support local causes and advocacies; or to simply help each other and other people when the need arises. Every Lodge can support whatever good works they want to support. Every member can bring in ideas and suggestions. One of the degrees of initiation in the Odd Fellows teaches its members that it is not the nature and size of the deed but the right attitude of love. Nationally or State-wide, Grand Lodges organize and support philanthropic causes and advocacies. Internationally, Odd Fellows and Rebekahs across the world raise and donate millions of dollars and render thousands of volunteer hours in support humanitarian projects. While the individual Grand Lodges and Lodges enjoy some autonomy on what projects to support, the Sovereign Grand Lodge of the Independent Order of Odd Fellows has identified several programs and projects that all members and lodges may join and support.

- **IOOF Arthritis Advisory Board**

In 1985, the Independent Order of Odd Fellows began supporting the Arthritis Foundation in the United States and the Arthritis Society in Canada based on their command to "relieve the distressed." Since that year, the Odd Fellows and Rebekahs have

In 2019, members under the Grand Lodge of Norway raised NOK 40 million to donate a third rescue boat to the Norwegian Rescue Society in celebration of the 200th anniversary of the Independent Order of Odd Fellows. Photo courtesty of Grand Lodge of Norway, 2020.

raised more than $8 million to support and fund research on arthritis. Every year, lodges across the United States and Canada raise over $500,000.00 to support arthritis research.

- **IOOF Educational Foundation**

    The Educational Foundation of the Independent Order of Odd Fellows began its operation on September 20, 1927. The purpose of the Foundation is to operate a revolving loan fund for qualified students dependent, wholly or in part, on their own efforts for an education. Since the opening of the Foundation, donations of approximately $3.5 million have made it possible for over 5,000 young people to receive student loans amounting to over $7.1 million. The Foundation has expanded its educational investment for deserving students by providing several scholarships: Christine Smith Scholarship, Ingstrom Scholarship, Wirz Scholarship, Vocation Technology Scholarship, Glenn Coursey Scholarship, Continuing Education Grants, Odd Fellows and Rebekahs Education Pilgrimage Tour Scholarship, Non-Traditional Scholarship, and Davis Odd Fellows Charities, Inc.

- **IOOF Living Legacy Program**

    This program began as the idea of Past Sovereign Grand

Master Wilson D. Berkey, who in 1989 noticed many dead trees in the jurisdictions that he was visiting. This aroused his concern for global tree loss, so he commissioned this worthy project as "The Living Legacy Program" of the IOOF. Planting trees has been advocated due to the ability of trees to absorb carbon dioxide, store the carbon, and release oxygen for human use. During its first implementation on June 1, 1990, members around the United States and Canada planted 162,772 trees. In 1992, exactly 420,000 trees were actually planted, hundreds of shrubs, at least two rose gardens, ten flower beds on public grounds, the perpetual care of several parks, and donations of close to $12,000 in cash and checks. Since the inception of the project, approximately 8 million trees have been planted by the Odd Fellows and Rebekahs in the United States and Canada.

• **Odd Fellows and Rebekahs Pilgrimage for Youth**

This program was established by the Sovereign Grand Lodge in 1949 to provide the youth with opportunity to exchange views on education, politics, and global relations, and to develop friendships among themselves. Annually, the IOOF brings together high school students from North America and Europe for a field trip to study and observe the United Nations and visit historical sites in the United States and Canada. Expenses including transportation, meals, lodging, and sightseeing are paid by the sponsoring Odd Fellows and Rebekah Lodges. Since it was established, over 50,000 students have participated in the Pilgrimage.

• **IOOF Visual Research Foundation**

Established in 1957, the Visual Research Foundation and World Eye Bank of the Independent Order of Odd Fellows and Rebekahs support and provide funds to advance eye research through professorships in ophthalmology at the Wilmer Eye Institute at John Hopkins School of Medicine in Baltimore, Maryland. Moreover, the World Eye Banks located in different state jurisdictions allow members of the IOOF to donate their eyes after death for corneal transplants and research.

In 1961, the Foundation's professorship in eye research was

established through an endowment of $625,000. With the subsequent challenge of more research needed and its rising costs, another $1 million was added to the fund in 1987. As of 2012, the IOOF had a total endowment of $2.5 million for this program, and continues to donate at least $500,000 annually. The IOOF support to this program has made it possible for many handicapped persons to be aided, whether through corneal transplant or research breakthrough to prevent blindness.

- **IOOF World Hunger and Disaster Fund**

    The IOOF World Hunger and Disaster Fund provides relief through any humanitarian project to assist a person, persons, or groups of people in need, or in rehabilitation of their damaged properties. It provides assistance in terms of food, clothing, shelter, medical expenses, or other needs that may arise. In 1976, this Program raised $50,000 to help feed the hungry, donated $35,000 to support the "Save the Rice" Congress in India, donated $5,500 to feed hungry children in Chile, and gave other amounts to the Salvation Army and International Red Cross to purchase food for destitute people. Its "Love Thy Neighbor" project served refreshments to weary travelers at highway rest stops and roadside parks during heavy-travel weekends and holidays. At present, this program allocates more than $7.5 million in support of relief projects annually.

- **Odd Fellows and Rebekahs Retirement Homes**

    The first Odd Fellows Home was built in 1872 in Pennsylvania. Eventually, almost all states and provinces in North America had a home. The endowments for and cost of operating these early homes ran in the millions and were entirely supported by the membership. These homes have provided care to thousands and afforded a home-like atmosphere and education for hundreds of orphans. Because of the works of the IOOF in the United States, then President Ronald Reagan invited Sovereign Grand Secretary Edward T. Rogers to the White House where he recognized the work of the IOOF in caring for the elderly and indigent.

    As times have changed, so has the concept of care-giving.

In 1962, the Odd Fellows and Rebekahs began building high rise apartments and skilled nursing facilities to take care of seniors. Photo of Rebekah Rehab & Extended Care in Bronx, New York.

In 1984, the Odd Fellows and Rebekahs of Ontario, through its Humanitarian Services, gave Camp Trillium a grant of $5,000 to hold a one-week camp. This has now grown to two permanent camps and numerous day camps and over 2,500 campers (Children with Cancer) per year. In 2000, the Grand Master of Ontario established the "Camp Trillium, Odd Fellows and Rebekahs Capital Fund," which received donations and helped the camp with a donation of around $100,000 per year. This fund paid off the mortgage on Trillium's Office building. Eventually, the Odd Fellows and Rebekahs awarded Camp Trillium $1 million to purchase Garratt's Island, which is now known as "Camp Trillium Odd Fellows and Rebekah Island." Photo courtesy of Camp Trillium.

The Odd Fellows hall, building, house, palace or lodge is the place where members hold their meetings, ceremonies, fund-raising and other social activities. There are thousands of Odd Fellows Lodges located in about 30 countries.

During the 19th century, the Odd Fellows literally "buried the dead" that almost all Odd Fellows' lodges owned cemeteries or burial plots. Many of these cemeteries are now considered historical sites. Photo shown is the Odd Fellows Cemetery in Tamaqua, Pennsylvania. Photo by the author, 2019.

Governments became involved in care-giving and Homes for the Aged are no longer considered charitable homes. The high-rise, the cottage, and the apartment complex type of living arrangements have replaced the original concept. Orphanages have been replaced by foster homes. Many jurisdictions under the Independent Order of Odd Fellows have become involved in remodeling Homes into:

- Retirement Homes

- Skilled Nursing Facilities

- Day care centers

Many of these Homes provide private rooms for residents, dining rooms, recreation rooms, hospital facilities nearby, and security and comfort in the twilight years of life. High-Rise Apartments for Senior Citizens who have retired and reached the age of 62 are also sponsored by the Odd Fellows and Rebekahs in several states and jurisdictions.

- **Odd Fellows and Rebekah Camps**

In some states and countries, the Odd Fellows and Rebekahs own and sponsor Youth Camps and Recreation Parks. These facilities aim to provide a healthy and entertaining outdoor experience for the youth and their families. Today, the IOOF still owns and manages several Camps in Alabama, Arizona, California, Colorado, Iowa, Kentucky, Maine, Minnesota, Michigan, New Hampshire, New Mexico, Ohio, Oregon, Washington, and Wisconsin.

- **Odd Fellows Cemeteries**

In some states or cities, Odd Fellows own cemeteries in line with their ancient command: "To Bury the Dead." While many of these cemeteries have already closed, some are still being utilized at present. Many are also registered as historic places or landmarks.

- **Odd Fellows Halls**

    Many Odd Fellows lodges across the world own buildings. Most of these halls are not just a place for lodge meetings but also serve as venue for various community and social events where people can organize fund-raising events or simply hang out and have fun. Many of these buildings are already registered as historic landmarks

- **Pilgrimage to the Tomb of the Unknown Soldier and the Canadian War Memorial**

    The first Sunday in May has been designated for the Annual Odd Fellows and Rebekahs Pilgrimage to the Tomb of the Unknowns in Arlington, Virginia. The yearly event developed from a privilege that was afforded to the Odd Fellows and Rebekahs by 32nd President of the United States and Odd Fellow Franklin D. Roosevelt, who was in the White House from 1933 to 1945. The first Pilgrimage was on June 17, 1934. Permission for this has been granted by the Department of Army, custodian of the Arlington National Cemetery. The purpose of this Pilgrimage was not only to honor the Unknown Soldier and the Nation's War Dead, but also the IOOF members who had made the supreme sacrifice in World War I and World War II. Moreover, Odd Fellows and Rebekahs also gather on the first Sunday of June at the *Canadian War Memorial* in Ottawa, Canada, to pay homage to those brave soldiers who gave their lives for their beloved country of Canada. In other countries, Odd Fellows and Rebekahs also participate in other solemn activities to pay tribute to those who made supreme sacrifices for their country.

- **S.O.S. Children's Village**

    In 2003, The Sovereign Grand Lodge voted to raise more than $2 million to build an S.O.S. Children's Village in Battambang, Cambodia. This consists of homes, a kindergarten, school, social center, and medical facility for children who have lost their biological family due to personal, national, or natural disaster. In 2016, another S.O.S. Children's Village was built in Malawi, Africa, through the generous donations by the IOOF Grand Lodge of Norway.

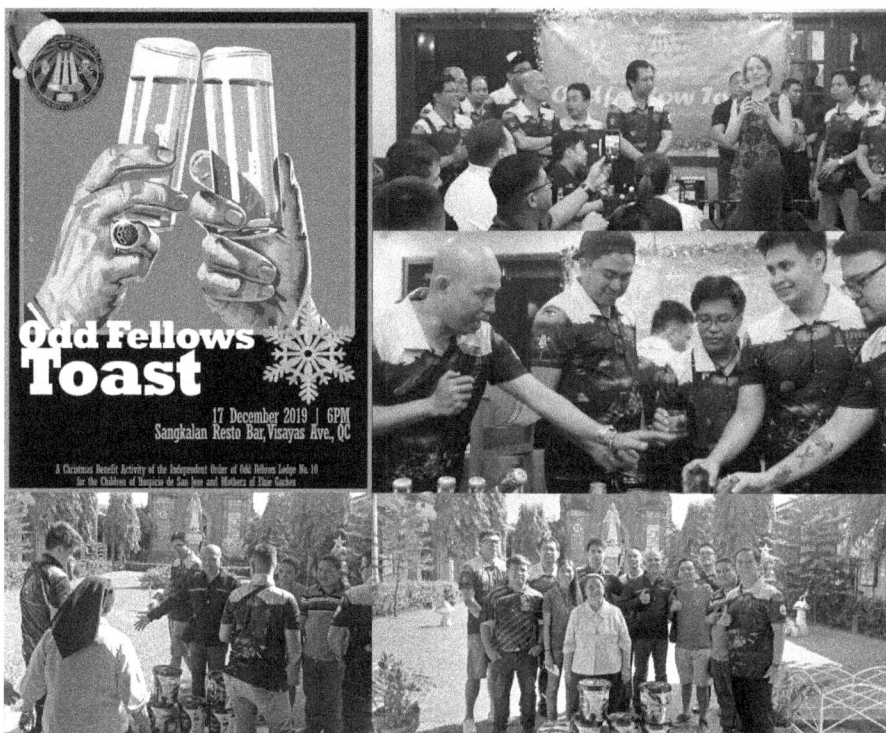

Quezon City Lodge No.10 organized the "Odd Fellows Toast", a social and fund-raising event at the same time. The proceeds raised during the event were donated to a particular charity. Photo courtesy of Quezon City Lodge No.10 in Manila, Philippines, 2019.

- **Odd Fellows Rebekahs Rose Parade Float**

Since 1908 and until the present, the Odd Fellows and Rebekahs participate in the *Annual Tournament of Roses Parade* in Pasadena, California. This project is now run and managed by the Odd Fellows and Rebekahs Rose Float Organization, which provides an educational experience for the public by teaching volunteers to create and display a work of art in the annual Tournament of Roses Parade.

4. Rewarding Social Life

The work of Odd Fellowship should not be all serious. Growing Odd Fellows Lodges also host or organize annual social or community fund-raising events that are fun and fulfilling. This kind of lodge activity provides an opportunity and time when the bonds of friendship between members can become stronger.

How do Odd Fellows raise funds to support their projects and activities?

Locally, mainly from:

- Membership application and Degree fees

- Annual dues from each member

- Donations and personal contributions from members

- Revenue from sales of merchandise, rent of its properties and other fund-raising activities

Nationally and Internationally:

- Grand Lodge dues

- Sovereign Grand Lodge dues

- Donations and personal contributions from members

- Revenue from sales of merchandise, rent of its properties and other fund-raising activities

At the close of each year, the total net funds received from Membership Fees, Annual Dues and other contributions raised by the Lodge, Grand Lodge and Sovereign Grand Lodge are usually budgeted to support programs and cover operational expenses.

WHAT ODD FELLOWS CANNOT OFFER?

The Odd Fellows cannot promise financial rewards. The Odd Fellows is a humble and grass-roots type of fraternal organization. As a service-oriented group, Odd Fellowship is a place for "givers." Anyone who will join out of curiosity or for the sake of financial gain will end-up disappointed.

Joining and Maintaining Membership

Qualifications for membership

The basic qualifications for membership in an Odd Fellows Lodge are the following:

- Must be male or female (depending on the jurisdiction, there are lodges for both men and women; there are lodges for men only and there are lodges for women only).

- Must be of age (minimum age to be determined by the Grand Lodge of the jurisdiction, either sixteen (16), eighteen (18) or twenty-one (21) years of age).

- Must hold a belief in a Supreme Being (Odd Fellowship strictly forbids any interference with one's religious beliefs)

- Must be of good character (the authority to determine character shall vest in each lodge, however, membership shall not be denied on the basis of their age, disability, ethnicity, gender, race, sex, sexual orientation, religion or other social identity.)

- Length of Residence (unless restricted by the Grand Lodge, each lodge shall have the authority to fix the length of residence in its by-laws before becoming eligible for membership)

Non-Discrimination Policy

The Independent Order of Odd Fellows will not exclude any individual based on disability, age, ethnicity, gender, race, sexual orientation, religion or other social identity from the full and equal enjoyment of its services and facilities, unless the individual poses a direct threat to the health or safety of others, or himself or herself, that cannot be eliminated by a modification of policies, practices, or procedures or by the provision of auxiliary aids or services. The IOOF will not exclude any individual from the full and equal enjoyment of its services and facilities because of the individual's association with a person of disability, age, ethnicity, gender, race, sexual orientation, religion or other social identity.[1] W.G. Nye, Grand Representative of the Grand Lodge of Minnesota (1897), shared:

Odd Fellowship is rendering service by teaching and developing the great principle of equality - not of an equality of character, ability, or wealth but an equality by virtue of common parentage and a common humanity. The doors to its Lodge rooms are open no wider to receive a king than a peasant; no more quickly for a millionaire than for the man of moderate means. The passport to its sacred precincts is not rank, but virtue; not money, but maturity; not power but character. Around its altar gather men of different grades of wealth and social standing, of varied opinions and beliefs, of every degree of education and culture, and with the clasping of hands and the touching of elbows each learns to regard the others for what they are, not for what they have.

What are the steps in Joining?

To become a member of an Odd Fellows Lodge, the path is similar - find a local lodge. Those interested simply would either contact the lodge via telephone or e-mail, meet a current member, come to an Odd Fellows' sponsored event and let the lodge know your intentions. Once the lodge is aware of your intention, it is strongly suggested that you do the following:

- Research about the Odd Fellows. Information is available in libraries and all over the internet.

- Attend a lodge dinner or other functions so that you have the opportunity to get to know the members and see first-hand some of the programs the Lodge are involved in.

- Visit other Odd Fellows Lodge in the area, if there are any.

- Consider the time and resources you have to offer. Odd Fellows are Odd Fellows 24/7 365 days. All members have to financially contribute to maintain and support the local, national and international projects and activities of the organization.

- If after you have contemplated the above and wish to proceed, you will need a sponsor who will recommend you to other lodge members of your eligibility for membership. If you don`t personally know someone in the lodge and wish to join and have made your intention to become a member, one will be appointed

WHAT HE IS

In the lodge room we do not ask a man who his father was; we simply inquire what he is.

We do not ask him what his father has done; we simply ask him if he is ready to do the work that falls to him.

We do not ask him whether he has received a diploma from some institution of learning; we simply ask him if he studied the science of How to Live; if he recognizes the ties that bind him to mankind.

We do not ask him how many acres of land he possesses; we ask him whether he is possesed of the spirit of brotherhood. The lodge room helps to draw us together, it helps us to unify the world.

William Jennings Bryan (1860-1925)
41st Secretary of the United States
Member, Independent Order of Odd Fellows

for you. Applications may be withdrawn by the sponsor, without permission of the Lodge, before the committee reports.[2]

- Fill-up and submit your membership application form together with the required fees. This becomes your official start.

- You will undergo a petitioning process which may vary per lodge and jurisdiction. Some lodges require that you will be educated on what is expected and you will be asked to be involved in various lodge functions and activities as well. Other lodges or jurisdictions require your membership application to be forwarded to the Grand Lodge which the Grand Lodge will circulate to other active lodges within its jurisdiction.

- Most lodges also require a background check by an Interviewing Committee.

- If the Interviewing Committee finds your petition to be favorable, your name will be balloted using a secret balloting procedure held during a scheduled regular or special lodge meeting. Customarily, some jurisdictions require that no rejected petitioner may re-apply in any lodge within a period of six (6) months from the date of said rejection.

- If the result of the secret ballot is favorable, the lodge will set a date for the Initiatory degree.

- Membership and dues start when the applicant signs the Members' Register during the Initiatory Degree.[3] There is no more secret balloting in the succeeding degrees. But you are expected to study and review what was taught to you in the prior degree because there is a required test or examination of the lessons, password, symbols and other unwritten work before you can proceed to the succeeding degrees: Degree of Friendship, Degree of Love and Degree of Truth.

No hazing, no sacrifice of your opinions and beliefs, no change of relations to your country, no loosening of the obligations which, as a good citizen, you owe to the laws and institutions under which you live, is required. The initiation and degrees are a time for reflection and meditation. Wise lessons will be taught and noble principles will be inculcated through the process in the different degrees of advancement. It is important for the lodge to confer each ceremony with utmost solemnity and respect. If a candidate is attentive and true to himself or herself, he or she will be morally better and consequently happier when all the teachings are given to him or her.

How much does it cost to be a member?

No organization can continue to exist, provide sensible activities and projects and maintain its buildings and facilities without the financial support of its members. Usually, there is an initiation fee and degree fee when you join and each lodge charges annual dues to cover administration and operation costs. Other lodges only charge an initiation fee. Other lodges require a new member to purchase his or her own regalia while some already provide the regalia for its members. But the cost for membership can vary per lodge because every lodge enjoys some level of financial autonomy. This lodge charges the following:

Membership Application or

Initiatory Degree Fee = _____

Degree of Friendship Fee (1st Degree) = _____

Degree of Love Fee (2nd Degree) = _____

Degree of Truth Fee (3rd Degree) = _____

Annual Dues = _____

Regalia = _____

GRAND TOTAL = _____

Meetings are usually followed by a dinner, with cost depending on the food and venue. But members are not required to attend dinner. Some lodges provide dinner for free using the revenue they raised from their property or projects. Members may also be encouraged to donate to a charity, but this is voluntary and should be based on your means.

Ballot Box and Balloting

A ballot box is a sealed container, usually with a narrow slot sufficient for a small ball or cube to enter. Balloting is a traditional form of secret ballot, where a white ball constitutes a vote in support and a black ball or cube signifies opposition. Generally, a majority of black ballots are cause to reject the applicant.[4] However, other jurisdictions require a smaller requirement usually a maximum of three black ballots can cause a rejection. At no time shall the number of black ballots cast be disclosed. No debate is also permitted upon the merits or demerits of any candidate at, or before, or after the time of balloting. The secret vote of each member is the legal expression of his or her opinion and he or she will not be asked to explain why he or she voted in that manner.

After the report of a committee is received by the Lodge, a ballot shall be taken upon the applicant.[5] More than one (1) application for membership may be acted upon by a collective ballot. Should the number of black ballots necessary to reject a candidate appear, and then the collective ballot shall be declared void and a separate ballot cast for each applicant.[6] The Noble Grand shall supervise the casting of ballots and the result. Once all members present have cast their ballot, the Noble Grand shall declare the balloting closed which seats the members except the Noble Grand, Vice Grand, Warden and Conductor, and direct the Warden to present the ballot box to the Vice Grand. This shall be carried out in a manner whereas only the Vice Grand views the ballot.

The Warden shall then present the ballot box to the Noble Grand ensuring access only to the Noble Grand. The Noble Grand, after viewing shall ask the Vice Grand, "Vice Grand, how find you the ballot?" The Vice Grand responds accordingly: "I find the ballot favorable" *or* "I find the ballot unfavorable." The Noble Grand shall state: "I too find the ballot favorable, and the applicant is elected to membership" *or* "I too find the ballot unfavorable", and the applicant not elected to membership.[7]

If a majority of black ballots are cast, the applicant shall be rejected. To verify the ballot and guard against errors the Noble Grand may immediately call for a second ballot. The secretary shall so note in the minutes the action of the lodge.[8] In all cases where a candidate for membership in a lodge shall have been elected to membership, and

An Odd Fellows Lodge ballot box with white and black balls.

prior to initiation, the Lodge shall discover the applicant is unworthy, such Lodge shall have the power, by majority ballot of two-thirds (2/3) of the members present at any regular meeting, to annul such election and declare the same void.[9] When the applicant is rejected, notice in writing must be sent to the Grand Secretary.[10] The applicant must also be informed of the decision. A subsequent application from a rejected applicant is usually not considered until after the expiration of six (6) months.[11] A rejected applicant must apply to the Lodge in which the applicant was rejected, or procure the Lodge's consent before applying to any other Lodge.[12]

Is there a waiting period for every degree?

It depends on the Lodge and Grand Lodge. The degrees were designed to be successive. Traditionally, there is a minimum waiting period between receiving the Initiatory Degree, the Degree of Friendship, and all other succeeding degrees. Historically, only one degree is allowed to be conferred on a candidate in one (1) day or evening and the next degree is given after three (3) or four (4) months. The candidate is expected to first familiarize or master the teachings, symbols and unwritten work of the degree he or she received before advancing to the next degree.

In some countries in Europe, there is a minimum waiting

period of six (6) months between receiving the Initiatory Degree, the First degree, and each succeeding degree. After the Initiation, the member must prove himself or herself as worthy to advance before being eligible to attain the next degree. In some countries, a minimum of two (2) years is required for a member to attain the Third Degree. During this period, a new member must attend lodge meetings regularly, serve on committees, and take a full and active part in the affairs of the lodge. This will give the new member time to reflect on the lessons received, learn how meetings are conducted, and get to know more the other members.

However, the waiting period had been relaxed in other countries especially in the United States and Canada where many lodges are experiencing a decline in membership or are still in the revival stage. There are even lodges that confer all the degrees in one (1) day, although this had been criticized and discouraged by many leaders of the IOOF.

Forming a New Lodge

If there is no Odd Fellows lodge in your location, you can petition to charter a new lodge by doing the following:

- Gather at least fifteen (15) or more qualified applicants or a minimum of five (5) Third Degree members in good standing who are willing to organize a lodge and dedicate themselves in promoting the principles of Odd Fellowship.

- Fill-up and submit the petition for charter and individual application forms and pay the required fees to the respective Grand Lodge or The Sovereign Grand Lodge.

- Once individual applications and petition for charter are approved, the Grand Lodge or The Sovereign Grand Lodge will send a degree team who will plan out a mutually convenient date, venue and location for the degrees and the institution of the new lodge.

- Traditionally, the new lodge will first work under a dispensation for one (1) year or so until a charter is approved and issued during the Grand Lodge or The Sovereign Grand Lodge Sessions.

OTHER TYPES OF MEMBERSHIP

Associate Membership

A member may not hold membership in two (2) Odd Fellows Lodges except by associate membership as provided by the Grand Lodge by-laws.[13] But a member is restricted from being an associate member in more than three (3) lodges under each Grand Lodge within the jurisdiction.[14] The Grand Lodge may grant further-associate memberships: [15]

- To those members who have moved ninety (90) miles or greater from their home Lodge (a sojourner)

- To assist a Lodge within the same district in which their Lodge is associated for the purpose of assisting the lodge to rebuild membership.

- To an Ancient and/or Historical Lodge which by reason of the economic conditions of its domicile, is in danger of losing its charter and it is desired to maintain such charter and thus perpetuate its historical and traditional worth to the Order and jurisdiction.

- To those members who desire to obtain membership in a jurisdiction other than the jurisdiction in which they reside.

Applications for associate membership must be made on regular forms and the applicant shall be interviewed and balloted on as in all other cases.[16] If an associate member desires to voluntarily withdraw from associate membership, the member shall submit a letter of resignation.[17] Most Grand Lodges prescribe minimum fees and minimum dues that lodges charge for associate membership.[18]

Non-participating Honorary Membership

Nonparticipating honorary membership may be conferred upon a person not a member of the Order but otherwise eligible for membership as recognition of achievement or prominence.[19] Membership shall be recommended by the Sovereign Grand Master and approved by The Sovereign Grand Lodge and be conferred only by the Immediate Past Sovereign Grand Master at a time and place that is proper and authorized by the Executive Committee.[20] But no more than one person shall receive recognition during any one (1) year. Recognition shall be an engraved plaque setting for the reason for conveying this honor.[21]

Beneficial and Non-beneficial Membership

Beneficial members have all the rights of other members of the IOOF.[22] On the other hand, non-beneficial members have all the rights of other members of the Order except the right to funeral and sick benefits for themselves, their dependents or beneficiaries.[23] Non-beneficial members are usually not entitled to be admitted to the Odd Fellows Home and may be exempt from payment of the Odd Fellows Home Tax; provided the Grand Lodge grants such exemption.[24] However, a member may change from either class of beneficial or non-beneficial by applying to his lodge as prescribed by its by-laws.

Non-contributing Membership

A Member who has been a contributing member of a Lodge for forty (40) consecutive years, or a minimum age of seventy-five (75) with at least ten (10) years of consecutive service and is unable to pay dues may be transferred to non-contributing membership without the loss of benefits if the Grand Lodge so provides.[25] Non-contributing membership must be approved by the Lodge and circumstances documented in the Lodge Minutes.[26]

The Lodge shall be exempt from paying the Grand Lodge or The Sovereign Grand Lodge per capita dues on Non-contributing members. A Grand Lodge may also provide that a non-contributing member is entitled to admission to a Home supported by Odd Fellows upon payment into the proper fund of such sums determined by the Grand Lodge.[27]

Life Membership

Grand Lodges may also provide for life membership in their by-laws. When so provided, the legislation shall apply to all lodges within its jurisdiction. [28]

A Grand Lodge shall prescribe the minimum amount of the life membership fee or may authorize the lodge to do so.[29] A member may become a life member upon application to the Lodge accompanied with advance payment of one (1) year's dues and life membership fee provided required by the Grand Lodge. Such membership fee shall be remitted to the Grand Secretary together with all information required for the proper administration of the Life Membership Fund.[30]

Having established life membership, the Grand Lodge, through a Board of Trustees or otherwise, provide for the investment of the Life Membership Fund and shall enact rules and regulations for the control of the Fund as necessary or advisable.[31] The Sovereign Grand Lodge require that such funds shall be invested only in government, state, provincial, or municipal bonds, or in first mortgage real estate loans and not in speculative securities.[32] The income from the Life Membership Fund shall then be used for the payment of annual dues. The Life Membership Fund and contributions thereto shall be held by the Grand Lodge as a trust fund for the sole purpose of maintaining the life membership for which contributed. A member having paid a life membership fee has no right to withdraw the same.[33] On the death of a Life Member, the life membership fee paid by each member shall be disposed of as provided for by the Grand Body having jurisdiction.[34]

Life members may transfer their membership in the same manner as in other cases. The proper office of the lodge to which transfer is made shall at once notify, under seal, the Grand Secretary having custody of the life membership fee.[35] The Grand Body Secretary shall remit to the Lodge with which the member has become affiliated, whether in the same or in another jurisdiction, the income from the life membership fee, which shall be accepted in full payment for annual dues of such member.[36] Said fee shall remain in the hands of the Grand Jurisdiction where it originated. If a Lodge to which said member belongs shall cease to exist, the status of such life member shall be the same as all other members who were in good standing in this Lodge at the time of the surrender of charter.[37]

If the life member is suspended or expelled, the Lodge must notify the Grand Secretary. The life membership fee shall be disposed of as in the case of the death of a member.[38] The card of said life member shall be void and shall be obtained, if possible, by the lodge and transmitted to the Grand Secretary. If a member expelled or resigned shall be later readmitted, the card shall be returned upon payment of the membership fee, which shall be transferred back to the Life Membership Fund from which it was taken. When a member is suspended for cause, the proper officer until the end of the suspension shall retain the card, when it shall be returned to the life member. An expelled or suspended member cannot be readmitted to active membership unless the life membership card has been surrendered as provided in this section.

MEMBER DUTIES AND RESPONSIBILITIES

To maintain membership, the member must fulfill his or her duties and responsibilities. Each member, whatever his rank or station in the IOOF, has certain duties to perform and obligations to discharge by virtue of his membership as an Odd Fellow.[39] These exist and surround him or her in every situation and condition in which he or she may be placed in life, public and private, in the Lodge and in the bosom of his family.[40] A member is an Odd Fellow, fist, middle, and last: an Odd Fellow always, whether a Grand Master or a mere initiate, wherever and whatever he may be.[41] And in consequence of these acknowledged duties and obligations, the lodge claim the privilege of observing the conduct of all members inside and outside the lodge for brotherly or sisterly approval, advice, admonition, or correction.[42]

Payment of Annual Dues and other Assessments

Non-payment of annual dues for one (1) year shall warrant suspension of membership from the Independent Order of Odd Fellows. A suspended member shall lose all rights, benefits and privileges of a *member in good standing* that the Independent Order of Odd Fellows offers, including disqualification from:

- Right to Vote and hold office

- Lodge mutual-benefit programs and use of facilities

- State-wide, national and international visitation and recognition

Whether the arrearages accumulate as unpaid dues, fines, or assessments, or all of them combined, the member may be suspended, providing proper notification of such arrearages provided by law. A member suspended shall be notified in writing by the Secretary and may appeal the suspension within three (3) years. Provided, a suspended member may have his or her membership reinstated upon settlement of his or her annual dues and other assessments. However, a member who has become mentally ill or sick shall not be suspended. The Lodge shall be relieved of dues during such illness by moving the member's status to Non-contributing. A member suspended for nonpayment of dues cannot resign membership, but has the right to apply for reinstatement.

Lodge Attendance and Participation

Other jurisdictions also require a minimum attendance in meetings but this is not true for all lodges. However, it should be noted that a member will fail to appreciate his or her membership if she or she does not attend meetings and participate in the activities of the lodge. Our early leaders have expressed their observation and left a reminder: [43]

> Some members are very faithful in Lodge attendance until they have "passed the Chairs" or until they find they cannot succeed in doing so, and then their zeal suddenly cools down, and they seldom attend, except to pay their dues, and even these they sometimes send by a neighbor! Be not one of these. And never vote for or aid in any way to elevate to the honors of the Order, any brother whom you have good reason to believe one of this class. They love not the principles – their hearts are not in the works of Odd Fellowship. It is time that those who united with us, not because they love to do good, but "for loaves and fishes", should learn that they have mistaken their aim, that we prefer honor, above all others, the workers in our ranks, the lovers of our principles.

Official Certificate and Annual Traveling Password

The Official Certificate, also known as the *Annual Dues or Annual Traveling Card*, is a documentary proof that a person is a member in good standing in his or her lodge for the whole year and eligible to receive all rights, benefits and privileges of an Odd Fellow.

Alleged Annual Traveling Card of Wyatt Earp, 1909. Photo from public domain

It is issued once (1) a year to members in good standing after payment in advance of their dues. Every Odd Fellow must be in possession of the Official Certificate and the Annual Traveling Password (ATP) when attending Lodge meetings and visiting other Lodges and jurisdictions. Annual dues are *payable in advance* to the Lodge and must be forwarded to the Grand Lodge on or before March 1st of each year. But the date of the deadline may vary per jurisdiction.

Good Character and Conduct

Good character is a continuing qualification in an Odd Fellows Lodge so any member may be suspended or expelled for *conduct unbecoming an Odd Fellow.* Alfred S. Pinkerton, Past Grand Sire of The Sovereign Grand Lodge and 58th President of Massachusetts State Senate, emphasized that:

> Fraternities, like men, are judged by what they do rather than what they profess; judged by material, as well as by spiritual things; judged by the ideal wrought into the actual. As a nation is measured by its citizenship, so is a fraternity, or a lodge, measured by the lives and conduct of those who compose it. Interest in a lodge means interest in its membership. Charity must be more than a name; it must be a living presence. Truth must ever be an abiding force. Brotherhood finds its broadest expression not within the

lodge room, but in those outward places where its devotees live, meet and strive in the world at large - all serving - all served.

Behavior in the Lodge

During the working hours of the Lodge, members should conduct themselves with propriety and decorum. It is the object of our ceremonies to make a good as well as indelible impression on the minds of those who would become Odd Fellows. Solemnity is a requirement during lodge meetings and more especially during the initiation degrees of the Lodge. It would seem to be a mere farce to ask a candidate to be serious, while all around him or her are talking and laughing.[44] The lodge room does not need to be serious and boring but members are expected to be courteous and respectful. But nobody will be encouraged to attend to a lodge when all he or she can witness is disharmony, confusion or noise.[45]

Members should also be attentive in the Lodge to its regular business. They should listen to whatever may be proceeding, in order that they may be able to vote upon it with correct apprehension of its propriety and importance. Neither should a brother "dodge" a question, or refuse or neglect to vote upon it, without a substantial reason.[46] Members are encouraged to participate in the discussions of the Lodge; not for the purpose of mere debate, contention or love for opposition, but to improve in suitably expressing their sentiments, and to render them useful to the lodge. For this purpose, members should acquaint himself or herself with the rules of order and debate.[47] Study well each subject he or she intends to discuss, in all its bearings and tendencies, so that he or she may have a well digested opinion to express. Avoid every appearance of disrespect for the opinions and motives of others, and strive, not to merely to repeat what others have said but try shedding new light upon the question. It is also important to express your opinions and suggestions in few words as possible, deliver them in a clear tone, in a calm but impressive manner, and then take you seat.[48] It is also very important for members to not lose their temper in the Lodge. Be sure to be always "in order."[49]

Further, members should keep clearly impressed on his or her mind and heart the lessons learned from the degrees of initiation.

Remember the signs and words imparted to enable a member to enter various Lodges and to recognize and be recognized by other brothers and sisters.[50] These are also a guide to the great principles of the IOOF.[51] Lastly, members should not hang-on to titles and positions because every member is important. If lodge leaders do not take time to recognize the contributions that each one is making to the organization, then the lodge will take a vital asset for granted. Remember: Odd Fellows is a voluntary organization and all members are volunteers. The lodge leaders must provide an environment that will offer its members moral, personal and social growth. If the lodge fails to do so, some members may eventually stop being active participants because they feel useless either because their ideas and voice are never heard or simply because the lodge does not provide activities that will result to feelings of fulfillment.

Behavior out of the Lodge

The founders and early leaders of the IOOF left a reminder that Odd Fellows should always be gentlepeople.[52] And by this term, Odd Fellowship mean precisely what the word itself means – persons of kind, gentle, affectionate hearts; conjoined, if possible, with refined tastes and cultivated minds, with courteous speech and easy manners.[53] Odd Fellowship absolutely requires that members whose motto is "Friendship, Love and truth" and whose work is the "diffusion of the principles of benevolence and charity," shall in all their intercourse with the world and each other (and especially in the Lodge), illustrate this motto and diffuse these principles by a living example.[54] The IOOF do not care what maybe be his or her descent, occupation in life, personal appearance, or dress: true gentility resides not in these fortuitous, fictitious, or external circumstances, but in the heart of the person.[55] And hence, every true Odd Fellow – he or she who is friendly, truthful, sympathizing and benevolent in soul, is, and will be always a gentleperson.[56]

Members should endeavor to convince the world, by their conduct as neighbors and citizens, that the teachings and objects of Odd Fellowship tend to make them wiser and better people. They should be honest and truthful in their dealings – should be charitable and benevolent – willing to relieve the distresses and wants of the poor, when they may do so consistently. Members should be industrious

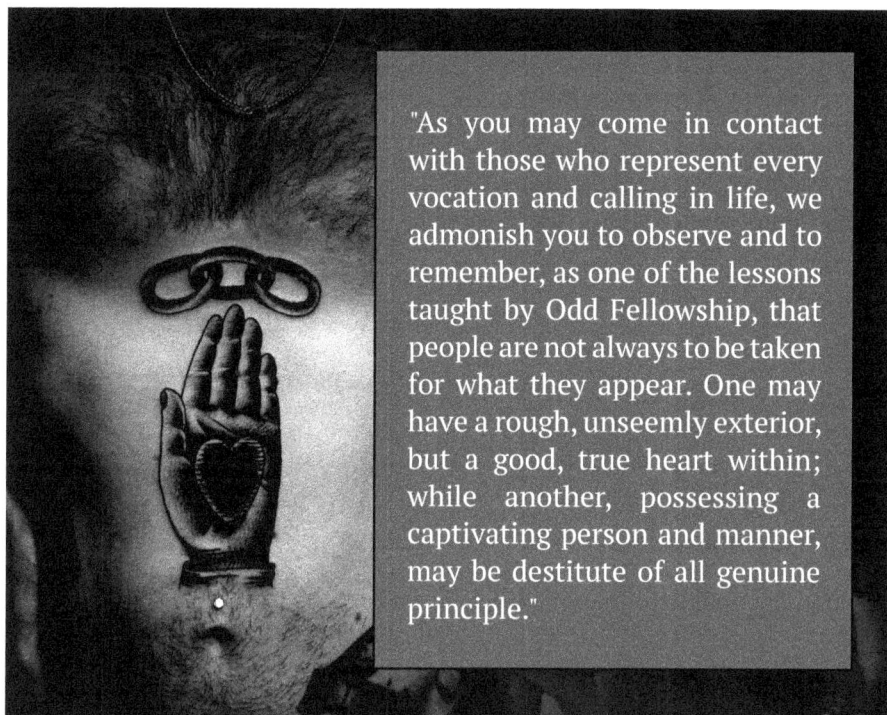

"As you may come in contact with those who represent every vocation and calling in life, we admonish you to observe and to remember, as one of the lessons taught by Odd Fellowship, that people are not always to be taken for what they appear. One may have a rough, unseemly exterior, but a good, true heart within; while another, possessing a captivating person and manner, may be destitute of all genuine principle."

and virtuous, and provide for those dependent upon them. The Odd Fellows who behave ill to his family, either personally in not providing for their wants, or idling away his time in dissipation and drunkenness, may be accused before his or her Lodge, and condemned for conduct unbecoming an Odd Fellows.[57]

Furthermore, members should be strictly cautious in their conversations and communications with others relative to any confidential matter discussed in the Lodge. They should not only not make any improper discovery to the uninitiated, but they should also not, by any hint or double entendre, excite their curiosity.[58]

Proposal of Candidate

The early leaders of Odd Fellowship have emphasized that this is one of the most essential matters in reference to Odd Fellowship. There was an old charge in the ancient ritual ceremonies which Odd Fellows were reminded to put into their mind, to wit:[59]

Should you, at any time, propose a friend to become a member of the Order, see that he be such a man as will be likely to conform to the rules and precepts of Odd Fellowship; for nothing is so painful to the feelings of faithful Odd Fellows as to see the requirements of the Institution trampled upon and profaned.

Members should not propose anybody for admission into Odd Fellowship anyone whom he or she does not have thorough knowledge and whose uprightness he or she does not have full confidence. There are lodges that have become weak and disharmonious because the lodge was not careful in admitting members. There are lodge funds and properties stolen or sold for selfish purposes because of unworthy members. There are lodges that were actually closed or whose charters were revoked because of members who joined with mercenary motives. Prevention is always better than cure.

Resignation and Restoration

A member of a lodge in good standing must resign membership in writing.[60] But a member having resigned may apply for a renewal either in the Lodge from which the member resigned or in another Lodge. Renewal can be done by presenting an application accompanied by a certificate of resignation and shall be entitled to the member's former rank.[61]

Other Branches of the IOOF

The Independent Order of Odd Fellows is analogous to a university composed of several colleges that offer different degrees under its wing. While the IOOF is a single entity, it consists of several official and unofficial branches or units that aim to serve specific interests among men, women, and youth. These branches have their own set of officers, regalia, membership fees and annual dues, degrees of initiation, symbolism, signs and passwords.

Rebekahs

In the days long gone, women were expected to just stay at home. They were not allowed to go to school, own a property, practice a profession, vote, hold public office, or join civic associations. In 1846, the IOOF allowed Odd Fellows Lodges to issue official identification cards to wives and widows of members. This led to a proposal to create a Degree for women, but this idea endured years of consideration because of the legal status of women at that time. Eventually, the IOOF deviated from the trends of those times; it became the first international fraternal organization to officially accept women when it adopted the *Rebekah Degree* on September 20, 1851. The degree was written by Schuyler Colfax, who later became the Vice President of the United States from 1869 to 1873.

The Rebekah Degree began as an honorary award only, which was conferred on wives and daughters of Odd Fellows at special lodge meetings, and recipients were known as *Daughters of Rebekah*. Later, the women were allowed to take parts in the ceremony and confer the degree on other women. The system further improved in 1868 when the Rebekahs were eventually given the right to vote and elect their own officers, charge for initiation fees, collect dues, and undertake charitable and benevolent activities. Eventually, women were given full freedom to manage the affairs of the Rebekah Lodges without need of attendance of any male member. This was way before the women's rights' movement and way before women were granted suffrage by the United States government. Its success encouraged many other fraternal organizations and clubs to follow the example of the IOOF and create women's branches within their organizations.

To be a Rebekah, one must be at least sixteen (16) years old and of good character. The name Rebekah was taken from one of the prominent women in history, Rebecca, whose story started when she gave water to a stranger and his camels. Hence, a character who was charitable, generous, and kind. The Rebekahs as a sisterhood pledge themselves to follow her example. The general duties of the Rebekahs are: "*To live peaceably, do good unto all, as we have opportunity and specially to obey the Golden Rule, Whatsoever ye would that others should do unto you, do ye even so unto them.*" Traditionally, there is only one degree as still practiced in most Rebekah Lodges in North America. In European countries, however, the Rebekah Lodge ritual was revised into four (4) degrees to resemble that of the Odd Fellows Lodge, although the branch continues to have their own regalia, signs, passwords, and symbols.[1] The regalia is a collar or badge of *pink and green.*

The basic unit is called a *Rebekah Lodge* or *Sister Lodge.* A Rebekah Lodge is organized upon receipt by a Rebekah Assembly, Grand Lodge or Sovereign Grand Lodge of a signed petition for a charter or dispensation which must be signed by at least five (5) members who have attained the Rebekah Degree and are in good standing or upon application by at least fifteen (15) persons who are eligible for membership. The elective officers are: Noble Grand, Vice Grand, Secretary, Financial Secretary, and Treasurer. The appointive officers are: Warden, Conductor, Right Supporter of the Noble Grand, Left Supporter of the Noble Grand, Chaplain, Inside Guardian, Outside Guardian, Musician, Color Bearer, Altar Bearers, Banner Bearers, Right Supporter of the Vice Grand and Left Supporter of the Vice Grand.

The governing body for all Rebekah Lodges in a particular state, province, country, or territory is called *Rebekah Assembly*, also referred to as *Rebekah Council* in European jurisdictions. A Rebekah Assembly may be organized upon petition to the Grand Lodge of the jurisdiction for a charter by five (5) or more Rebekah Lodges, having an aggregate of seven (7) or more Past Noble Grands, in a state, province, country, or territory, but no more than one Rebekah Assembly may be chartered in the same state, province, country, or territory. When authorized by the Grand Lodge, the Rebekah Assembly has power to grant charters or dispensations for Rebekah Lodges in their jurisdiction and shall adopt legislation prescribing the methods and procedures. The elective officers of a Rebekah assembly are: President, Vice President, Warden,

Rebekah Council meeting in Sweden. Photo courtesy of the Rebekah Council of Sweden, 2011.

Secretary, Treasurer, and Representative. The appointive officers are: Marshal, Conductor, Chaplain, Musician, Inside Guardian and Outside Guardian. All the officers and members of the Rebekah Assembly shall be Past Presidents who have received the *Rebekah Assembly Degree*.

The *International Association of Rebekah Assemblies* (IARA) is the international governing body composed of representatives from all the Rebekah Assemblies within the jurisdiction of the Sovereign Grand Lodge. The purpose of this body is to promote Rebekahship in partnership with the Sovereign Grand Lodge. The elective officers are: President, Vice President, Warden, Secretary, and Treasurer. The appointive officers are: Marshal, Conductor, Chaplain, Musician, and two Guardians.

The peak of membership in the Rebekahs was in 1922 when they had more than 1 million active members belonging to 9,793 Rebekah Lodges. Today, the Rebekahs still continue to exist as a separate branch within the IOOF, with their own set of local, national, and international officers. Like a number of Odd Fellows' Lodges in the United States that have become co-ed, membership in the Rebekahs are also open to both women and men. However, majority of the Rebekah Lodges in Europe and Latin America still limit their membership to women. In fact, only the Grand Sire of a particular Grand Lodge in Europe can join the Rebekahs.

As of this writing, there are more or less 80,000 members belonging to 1,304 Rebekah Lodges located in approximately 20 countries. A Rebekah member in good standing may also join higher branches for women such as the *Ladies Encampment Auxiliary* (LEA) and the *Ladies Auxiliary Patriarchs Militant* (LAPM), otherwise known as the *Matriarchs Militant* (MM) in Denmark and Iceland.

Encampment

The Encampment is a higher branch in the Independent Order of Odd Fellows that confers three additional degrees to Third Degree Members in good standing in an Odd Fellows Lodge. The degree work in this branch is a result of evolution from additional degrees that were once conferred only to Past Grands of an Odd Fellows Lodge and only during sessions of Grand Lodges. These degrees originated from both England and the United States and fragmentary records would indicate that these belonged to earlier Odd Fellows groups. A ritual of the *Loyal Ancient Order of Odd Fellows*, which existed many years prior to the IOOF, opened its lodge meetings in the *Golden Rule Degree*. The same ritual has the Purple Degree and its tent emblem appeared as early as 1805.[2]

These degrees were conferred and adopted by the Grand Lodge of Maryland at different times. The *Golden Rule Degree* was first conferred to five Past Grands in the United States by one Past Grand Larkham on February 22, 1821.[3] This was followed by the introduction of the *Royal Purple Degree* and the *Patriarchal Degree* in the United States in 1825. On July 6, 1827, these three additional degrees were eventually conferred in a separate branch called *Jerusalem Encampment No.1* that had 524 members at this time. The Encampment degrees are based on the teachings of *Hospitality*, *Toleration*, and *Fortitude*. The motto is: *Faith, Hope*, and *Charity*.

To be eligible for the Encampment, one must be a Third Degree member in good standing in his or her Lodge. In European countries, conferral of the Encampment Degrees is reserved for dedicated members. Third degree members have to actively participate in lodge meetings and activities for at least 3 to 10 years to be invited in the Encampment. At least two years is required for a member to receive all his Encampment degrees. Upon receiving his Royal Purple Degree, the Patriarch or Matriarch is presented an Encampment ring, nearly identical for all European Jurisdictions, indicating that he or she is an active and devoted member of the Independent Order of Odd Fellows.[4] The Rebekahs also have their own higher branch called the *Ladies Encampment Auxiliary* (LEA). But since 2003, Rebekah members in North America were made eligible to join and receive the degrees in the Encampment.[5] Male members are called *Patriarchs* while female members are called *Matriarchs*.

ENCAMPMENT DEGREES

Patriarchal Degree

This degree is based on the principle of *Hospitality,* and teaches transparent honesty, domestic purity, and unfeigned righteousness. The regalia is a b*lack collar* with a *black lining*.

Golden Rule Degree

This degree is based on the principle of *Toleration*, and teaches good will, and true brotherhood. It teaches that members should unite with the virtuous and good irrespective of race, religion, politics or country in the discharge of duties which all agree are paramount to universal peace and cooperation. The regalia is a b*lack collar* with a *golden yellow lining*.

Royal Purple Degree

This degree is based on the principle of *Fortitude*, and teaches, among others, alertness and determination as basis for a possible success in the journey called life. This degree is a derivation of the 1797 initiatory ceremony of the Patriotic Order. The regalia is a *purple collar* with a *golden yellow* lining.

The local branch is called an *Encampment*. A charter or dispensation for an Encampment may be issued upon a petition signed by at least five (5) Royal Purple Degree members of good standing or by at least five (5) Third Degree members. The elective officers are: Chief Patriarch or Chief Matriarch, High Priest or High Priestess, Senior Warden, Scribe, Financial Scribe, Treasurer, and Junior Warden.

The appointive officers are: Guide, Inside Sentinel, Outside Sentinel, First and Second Watch, Third and Fourth Watch, and the First and Second Guard of the Tent.

The state or provincial governing body for the Encampments is called a *Grand Encampment*. A Grand Encampment may be organized upon receipt by the Sovereign Grand Lodge of a signed petition for a charter by seven (7) or more Past Chief Patriarchs of the Grand Encampment Degree from not less than three (3) Encampments within a jurisdiction of the Sovereign Grand Lodge. The petition must be accompanied by the sealed letters from the encampments certifying the rank of the Past Chief Patriarchs. Each Grand Encampment has exclusive jurisdiction over all Encampments within its jurisdiction, and may exercise all power and authority not reserved by the Sovereign Grand Lodge. The elective officers are Grand Patriarch or Grand Matriarch, Grand High Priest or Grand High Priestess, Grand Senior Warden, Grand Scribe, Grand Treasurer, Grand Junior Warden, and Grand Representatives. The appointive officers are the Grand Marshal, Grand Inside Sentinel, Grand Outside Sentinel, and such other officers as may be provided, who are appointed by the Grand Patriarch or Grand Matriarch. In Europe, however, all Encampments fall directly under the authority of their Grand Lodge. As of writing, there are more or less 35,000 Patriarchs and Matriarchs belonging to 513 Encampments located in about 26 countries.

Patriarchs Militant

The Patriarchs Militant (PM) is the uniformed branch of the Independent Order of Odd Fellows, first founded by veterans as the "Patriarchal Circle" right after the American Civil War in 1865. It was a part of the Encampment for several years until it became a separate branch of the IOOF when the Sovereign Grand Lodge granted its approval in 1885. General John Cox Underwood, revered as founder, was instrumental in revising its rituals and formulating its rules and regulations.

Traditionally, membership in the Patriarchs Militant is open to Royal Purple Degree members of good standing. Beginning 2018, the qualification was lowered to Third Degree members and Rebekah Degree members of good standing. Male members are called *Chevaliers* while the female members are called *Ladies*. There are two mottoes:

Traditionally, the Encampment degrees were designed and conferred as merit degrees for past presiding officers. They were conferred during Grand Lodge sessions to the most enthusiastic, the most active and the most interested leaders of the Odd Fellows or Rebekah Lodge. Photo from the Grand Lodge of Sweden.

The Patriarchs Militant (PM) and Ladies Auxiliary Patriarchs Militant (LAPM) are the chivalric units of the IOOF. Photo by author, 2014.

The first one, *Justitia Universalis*, means *"Universal Justice;"* this is the central idea of the Patriarchs Militant. The second, *Pax Aut Bellum*, means *"Peace or War"* and represents the commitment of the Patriarchs Militant to seek "Universal Justice" by peaceful means as well as the more forceful ones commemorated in our symbolism. Therefore, the interpretation of the name Patriarchs Militant is a *"peaceful ruler, serving as a soldier."*

The basic unit is called a *Canton* with one degree. A Canton is organized upon receipt by the Department Council or the General Military Council of a signed petition for a warrant by five (5) or more members of the Patriarchs Militant Degree or ten (10) persons qualified to become members. The elective officers are: Captain, Lieutenant, Ensign, Clerk, and Accountant. The appointive officers are: Color or Banner Bearer, Guard, Chaplain, Picket, and Sentinel.

Four (4) or more Cantons, having an aggregate of seven (7) or more Past Commandants may form a *Department Council*. The Department is organized into battalions, regiments, brigades or divisions, as the strength of the forces will permit. A battalion shall consist of two (2) to six (6) cantons, a regiment of two (2) to six (6) battalions, a brigade of two (2) or more regiments and a division of two (2) or more brigades. The officers of a Battalion are: Battalion Commander shall have the rank of Major, Chief of Staff and Aide, Adjutant, Quartermaster, Inspector, Judge Advocate, Chaplain and Color Sergeant. The officers of a Regiment are: Regimental Commander with the rank of Colonel, Lieutenant Colonel, Adjutant, and optionally, Inspector, Quartermaster, Equipment Officer, Surgeon or First Aid Officer, Chaplain, Color Sergeant and Bugler. The officers of a Brigade are: Brigade Commander with the rank of Brigadier General, Chief of Staff, Military Advisor, Adjutant and optionally Inspector, Quartermaster, Judge Advocate, Equipment Officer, Surgeon or First Aid Officer, Chaplain, Bannerette and two (2) Aides. The officers of a Division are: Division Commander with the rank of Major General, Chief of Staff, Military Advisor, Adjutant, and optionally Inspector, Quartermaster, Judge Advocate, Equipment Officer, Chaplain, Surgeon or First Aid Officer, Bannerette, and four (4) Aides.

Internationally, the *General Military Council* has general supervision over the Patriarchs Militant Army. The elective officers are: General Commanding, Deputy General Commanding, Executive Officer, Adjutant General and Quartermaster General. The Sovereign Grand Master shall be the Commander-in-Chief and the Sovereign

Grand Secretary shall be the Executive Adjutant General.

Ladies Auxiliary Patriarchs Militant

On November 4, 1901, Chevalier Joseph Fairhall, together with his wife and some Rebekahs, launched the *Ladies Militant Auxiliary Association*. This group established several units across the United States called Fortresses. After much consideration, the group was eventually approved by the Sovereign Grand Lodge in 1915 as the Ladies Auxiliary Patriarchs Militant (LAPM). In Denmark and Iceland, the women's branch is called the *Matriarchs Militant* (MM). The emblem of the LAPM is a *purple cross and a white rose*. The white rose symbolizes purity of thoughts and actions. The Purple cross, on the other hand, represents the cross of St. John, which signifies help and shelter and tells members to be ready to offer assistance whenever there is suffering. In 2000, the Sovereign Grand Lodge passed a legislation allowing women to directly join the Patriarchs Militant. But surprisingly, many of the women still want to retain a separate LAPM branch.

Both the PM and LAPM are purely semi-military in its character, organized for purposes of chivalric display, and are admirably fulfilling their mission through the annual *"Pilgrimage to the Tomb of the Unknown Soldier"* ceremonies held in Washington D.C., and the *"Canadian War Memorial"* in Ottawa, Ontario, Canada. Today, there is an estimated 6,000 Chevaliers and Ladies belonging to 211 Cantons located in the United States, Canada, Cuba, Denmark, Iceland, and the Philippines.

Branches for the Youth

The first proposal to form an Odd Fellows branch for the youth began in 1830 but, owing to the standing of minors in society at the time, the Grand Lodge of the United States found themselves "not yet ready for a separate Order for the youth." But due to succeeding wars in the past, a number of boys and girls in Europe and North America were growing up without fathers. This encouraged several members of the IOOF to establish unofficial clubs for the youth. The first attempt to establish a branch for sons and daughters of

Odd Fellows began in Copenhagen, Denmark, when a club called *Esperanca* was established in 1887. In the Netherlands, *Jonge* (Young) *Odd Fellows Club* was formed in 1918. Other countries such as Norway and Sweden also formed groups for the youth. Sadly, very little is known about these European youth clubs. It seems that these groups did not flourish, perhaps no longer exist today, or exist in very small numbers. At present, there are four (4) youth branches officially recognized by the Sovereign Grand Lodge.

Junior Odd Fellows Lodge

The IOOF in Australia was the first to introduce the idea of Junior Lodges in 1898. The group was first organized with a crude organizational structure until a more formal structure paralleling the lodge system was established in 1901. In 1920, the Sovereign Grand Lodge in the United States and Canada finally passed a legislation to officially establish a youth branch. On November 21, 1921, a boy's club for the youth called *Supreme Fireside, Loyal Sons of Odd Fellows* was founded by one J.H. Stotler in Kansas City, Missouri.

J. H. Stotler's boys club has four degrees and each degree is devoted to a distinct lesson for the youth. The first degree teaches *fraternity*. The second degree places an emphasis on home and *devotion to parents*. The third degree teaches *patriotism* and devotion to flag and country. The fourth degree teaches the lesson of *devotion to a Deity or God*. In addition to these, there is another degree called the "Knight Degree" which is an honorary degree conferred based on actual service. The four degrees are secret while the knight degree can be conferred publicly in the presence of parents, Rebekahs, and Odd Fellows.

On April 18, 1922, another group called *The Sons of Wildey for Boys* was formed in Bonham, Texas, organized by Odd Fellows for the youth but they claim that they are not totally connected with the Independent Order of Odd Fellows. These two early groups eventually became the nucleus for what became the Junior Odd Fellows Lodge.

To be a member of the Junior Odd Fellows Lodge, one must be between eight (8) to eighteen (18) years old. Members who have attained the age of eighteen (18) years may receive the graduate degree and retain all rights and privileges of a member until age twenty-one

Officers of the Grand Junior Lodge of California. Photo from the Grand Lodge of California, 1993.

(21). A member of a Junior Lodge who acquires membership in an Odd Fellows Lodge shall be a life member of the Junior Lodge so long as he remains an Odd Fellow in good standing. Adult Odd Fellows may also be elected by ballot to Senior Membership on petition accompanied by the required fees and dues. The Junior Odd Fellows participate in their own degree and meetings similar to the Odd Fellows Lodges. Their watchwords are *Fidelity, Honor and Loyalty*. Their symbolic colors are *silver and dark blue*.

The basic unit is called a *Junior Lodge,* which shall be organized upon receipt by the Grand Junior Lodge, Grand Lodge or Sovereign Grand Lodge of a signed petition for a charter by five (5) or more members of the Junior Lodge Degree or ten (10) persons qualified to become members. The elective officers of the Junior Lodge are: Chief Ruler, Deputy Ruler; Recorder, Accountant, and Treasurer. The appointive officers are: Chaplain, Warden, Conductor, Marshal, Color Bearer, Right Supporter of the Chief Ruler, Left Supporter of the Chief Ruler, Inner Sentinel, Outer Sentinel, Right Supporter of the Deputy Ruler and Left Supporter of the Deputy Ruler, Right Supporter of the Chaplain, Left Supporter of the Chaplain, Right Supporter of the Past Chief Ruler, Left Supporter of the Past Chief Ruler. At least two (2) adult Advisory Officers shall be present at all times for safety and welfare.

The state or provincial governing body is called the *Grand Junior Lodge.* A Grand Junior Lodge shall be organized upon receipt by the Grand Lodge or Sovereign Grand Lodge of a signed petition for a charter by at least three (3) Junior Lodges in good standing with the approval of the Jurisdictional Youth Committee (JYC). The elective officers of the Grand Junior Lodge are: Grand Ruler, Deputy Grand Ruler, Grand Warden, Grand Recorder, and Grand Treasurer. The appointive officers are the Grand Marshal, Grand Conductor, Grand Chaplain, Grand Musician, Grand Inner Sentinel, Grand Outer Sentinel, Right and Left Supporters for the Grand Ruler, Past Grand Ruler and Grand Chaplain.

Theta Rho Girls' Club

In 1929, the Sovereign Grand Lodge approved the formation of *Junior Rebekah Lodges* for girls. This group was ultimately renamed as the Theta Rho Girls in 1931.

To be a member, one must be between eight (8) to eighteen (18) years old. Members who have attained the age of eighteen (18) years may receive the graduate degree and retain all rights privileges of a member until age twenty-one (21). The Theta Rho has one degree which encourages the girls to exert effort to improve oneself physically and mentally, build a character necessary for happiness in the home, and create an influence for good in the community. The degree seeks to teach unselfishness, morality, and patriotism; to encourage mental and physical development; to develop character; to promote the sentiment that happiness is obtained only through service to God and man, and that obedience to law is necessary for preservation of government and protection of home and country. Their motto is *"Happiness through Service"* and the symbolic colors of the degree are *peach and Yale blue*.

The local branch is called a *Club* which shall be organized upon receipt of a signed petition for a charter by five (5) or more members of the Theta Rho Degree or ten (10) persons qualified to become members. But no Theta Rho Girls' Club can exist therein without the sanction of the Rebekah Assembly within that jurisdiction. The elective officers of the Theta Rho Girls' Club are: President, Vice President, Secretary, Financial Secretary, and Treasurer. The appointive officers are: Chaplain, Warden, Conductor, Marshal, Right Supporter of the President, Left Supporter of the President, First Herald, Second Herald, Third Herald, Fourth Herald, Right Supporter of the Vice President and Left Supporter of the Vice President, Inside Guardian, and Outside

Guardian. At least two (2) Advisory Officers shall be present at all times for safety and welfare.

The state or provincial governing body is called the *Theta Rho Assembly* which shall be organized upon receipt of a signed petition for a charter by at least three (3) Theta Rho Girls' Clubs in good standing with the approval of the Jurisdictional Youth Committee (JYC). The elective officers of the Theta Rho Assembly are: President, Vice President, Warden, Secretary, and Treasurer. The appointive officers are: Marshal, Conductor, Chaplain, Musician, Inside Guardian, Outside Guardian, Right and Left Supporters to the President, Right and Left Supporters to the Vice President, First, Second, Third and Fourth Herald, and Color Bearer. All the officers and members of the Theta Rho Assembly shall be Past Presidents who have received the *Theta Rho Assembly Degree*.

United Youth Group

The first attempt to form a co-ed fraternal organization for the youth began in 1941 when the IOOF formed the *Alpha Rho*. The purpose was to allow the youth of both sexes an opportunity to cultivate understanding between the two sexes. But because it was not yet generally acceptable to see both boys and girls in one club, the group did not flourish. Nevertheless, when the Sovereign Grand Lodge permitted the Odd Fellows Lodge to become co-ed, a second desire for a co-ed youth organization led to the formation of the *United Youth Group* (UYG).

Membership in the United Youth Group is open to all persons who believe in a Supreme Being, of good character, and are between the ages of eight (8) and eighteen (18) years. Members who have attained the age of eighteen (18) years may receive the graduate degree and retain all rights privileges of a member until age twenty-one (21). All members in good standing in an Odd Fellows Lodge or Rebekah Lodge may attend any UYG meeting. They may be elected by ballot to *Senior Membership* in the group on a petition accompanied by the required fee, dues, and being obligated in keeping with the ritual. However, adult members have no right to vote, and may speak only upon request or by invitation of the presiding officer. The United Youth Group seeks to teach leadership, community service, and responsibility.

The basic unit is called a *United Youth Group* formed upon a petition signed by not less than five (5) applicants, sponsored by any chartered adult branch of the IOOF. This follows a co-ed lodge setting. The elective officers of a group are: President, Vice-President, Secretary, and Treasurer. The appointive officers of a group are: Warden, Chaplain, Conductor, Guardian, Right and Left Supporters to the President who shall be appointed by the President, and Right and Left Supporters to the Vice-President who shall be appointed by the Vice-President. Meetings must be attended by an adult Advisor and Assistant Advisor to constitute a quorum for the transaction of business. The number of United Youth Groups have recently increased because several lodges in the United States, particularly in Texas and Illinois, were able to establish them.

Patriarchs Militant Cadet Corps

On September 17, 2016, the *Department Council of Virginia of the Patriarchs Militant* approved the formation of the Patriarchs Militant Cadet Corps for the Youth. This branch is connected to the Patriarchs Militant branch. The program aims to promote dignity and pride, teach the value of service to others, and prepare the youth to be useful citizens and help them grow into responsible adults and be a credit to their community. Its creed is: "*We the Cadet Corps are youth working together to reach out and do community service.*" Its motto is: "*Service is honor.*"

In establishing these youth branches, the IOOF wanted to project an atmosphere that it is a family-oriented fraternity encouraging all family members to join. The communal goal of establishing these youth branches was to teach children and youth how lodges operate, the democratic process, leadership abilities, poise, social graces, and community service. For many years, the youth branches provided boys and girls with a social support system with other boys and girls of their age bracket and a moral guide as taught in the initiations. It has also been thought that these young people are an important part of the organization's "Present" because they will eventually find involvement with Odd Fellowship meaningful and enriching so that they will become an important part of its "Future" by joining the adult lodges. Indeed, many of the dedicated leaders of the Odd Fellows and Rebekahs today began as members of these youth branches.

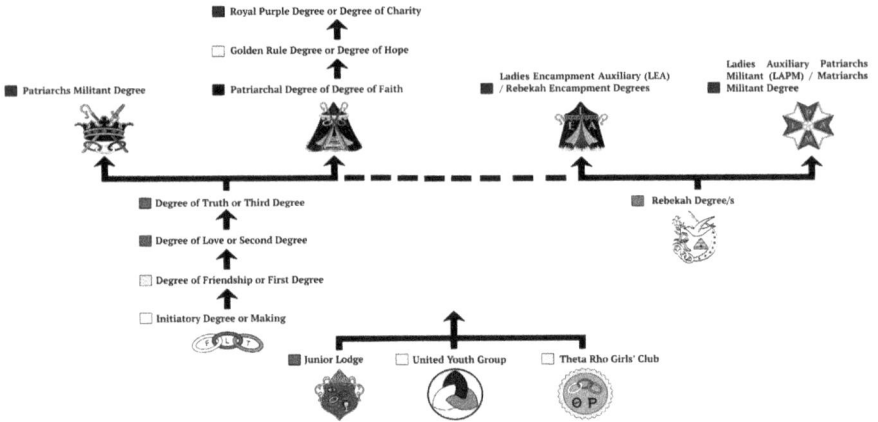

Diagram of the different official branches and degrees of the Independent Order of Odd Fellows. In Europe, however, both the Rebekah Lodge and the Rebekah Encampment have three degrees. Diagram by the author, 2020.

Unofficial Fun Degrees

Records with the Sovereign Grand Lodge show proof that some Odd Fellows were initiating people into a fun degree known as the *Oriental Order of Humility* (OOH) as early as 1868 - a group which predated the Masonic Shriners.[6] This degree was created for the purpose of fun, recreation, and amusement as an enjoyable diversion from the serious initiation ceremonies of the lodge and encampment. However, this deviation from the seriousness of the Odd Fellows' Lodge and Encampment degrees was considered unacceptable by the leaders of the IOOF. On July 5, 1870, Grand Sire E.D. Farnsworth of the Sovereign Grand Lodge sent a circular to all Grand Lodges as transcribed below:[7]

> Dear Sir and Brother: It has been presented to me that in some of the State jurisdictions thoughtless and inconsiderate brethren have used the Subordinate Lodge rooms for the purpose of conferring degrees, so called, laying no connection whatever with the Order, and, if not positively indecent and contrary to morals, certainly of an unbecoming and discreditable character, one of which is known as the degree of "*The Oriental Order of Humility.*"
>
> As such practices are in gross violation of our laws and calculated to bring the Order into disrepute, you are hereby required to suppress them promptly within your jurisdiction, if any such should exist, and to take such measures as may be proper and necessary to give to this

circular general publicity.

For how many years, it was the opinion of the Sovereign Grand Lodge that the fun degrees can ruin the public image of fraternal orders because they involved horseplay and some mirth. While the Masonic Shriners prospered within Freemasonry, the Sovereign Grand Lodge banned Odd Fellows from creating and performing what the leaders call as "spurious degrees" within Odd Fellowship. Yet, many fun degrees for Odd Fellows were still informally created. The OOH even added a second degree and changed its name to the Oriental Order of Humility and Perfection (OOH&P) in 1901. A number of SGL resolutions were passed declaring these fun groups illegal and demanding them to disband. The suppression continued periodically for about 50 years until the Sovereign Grand Lodge finally yielded and recognized the Ancient Mystic Order of Samaritans (AMOS) as a private club for Odd Fellows in 1951. But because this group opted not to come under the authority of the Sovereign Grand Lodge, they do not have representation in the international governing body.

Ancient Mystic Order of Samaritans

AMOS is an unofficial branch for male Odd Fellows formed as a merger of six fun groups. In 1924, the *Oriental Order of Humility and Perfection* merged with the *Imperial Order of Muscovites*, the *Pilgrim Knights of Oriental Splendor*, and the *Ancient Mystic Order of Cabiri* to form the *United Order of Splendor and Perfection*. They were joined by the *Veiled Prophets of Baghdad* in 1925 at which point the name was changed to AMOS and was subsequently joined by the *Improved Order of Muscovites* in 1927. AMOS experienced substantial growth for several years, reaching more than 100,000 members. But membership eventually declined when all fraternal organizations began losing its popularity.

Membership is open to all Odd Fellows, whether affiliated with the IOOF, MUIOOF, or the GUOOF. The first degree, known as *Humility Degree*, is conferred by the basic unit of AMOS called a *Sanctorum*. Those who have received this degree are referred to as "*Samaritans*." The elective officers of a local Sanctorum are: Grand Monarch, Vice-Grand Monarch, Grand Counsellor, Registrar, Collector, and Banker. The appointive officers are: Grand High Executioner, Grand Chief Guide, Venerable Friar, Grand Monitor, Grand Stentoros, and Grand

Herald. The second or *Perfection Degree* is usually conferred only at a Divisional or Supreme Convention held once a year confers the title of "*Sheik.*" The officers of a *Supreme Sanctorum* are: Supreme Monarchos, Supreme Khalifah, Supreme Counsellor, Supreme Prince, Supreme Secretary, Supreme Treasurer, Supreme Vizier, Supreme Muezzin, and Supreme Stentoros. The regalia is a *dark red fez* with *yellow tassel* for Samaritans and a *red tassel* for Sheiks. Recently, a number of new Sanctorums have been established across the United States but the total membership is still alarmingly low, which is below a thousand all over the United states and Canada.

Ladies of the Orient

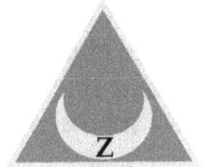

The Ladies of the Orient (LOTO) is a women's fraternal organization in the United States and Canada, which had its origins as an appendant body of the Rebekahs. It was founded in Syracuse, New York, in 1915 by Emily Voorheis for the purpose of having a group dedicated to recreation and amusement as a pleasant diversion from the serious charitable work done by other groups to which the ladies already belonged. The group still exists today with a handful of members and is now open to non-Rebekahs.

The basic unit is called a *Zuanna*. The elected officers are: Great Ashayhi, Queen Ashayhi, Keeper of Traditions, Collector of Shekels, Prelate and Oriental Guide. The appointive officers are: Syndic, Guard of Zuanna, Musician, Color Bearers, Detector, Executioner, Assistant Detector, Assistant Executioner, and Captain of Degree. The regalia is a *white fez* with a variety of different tassel colors to denote different officer positions.

Noble Order of Muscovites

In 1893, a group of Odd Fellows in Ohio formed the *Imperial Order of Muscovites* (IOM). Unlike most fun branches of other fraternal groups, the Muscovites opted for a Russian theme instead of the standard Middle-Eastern. The IOM additionally spawned an affiliated appendant body for women who were Rebekahs known as the *Lady Muscovites* in June of 1925. The Imperial Order was active in different states throughout the Midwest and Western United

The origin of the Ancient Mystic Order of Samaritans can be traced to a side degree known as the *Oriental Order of Humility* (OOH) first introduced sometime in 1865. The group added a second degree, the *Degree of Perfection*, and changed its name into the *Oriental Order of Humility and Perfection* (OOH&P) in 1901. The OOH&P later merged with other fun groups to form the *Ancient Mystic Order of Samaritans* (AMOS). Recently, there has been a revival of interest in the fun degrees and a number of Sanctorums are being revived in the United States and Canada. Photo of Cyzicus Sanctorum No.24 and Jackalope Sanctorum No.333 in Waxahachie, Texas, 2018.

The members of the Kremlin Baku of the *Imperial Order of Muscovites* (IOM) left AMOS and re-organized as the *Royal Order of Muscovites* in the 1930s. In 2016, the Muscovites was reformed as the *Noble Order of Muscovites* and membership was opened to both men and women who are members of any fraternal organization, service club or civic organization. Photo courtesy of Kremlin Baku (Oregon) and Kremlin Tubabao (Philippines), 2021.

States, but was disbanded in 1909 due to pressure from the Sovereign Grand Lodge.

Remaining members in Eastern states re-formed and operated separately under the name *Improved Order of Muscovites*. This group continued until it merged into AMOS in 1927 under an agreement that the Muscovite Degree will be included in the AMOS. However, the incorporation of the Muscovite Degree

Late-1800s original "Busby" of the Imperial Order of Musco-vites. From the collection of the author.

did not happen so a portion of the membership in Oregon became unhappy with the results of the merger. This group left and revived the Muscovites under a new name, *The Royal Order of Muscovites*. One of the last surviving members of the Royal Order, together with younger candidates, reorganized the group as the *Noble Order of Muscovites* in 2016. This branch is now open to both men and women and no longer restrict its membership to Odd Fellows and Rebekahs. It is not an organization per se but a mere social group that will gather to put on the degree and raise some money from time to time. There are no annual dues as well. Their mission is: "*To have fun while saving the world*". The regalia of the Imperial Order was a *charcoal grey hat with a black band of fur* around the brim called by the members as a "*Busby*." The Improved, Royal, and Noble Order instead have a *dark red busby* with a *black band of fur* around the brim.

The basic unit of the Noble Order are called *Duchies*, which are chartered by a *Kremlin*. The officers of a Kremlin are: Czar, Commandant, Royal Inspector, Grand Counselor, Grand Duke, Chronicler, Minister of Finance, Royal Inner Guard, and Royal Outer Guard. There are no national or international governing body. Once a Kremlin is chartered, each state can then operate in the best way for them, provided they follow the rules about who can be a member and the ban on hazing.

- END -

Glossary

Annual Traveling Password: This is a password used to visit lodges in various countries and changed once (1) every year.

Anteroom: Most lodges have a room called an anteroom leading into the lodge room. The purpose is to have a place where candidates for degrees, members waiting to enter the lodge room and visitors to be introduced can wait until they enter the lodge room. The door from the anteroom to the lodge room is usually provided with a small opening called a wicket, through which the Inside Guardian can converse with a member in the anteroom.

Associate Member: Associate membership provides for a member of an Odd Fellow or Rebekah lodge to become a member of a second lodge as an associate member. Such associate member has the rights of any Non-beneficial member, except that an Associate member shall not hold the office of Noble Grand and/or Vice Grand in two Odd Fellow lodges concurrently.

Brother: Term of address to a fellow male member. The Odd Fellows is a fraternal organization. Membership is likened to belong to a family.

Charge Book: Often referred to as pocket rituals, Charge Books are loose-leaf books which Third degree members may purchase, containing all of the material in the Lodge Ritual Books.

Ciphers: The Ciphers are also known as the Keys to the Unwritten Work. These are very small manuals which may be owned by lodges and members alike, containing the Unwritten Work in coded form, consisting of the first letter of a word and as many dashes as there are additional letters. For example, the word Truth would be written as T_ _ _ _.

Code of General Laws: The Sovereign Grand Lodge issues a loose-leaf book, the Code of General Laws, which provides laws, rules, regulations, guidelines, etc., to be observed by all organizations which operate under its authority. Each lodge is required to have a Code of General Laws, which should be in the lodge room during meetings. Any member in good standing may purchase or see the Code of General Laws.

Dues: Each member is required to pay annual dues to his or her local lodge, with the amount specified in the lodge by-laws. The payment of dues provides the funds for the operation of the local lodge, the Grand Lodge or Rebekah Assembly, along with the Sovereign Grand Lodge. With the payment of dues, the member may avail certain rights and privileges such as the Annual Travelling Password used to visit lodges in various countries. Non-payment may lead to suspension and losing all the rights and privileges of a member in good standing such as inter-lodge visitation.

Elevated: refers to the progression or advancement of an initiate or candidate to the succeeding degree/s. Odd Fellowship do not use the term "raised."

Good Standing: A member is in good standing if he or she is current in reference to payment of dues and assessment due to the lodge.

Grand Lodge: The State or National organization of the Odd Fellows. For example, the Grand Lodge of Denmark. This body presides the national events and projects of the organization and holds annual meeting (sessions) at least once (1) a year where representatives from various lodges would meet. A Grand Lodge can only be formed if a country or state has five or more lodges.

Grand Lodge Officers: A Grand Lodge is headed by an elective officer, the Grand Master or Grand Sire. Other elective officers are the Deputy Grand Master, Grand Warden, Grand Secretary, who manages the office, and the Grand Treasurer, who is responsible for some of the financial aspects of the Grand Lodge. Election of these officers is held during the Grand Lodge Sessions, and all serve one (1) year term with the exception of the Grand Secretary and Grand Treasurer who are elected for five year terms after an initial one year term. It is customary for the Deputy Grand Master to be elected as Grand Master and for the Grand Warden to be elected Deputy Grand Warden to be elected as Deputy Grand Master, this providing a two-year "growth ladder" for the newly elected Grand Warden. However, a brother or sister can be elected Grand Master without serving as Grand Warden or Deputy Grand Master. There are also appointed Grand Lodge officers, who serve at the request of the Grand Master and officers during his or her term of office. They are the Grand Marshall, Grand Conductor, Grand Chaplain, Grand Guardian, Grand Herald, Grand Color Bearer, Grand Musician and Grand Instructor.

Honors of the Order: New members receive instructions in giving the Honors of the Order when initiated into an Odd Fellow and/or Rebekah Lodge. They are a formal way of honoring certain officers and members. Because they are a part of the 'Unwritten Work", ask a member to explain the procedure to you.

International Advisory Board: Tri-Annual sessions of the International Advisory Board are held alternately in North America, prior to the Sovereign Grand Lodge sessions, and in Europe. The Sovereign Grand Lodge furnishes four representatives and the Board secretary. Other jurisdictions, with three representatives each, include Australasia, Denmark, Finland, Germany, Iceland, The Netherlands and Belgium, Norway, Sweden and Switzerland.

Installation: Refers to the formal induction or ceremony of officers to their respective positions.

Institution: Refers to the formal opening of a new lodge, encampment or canton.

Jurisdiction: The term is commonly used to identify a state, country or provincial unit of the IOOF.

Journal of Proceedings: Both the Grand Lodge and Rebekah Assembly provide a Journal of Proceedings following their annual sessions. These include the minutes of the session, the text of all material considered by both bodies, as well as lists of appointments and committee members, and others. Each Lodge much receive a copy of the proceedings following the annual sessions, and individual members may also purchase a copy for their own use.

Member: When referring to Member, you are referring to those holding membership in the Independent Order of Odd Fellows. Several members, five or more, form a Lodge.

Official Certificate or Traveling Card: An official certificate is the wallet-sized card which shows that a member has paid dues in his or her lodge, expiring on a certain date. It is commonly called a receipt or a dues card by members and will be used when visiting other lodges.

Open Lodge: The term Open Lodge refers to the part of a lodge meeting after the Noble Grand directs that the meeting be proclaimed open.

Open and Closed Meetings: Open meetings may be attended by non-members as well as members, and official business is not conducted; gavels, signs and passwords are not used, and Rituals are not present. Closed meetings are meetings which may be attended only by members, which is normally the case with the lodge meetings; gavels, signs and passwords are used, the Rituals are present.

Past Grand: Past presiding officer of an Odd Fellows Lodge.

Past Noble Grand: Past presiding officer of a Rebekah Lodge.

Per Capita Tax: An assessment on members levied by the Grand Lodge and Rebekah Assembly at its annual session is called a Per Capita Tax. The Odd Fellows Lodge provide funds for operating the Grand Lodge office, assistance with the costs of printing and mailing letters, reports, certificates and publication, and the annual tax paid to the Sovereign Grand Lodge. The Per Capita Tax is paid semi-annually by each lodge from the member's dues.

Past Chief Patriarch/Matriarch: Past presiding officer of an Odd Fellows Encampment or Ladies Encampment Auxiliary.

Quasi-Independent Jurisdictions: Numerous countries where Odd Fellow Lodges exists form quasi-independent jurisdictions. These Grand Lodges include Australasia for lodges in Australia and New Zealand, Denmark, Finland, Germany, Iceland, Cuba, The Netherlands for lodges in Holland and Belgium, Norway, Sweden and Switzerland and Italy. Lodges are also located in Chile, Hawaii, Puerto Rico, Uruguay, Spain, Nigeria, Togo, Philippines and Venezuela.

A Country or State without a Grand Lodge may work under a Grand Lodge of a different country or directly with the Sovereign Grand Lodge and will be represented by a District Deputy Grand Master (DDGM) if under a Grand Lodge of another country or a District Deputy Sovereign Grand Master (DDSGM) if under the Sovereign Grand Lodge. Both are under the leadership of the Grand Master of a Grand Lodge of another country or the Sovereign Grand Master of the Sovereign Grand Lodge.

Quorum: the number of members necessary to hold a legal meeting is called a quorum. In all units, a minimum of five (5) members are required to form a quorum.

Rebekah Assembly: The Rebekah Assembly is headed by an elective officer, the President, Vice-President, Warden, Secretary, and Treasurer. There are also appointive officers who serve during the term. They are the Marshal, Conductor, Chaplain, Inside Guardian, Outside Guardian, Color Bearer and Musician.

Regalia: All members present during a lodge meeting are required to wear what is collectively called a 'regalia', and it is also worn at all sessions of the Grand Lodge or Sovereign Grand Lodge. It is also worn at some social functions and sometimes worn during funerals or memorial services for members. Odd Fellows regalia are color-coded to show the highest degree received. The various types of regalia includes: Collars (made of cloth or leather and worn over the neck), Cord regalia (consist of rope with a jewel connecting the ends), Chain regalia (uses a metal chain, rather than rope, again with a jewel connecting the ends) and Sash Regalia (consist of cloth sash and worn over one shoulder and under the other arm).

Sister: Term of address to a fellow female member in the Odd Fellows and/or Rebekah Lodge. The Odd Fellows and Rebekahs is a fraternal organization. Membership is likened to belong to a family.

Sovereign Grand Lodge: Like the Grand Lodge, this term refers to two things including the international organization of the Odd Fellows, and, more specifically, the annual meetings or sessions of the Sovereign Grand Lodge, held somewhere in the United States or Canada for a full week each August. The Sovereign Grand Lodge is headed by elective officers, the Sovereign Grand Master, Sovereign Grand Warden, Sovereign Grand Secretary and Sovereign Grand Treasurer. There are also appointed officers, similar to those of the Grand Lodge.

The Sovereign Grand Lodge has an office operated by the Sovereign Grand Secretary located in 422 Trade Street, Winston-Salem, North Carolina. Also located in the International Headquarters Building are the offices for the International Association of Rebekah Assemblies, the Schuyler Colfax Museum, and Thomas Wildey Museum.

Symbols: The emblems utilized in the Odd Fellow and Rebekah Lodges are referred to as Symbols, and they are used to present the teachings of the

Three Link Fraternity.

Unwritten Work: The unwritten work in Odd Fellowship is material which is never printed in full except in special albums in possession of the Grand Lodge and/or Rebekah Assembly. It includes the signs, passwords, tokens, etc. of various degrees. The material is kept secret in a manner so that non-members cannot have access to it, and thus be able to pretend as members. Secrecy was particularly important in the past, when Odd Fellow lodges routinely provided financial benefits to sick, distressed and travelling members, and prevention of fraud by non-members or former members was necessary to protect the funds of the lodge.

Voting: A member in good standing is required to vote, unless he or she has a conflict of interest in the outcome of the vote, or has been excused from voting by the presiding officer. The presiding officer is normally the Noble Grand, unless the vote directly affects him or her (such as when he is a candidate for office), in which case the Right Supporter would preside temporarily. You will participate in three types of voting:

Voting on motion: Which is before the Lodge is done in the way you were instructed in the Initiatory Degree. The presiding officer does not vote on motion unless it will change the outcome of the vote, such as to make a tie or break a tie.

Balloting on an application for membership: Done by ball ballot. There is a closed box located in the middle of the lodge room and each member will vote. White ball for accept and Black ball or cube for reject. Traditionally, three black balls would mean that the application for membership is rejected. Two black balls would mean that the application will be voted next meeting and applicant will not receive any degree yet. One or zero black ball would mean that applicant may continue with the degree. However, other jurisdictions require a majority of ballots for approval or rejection. This may be confusing at first so read the book of instructions regarding balloting first. Be sure not to walk between the Noble Grand and the Ballot box when voting or returning to your seat.

Voting in an election for an officer: Done by secret paper ballot, if there is more than one candidate for the office. If there is only one candidate, the candidate may be elected by acclamation. You will find election by acclamation handled in several ways, depending on the presiding officer and custom of the Lodge.

About the Author

Louie Blake Saile Sarmiento finished his Associate in Health Science Education in 2007; Bachelor of Science in Psychology with Certificate in Human Resource Management and Certificate in Women's Studies in 2010; Master of Arts in Industrial/ Organizational Psychology in 2013; and Juris Doctor (law) degree in 2020. With a wide range of academic backgrounds, he uses various quantitative and qualitative research methodologies in his writings. He does not rely solely on old history books and manuals written many years ago but also conducts interviews, surveys, SWOT analysis, case studies and consults the most recent dissertations, thesis and expert opinions of historians, sociologists, psychologists, lawyers and other academic scholars.

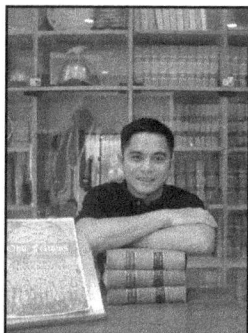

He is instrumental in re-establishing Odd Fellowship in the Philippines. He is a Past Grand and Past District Deputy Sovereign Grand Master of the Independent Order of Odd Fellows. He is credited for connecting thousands of members from various countries when he created and managed the first social media groups and pages of the Independent Order of Odd Fellows from 2009-2019. He is also credited for writing and creating most of the modern literature and infographics about Odd Fellowship on the internet at a time when the organization had almost zero presence online, including the first YouTube videos and the Wikipedia entries about the Odd Fellows. Because of his contributions, he was appointed as Public Relations Coordinator and member of both the Communications Committee and the Revitalization Committee of the Sovereign Grand Lodge from 2012-2015. He was based at the Odd Fellows International Headquarters in North Carolina for an aggregate period of three years where he had full access and was able to read from cover-to-cover all available journals, history books, manuals, rituals and secret works of the Odd Fellows. He traveled widely for more than six years to conduct research and case studies about Odd Fellowship and similar fraternal organizations; visited over a hundred Lodges and several Grand Lodges across the United States and Canada; read and reviewed volumes of records, books and artifacts; observed meetings and initiations; and interviewed local, national and international leaders.

He is an advocate for the preservation of historical fraternal organizations, service clubs and civic associations. He is a member of all branches of the Independent Order of Odd Fellows (IOOF), including the Rebekah Lodge, Encampment and Patriarchs Militant. He is also affiliated with the Grand United Order of Odd Fellows (GUOOF); Ancient Mystic Order of Samaritans (AMOS); Noble Order of Muscovites (Muscovites); International Order of DeMolay (IOD); International Order of Free Gardeners (IOFG); Universal Druid Order (UDO); Ordo Supremus Militaris Templi Hierosolymitani - Regency (OSMTH); Knights of Rizal (KOR); The Fraternal Order of Eagles - Philippine Eagles (TFOE-PE); and Tau Gamma Phi or Triskelion Grand Fraternity (TGP). He now enjoys living a secluded and peaceful life while focusing on his career. As a hobby, he writes and collects books, antiques and artifacts related to fraternal organizations, service clubs and other civic associations.

Other Books by the Author

Title: Odd Fellows - Rediscovering More Than 200 Years of History, Traditions and Community Service

Publication date: April 26, 2019 (Last updated on March 18, 2021)

Title: Odd Fellows - Brief History and Introduction to the Degrees, Symbols, Teachings, and Organization of Patriarchal Odd Fellowship

Publication date: October 6, 2020 (Last updated on March 18, 2021)

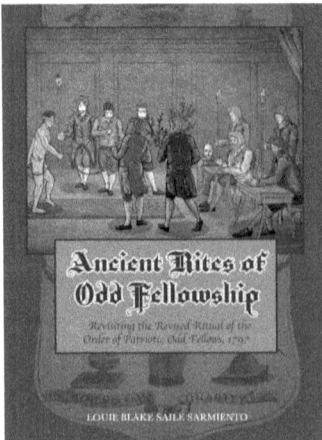

Title: Ancient Rites of Odd Fellowship - Revisiting the Revised Ritual of the Order of Patriotic Odd Fellows, 1797

Publication date: October 6, 2020 (Last updated on March 18, 2021)

Notes

From Right: With Sovereign Grand Secretary Bro. Terry Barrett, Past District Deputy Sovereign Grand Master Bro. Rex Boyson Olpoc and SGL staff Kelly Westbrook and Brenda Nelson at the International Headquarters of The Sove -reign Grand Lodge of the Independent Order of Odd Fellows in Winston- Salem, North Carolina, USA. Photo courtesy of Rex Boyson Olpoc, 2019.

I. Introduction
1.The IOOF have at least 250,000; IOOFMU have 304,000; GUOOF have at least 50,000; COOF have less than 100 members.

II. Philosophy and Purpose
1. Daniel Weinbren, *The Oddfellows 1810-2010*, 211.
2. Sovereign Grand Lodge, Members Handbook: Independent Order of Odd Fellows (North Carolina: Sovereign Grand Lodge, 2013), 11.
3. Grand Lodge of Ontario and J.B. King, *Odd Fellowship* (Toronto: Independent Odd Fellow Print, 1907), 4-5.
4. Elvin James Curry, *The Red Blood of Odd Fellowship* (Maryland: Elvin Curry, 1903), 209-253
5. Independent Order of Odd Fellows, Manchester Unity, A Manual of Ritual for the Use of Provincial and Lodge Officers, 5.
6.Powley, Concise History of Odd Fellowship, 71-72.
7.Powley, *Concise History of Odd Fellowship*, 73.

8. Ibid.

9. Sovereign Grand Lodge Independent Order of Odd Fellows, *Ritual of a Lodge of Odd Fellows of The Sovereign Grand Lodge of the Independent Order of Odd Fellows* (North Carolina: Sovereign Grand Lodge, I.O.O.F., 2004), 65.

10. Rita Cooper

11. Ibid.

12. Claude Enoch Sayre, *The Religion of Odd Fellowship*, 13.

13. Danial Weinbren, *The Oddfellows 1810-2010: 200 Years of Making Friends and Helping People* (Lancaster: Carnegie Publishing, 2012), 61.

14. Sovereign Grand Lodge Independent Order of Odd Fellows, *Ritual of a Lodge of Odd Fellows of The Sovereign Grand Lodge of the Independent Order of Odd Fellows* (North Carolina: Sovereign Grand Lodge, I.O.O.F., 2004), 56.

15. Ibid, 65.

16. Ibid, 65.

17. *Ibid.*

18. Sovereign Grand Lodge of the Independent Order of Odd Fellows, *Journal of Proceedings of the One Hundred and Forty-Eight Annual Communication of the Sovereign Grand Lodge of the Independent Order of Odd Fellows, 1974 (Volume LXII)* (Baltimore: The Sovereign Grand Lodge of the I.O.O.F., 1975), 246.

19. Sovereign Grand Lodge of the Independent Order of Odd Fellows, *Journal of Proceedings of the One Hundred and Sixty-Seventh Annual Communication of the Sovereign Grand Lodge of the Independent Order of Odd Fellows, 1993 (Volume LXXXI).* (Winston-Salem: The Sovereign Grand Lodge of the I.O.O.F., 1994), 51.

20. Mary Ann Clawson, Constructing Brotherhood: Class, Gender, and Fraternalism, 15.

II. The Name

1. Elvin James Curry, *The Red Blood of Odd Fellowship* (Maryland: Elvin Curry, 1903), 66.

2. Daniel Weinbren, *The Oddfellows 1810-2010: 200 years of making friends and helping people* (Lancaster: Carnegie Publishing, 2012), 33-34.

Etymological Perspective

1. Ward-Stillson Co., *Ancient Ritual of the Order of Patriotic Odd Fellows: Revised and agreed to in the Grand Lodge held at London, England, March 12, 1797* (Michigan: Kalamazoo Publishing, n.d.), 23.

IV. Origin and Early History

1. The Union Order or Grand United Order embraced all Lodges in England until 1813, when the first split or secession occurred. The seceding Lodges formed a union and styled themselves "Independent Order of Odd Fellows, Manchester Unity".

2. Brooks, *The Official History and Manual of the Grand United Order of Odd Fellows in America*, 12.

3. "Oddfellows Welcome", *Grand United Order of Oddfellows*, accessed October 25, 2017, https://www.guoofs.com/.

V. Rise of the Manchester Unity

1. Henry Leonard Stillson, *The Official History of Odd Fellowship* (Massachusetts: Fraternity Publishing Company, 1900), 50.

2. Don R. Smith and Wayne Roberts, The *Three Link fraternity* (California: Linden Publications, 1993), 6. See also Henry Leonard Stillson, *The Official History of Odd Fellowship* (Massachusetts: Fraternity Publishing Company, 1900), 50-51.

3. R.H. Moffrey, *A Century of Odd Fellowship* (United Kingdom: Manchester Unity Independent Order of

Oddfellows, 1910), 65-67.
4. *The Times*, January 4, 1944.
5. Sovereign Grand Lodge, *Journal of Proceedings of the International Council, Independent Order of Odd Fellows, 1999-2001* (U.S.A: Sovereign Grand Lodge, 2001), 49.
6. Ibid.
7. Daniel Weinbren, *The Oddfellows 1810-2010: 200 years of making friends and helping people.* See also official website of the Manchester Unity www.oddfellows.co.uk

VI. Independent Order of Odd Fellows
1. Robert Macoy, *A Dictionary of Freemasonry*, 271-272.
2. Ibid.
3. Powley, Concise History of Odd Fellowship, 5-6.
4. Ibid.
5. Stillson, *The official History of Odd Fellows*, 70. See also Grosh, *The Odd Fellows Improved Manual*, 30.
8 Journal of Proceedings of the Annual Sessions of the Grand Lodge of Massachusetts, I.O. of O.F., held at the City of Boston, August 3, 1818.
6. See Grosh, *A Manual of Odd Fellowship*, 40. Grosh (1882) mentioned that one of the first acts of the Grand Lodge of the United States was to step out in advance of nearly all social organizations of that period by decreeing that in no case should any refreshment except water be used in any of the lodge rooms.
7. Powley, Concise History of Odd Fellowship, 51-64.
8. Ibid.
9. Ibid.
10. Ibid.
11. Ibid.
12. Grosh, *A Manual of Odd Fellowship*, 31-36.
13. Curry, *The Red Blood of Odd Fellowship*, 80.
14. Powley, *Concise History of Odd Fellowship*, 20.
15. Ibid.
16. Streeter, *Behind Closed Doors*, 153-155.
17. Moffrey, *A Century of Odd Fellowship*, 46.
18. Powley, *Concise History of Odd Fellowship (Revised edition)*, 17.
19. Stillson, *Official History of Odd Fellowship: The Three Link Fraternity*, 99-100. Stillson (1900) mentioned that a resolution to dissolved ties with Manchester Unity was adopted on Spetember 23, 1842, and was reaffirmed on September 22, 1843. See also Powley, *Concise History of Odd Fellowship. (Revised edition)*, 17-18.
20. Sovereign Grand Lodge, *Journal of Proceedings of the I.O.O.F* (North Carolina: Sovereign Grand Lodge, 1987), 35.
21. Sovereign Grand Lodge, *Journal of Proceedings of the I.O.O.F* (North Carolina: Sovereign Grand Lodge, 1987), 35.
22. Ibid.
23. Sovereign Grand Lodge, *Journal of Proceedings of the I.O.O.F* (North Carolina: Sovereign Grand Lodge, 1944), 1130.
24. Ibid, 1131.
25. Ibid, 1132.
26. Charles Brooks, *The Official History ad Manual of the Grand United Order of Odd Fellows* (Pennsylvania: Odd Fellows Journal Print, 1903), 12.
27. Ibid, 12-14.
28. Ibid, 12-14.
29. *Odd Fellows Journal*, Vol.3, January 11, 1900.
30. Ibid.
31. *Journal of Proceedings of the International Council, I.O.O.F* (1993), 75.
32. *Journal of Proceedings of the International Council, I.O.O.F* (1993), 75.

VII. Growth and Decline of Fraternalism

1. Stillson, *Official History of Odd Fellowship: The Three Link Fraternity*, 525.
2. Stillson, *Official History of Odd Fellowship: The Three Link Fraternity*, 482.
3. See Annual Reports of the Grand Lodges to the Sovereign Grand Lodge ending December 31 from 1900 to 1910.
4. Sovereign Grand Lodge, *Journal Proceedings 1911-1912*, 184-185.
5. Sovereign Grand Lodge, *Journal of Proceedings 1921-1922*, 404-409
6. In 1921, Manchester Unity Independent Order of Odd Fellows report around 928,003 members and the Grand United Order of Odd Fellows estimated more than 300,000 members.
7. Sovereign Grand Lodge, *Journal of Proceedings 1921-1922*, 418-424.
8. *Journal of Proceedings of the Sovereign Grand Lodge, I.O.O.F* (1929), 55.
9. Ibid, 60.
10. David Beito, *From Mutual Aid to the Welfare State: Fraternal Societies and Social Services, 1890-1967* (Chapel Hill: University of North Carolina Press, 2000), 17.
11. W.S. Harwood, *Secret Societies in America*, North American Review, 164, (May 1897), 617-624.
12. Ibid.
13. Ibid.
14. Ibid.
15. Noel Gist, *Structure and Process in Secret Societies*, Social Forces 16(3), March 1938, 349-357.
16. Ibid.
17. W.S. Harwood,, *Secret Societies in America*, North American Review, 164, (May 1897), 617-624.
18. W.S. Harwood,, *Secret Societies in America*, North American Review, 164, (May 1897), 617-624.
19. David Beito, *From Mutual Aid to the Welfare State: Fraternal Societies and Social Services, 1890-1967* (Chapel Hill: University of North Carolina Press, 2000), 9-12.
20. Ibid.
21. Ibid.
22. Annual Reports of the Grand Lodges to the Sovereign Grand Lodge ending December 31 from 1900 to 1910.
23. Annual Reports of the Grand Lodges to the Sovereign Grand Lodge ending December 31 from 1900 to 1910.
24. Sovereign Grand Lodge, *Journal Proceedings 1911-1912*, 206.
25. David Beito, *From Mutual Aid to the Welfare State: Fraternal Societies and Social Services, 1890-1967* (Chapel Hill: University of North Carolina Press, 2000).
26. Wolfe, *Album of Odd Fellows Home (12th Rev. Ed.)*, 12
27. Sovereign Grand Lodge, *Journal of Proceedings 1931-1932*, 723.
28. Jason Kaufman, *For the Common Good? American Civic Life and the Golden Age of Fraternity* (New York: Oxford University Press, 2002), 29.
29. Robert Stewart, *The Illustrated Encyclopedia of Historical Facts from the Dawn of Christian Era to the Present Day* (United States: Barnes and Noble, 2002), 231.
30. Amy Gutmann, *Democracy and the Welfare State* (New Jersey: Princeton University Press, 1988), 3.
31. *Journal of Proceedings of the Sovereign Grand Lodge, I.O.O.F* (1917), 70.
32. Lynn Dumenil, *The Oxford Encyclopedia of American Social History* (United States: Oxford University Press, 2012), 415.
33. George Emery and JC Emery, A Young Man's Benefit, 116-
34. *Journal of Proceedings of the Sovereign Grand Lodge, I.O.O.F* (1968), 83.

35. *Journal of Proceedings of the Sovereign Grand Lodge, I.O.O.F* (1989), 139.

36. *Journal of Proceedings of the Sovereign Grand Lodge, I.O.O.F* (1994), 599.

37. *Journal of Proceedings of the Sovereign Grand Lodge, I.O.O.F* (1983), 390.

38. Dave Rosenberg, *The Future of Odd Fellowship: Evolution and Change* (2015), 230.

39. Dave Rosenberg, *The Future of Odd Fellowship: Evolution and Change* (2015), 10.

40. *Journal of Proceedings of the Sovereign Grand Lodge, I.O.O.F* (1932), 746.

41. *Journal of Proceedings of the Sovereign Grand Lodge, I.O.O.F* (1933), 16-17.

VIII. Signs of Revival

1. Lisa Hix, Decoding Secret Societies: What are those Old Boys' Clubs Hiding? https://www.collectorsweekly.com/articles/decoding-secret-societies/

2. Journal of Proceedings of the Sovereign Grand Lodge, I.O.O.F (2003), 121.

3. Sergio Paredes, *Why I joined*? Accessed on 17 November 2020 from https://oddfellowsguide.com/2020/10/31/why-i-joined-by-sergio-paredes/

4. Ibid.

5. Journal of Proceedings of the Sovereign Grand Lodge, I.O.O.F (1989), 452.

6. Sergio Paredes, *Why I joined*? Accessed on 17 November 2020 from https://oddfellowsguide.com/2020/10/31/why-i-joined-by-sergio-paredes/

7. Journal of Proceedings of the Sovereign Grand Lodge, I.O.O.F (2001), 310.

8. Journal of Proceedings of the Sovereign Grand Lodge, I.O.O.F (2001), 319

9. Journal of Proceedings of the Sovereign Grand Lodge, I.O.O.F (1981), 2.

10. Dave Rosenberg, *The Future of Odd Fellowship: Evolution and Change* (2015), 172.

11. Journal of Proceedings of the Sovereign Grand Lodge, I.O.O.F (2002),34.

12. Journal of Proceedings of the Sovereign Grand Lodge, I.O.O.F (2002),34.

13. Dave Rosenberg, 9 Steps to Help Resuscitate a Failing Lodge http://davislodge.org/9-steps-help-resuscitate-failing-lodge/

14. Dave Rosenberg, *The Future of Odd Fellowship: Evolution and Change* (2015), 32.

15. The Sovereign Grand Lodge, *Hand Book of Suggestions for Grand and Subordinate Bodies*, 12-13.

16. Journal of Proceedings of the Sovereign Grand Lodge, I.O.O.F (1969), 532.

17. Dave Rosenberg, *The Future of Odd Fellowship: Evolution and Change* (2015), 142.

18. Journal of Proceedings of the Sovereign Grand Lodge, I.O.O.F (1991), 285.

19. Dave Rosenberg, *The Future of Odd Fellowship: Evolution and Change* (2015), 264.

20. Journal of Proceedings of the Sovereign Grand Lodge, I.O.O.F (1977), 47.

21. Journal of Proceedings of the Sovereign Grand Lodge, I.O.O.F (1977), 47.

22. Chris Saur, Centennial: Odd Fellows Lodge is a Community Powerhouse https://www.davisenterprise.com/local-news/centennial-odd-fellows-lodge-is-a-community-service-powerhouse/

23. Dave Rosenberg, *The Future of Odd Fellowship: Evolution and Change* (2015), 58.

24. Rachel Watts, The Experienced Three Links Owners Get Their Priorities from the Odd Fellows http://www.dallasobserver.com/music/the-experienced-three-links-owners-get-their-priorities-from-the-odd-fellows-6430224

25. Robyn Ross, Antiques and 'Ink Master' Play Roles in Renaissance of Fading Fraternal Order https://www.nytimes.com/2014/05/11/us/antiques-and-ink-master-play-roles-in-renaissance-of-fading-fraternal-order.html

26. Dave Rosenberg, *The Future of Odd Fellowship: Evolution and Change* (2015), 92.

27. Dave Rosenberg, *The Future of Odd Fellowship: Evolution and Change* (2015), p.28

28. Linda Sailer, Restoring the Odd Fellows Lodge: Members helping do the work, one room at a time, http://www.thedickinsonpress.com/lifestyle/3947511-restoring-odd-fellows-lodge-members-helping-do-work-one-room-time

29. Journal of Proceedings of the Sovereign Grand Lodge, I.O.O.F (2000), 43.

30. Journal of Proceedings of the Sovereign Grand Lodge, I.O.O.F (2000), 44.

31. Dave Rosenberg, *The Future of Odd Fellowship: Evolution and Change* (2015), 63.

32. Journal of Proceedings of the Sovereign Grand Lodge, I.O.O.F (1993), 35.

33. Robyn Ross, Antiques and 'Ink Master' Play Roles in Renaissance of Fading Fraternal Order https://www.nytimes.com/2014/05/11/us/antiques-and-ink-master-play-roles-in-renaissance-of-fading-fraternal-order.html

34.

35. Journal of Proceedings of the Sovereign Grand Lodge, I.O.O.F (1969), 72.

36. Dave Rosenberg, *The Future of Odd Fellowship: Evolution and Change* (2015), 132.

37. Dave Rosenberg, *The Future of Odd Fellowship: Evolution and Change* (2015), 264.

38. Journal of Proceedings of the International Council, 1999.

39. Dave Rosenberg, *The Future of Odd Fellowship: Evolution and Change* (2015), 237-238.

40. Dave Rosenberg, *The Future of Odd Fellowship: Evolution and Change* (2015), 237-238.

41. Dave Rosenberg, *The Future of Odd Fellowship: Evolution and Change* (2015), 41.

42. Dave Rosenberg, *The Future of Odd Fellowship: Evolution and Change* (2015), 61.

43. Jynnette Neal, Join the Club: Old-School Networking Made Cool Again https://oakcliff.advocatemag.com/2017/09/join-club-old-school-networking-made-cool/

44. Amy Smart, For First Time in 151 Years, Woman Leads Victoria Odd Fellows http://www.timescolonist.com/news/local/for-first-time-in-151-years-woman-leads-victoria-odd-fellows-1.1734684

45. Sara Hayden, Odd Fellows Ensure No One is Odd Man Out https://www.hmbreview.com/news/odd-fellows-ensures-no-one-is-odd-man-out/article_b6e4da60-eaa0-11e7-9421-3b5f60770def.html

IX. Rituals, Secret Handshakes and Regalia

1. Clawson, 24-25.

2. Sovereign Grand Lodge of the IOOF, *Journal of Proceedings of the One Hundred and Sixty-Eight Annual Communication of the Sovereign Grand Lodge of the Independent Order of Odd Fellows, 1994 (Volume LXXXII)*, 607.

3. Sovereign Grand Lodge of the IOOF, *Journal of Proceedings of the*

One Hundred and Forty-Third Annual Communication of the Sovereign Grand Lodge of the Independent Order of Odd Fellows, 1969 (Volume LVII), 533.
4. Sovereign Grand Lodge of the IOOF, *Journal of Proceedings of the One Hundred and Fifty-Fifth Annual Communication of the Sovereign Grand Lodge of the Independent Order of Odd Fellows, 1981 (Volume LXVIX)*, 23.
5. Victoria Solt Dennis, *Discovering Friendly and Fraternal Societies* (United Kingdom: Shire Publications, 2008).

Evolution of the IOOF Rituals
1. Henry Leonard Stillson, *The Official History of Odd Fellowship* (Massachusetts: Fraternity Publishing Company, 1900), 739.
2. Stillson, *The Official History of Odd Fellowship*, 740.
3. Ibid.
4. Ancient Ritual of the Order of Patriotic Odd Fellows: Revised and agreed to in the Grand Lodge held at London, England, March 12, 1797.
5. Henry Leonard Stillson, *The Official History of Odd Fellowship, 745*.
6. Stillson, *The Official History of Odd Fellowship, 745*.
7. Stillson, *The Official History of Odd Fellowship, 746*.
8. Ibid.
9. Stillson, 746-747.
10. T.G. Beharrell, *Odd Fellows Monitor and Guide*, 43-59.
11. Ibid.

X. Initiatory Degree
1. T.G. Beharrell, *Odd Fellows Monitor and Guide*, 43.
2. T.G. Beharrell, *Odd Fellows Monitor and Guide*, 130-133.

XI. Degree of Friendship
1. T.G. Beharrell, *Odd Fellows Monitor and Guide*, 50.

2. Ibid, 52.

XII. Degree of Love
1. B.M. Powell, *The Triple Links*, 109.
2. B.M. Powell, *The Triple Links*, 110.

XIII. Degree of Truth
1. The Sovereign Grand Lodge, *Ritual of a Lodge of Odd Fellows*, 136.
2. Ibid.
3. T.G. Beharrel, *Odd Fellows Monitor and Guide*, 77.
4. Ibid.
5. T.G. Beharrel, *Odd Fellows Monitor and Guide*, 79.
6. T.G. Beharrel, *Odd Fellows Monitor and Guide*, 80.

XIV. Lodge, its Officers and their Functions
1. IOOF Code of General Laws
2. IOOF Code of General Laws
3. IOOF Code of General Laws
4. Ibid.
5. Ibid.
6. Ibid.
7. Ibid.
8. The Sovereign Grand Lodge, *Ritual of a Lodge of Odd Fellows*
9. Ibid.
10. Ibid.
11. Ibid.
12. Ibid.
13. Ibid.
14. Ibid.
15. Ibid.
16. Ibid.
17. Ibid.
18. Ibid.
19. Ibid.
20. IOOF Code of General Laws
21. Ibid.
22. Ibid.
23. Ibid.
24. Ibid.
25. Ibid.
26. Ibid.
27. Ibid.
28. Ibid.
29. Ibid.

30. Ibid.
31. The Sovereign Grand Lodge, *Ritual of a Lodge of Odd Fellows*.
32. The Sovereign Grand Lodge, *Ritual of a Lodge of Odd Fellows*.
33. The Sovereign Grand Lodge, *Ritual of a Lodge of Odd Fellows*.
34. IOOF Code of General Laws
35. Ibid.
36. IOOF Code of General Laws
37. Ibid.
38. Ibid.
39. Ibid.
40. IOOF Code of General Laws
41. Ibid.
42. Ibid.
43. Ibid.
44. Ibid.
45. Ibid.
46. Ibid.
47. Ibid.
48. Ibid.
49. Ibid.
50. Ibid.
51. Ibid.
52. Ibid.
53. Ibid.
54. Ibid.
55. Ibid.
56. Ibid.
57. Ibid.
58. Ibid.
59. Ibid.
60. Ibid.

The Lodge Gavel
1. Rev. A.B. Grosh, *The Odd Fellows Improved Pocket Manual*, 339-341.
2. The Sovereign Grand Lodge, *Ritual of a Lodge of Odd Fellows*
3. Ibid.
4. Ibid.

Committees
1. IOOF Code of General Laws

XV. Grand Lodge, its Officers and their Functions
1. IOOF Code of General Laws
2. Theo A. Ross, *Odd Fellowship: Its History and Manual*, 2-4.
3. IOOF Code of General Laws
4. Theo A. Ross, *Odd Fellowship: Its History and Manual*, 2-4.
5. IOOF Code of General Laws
6. Ibid.
7. Ibid.
8. Ibid.
9. Ibid.
10. Ibid.
11. Ibid.
12. Ibid.
13. IOOF Code of General Laws
14. IOOF Code of General Laws
15. IOOF Code of General Laws
16. IOOF Code of General Laws
17. IOOF Code of General Laws
18. IOOF Code of General Laws
19. IOOF Code of General Laws
20. IOOF Code of General Laws
21. IOOF Code of General Laws
22. IOOF Code of General Laws
23. IOOF Code of General Laws
24. Ibid.
25. IOOF Code of General Laws
26. Ibid.
27. Ibid.
28. IOOF Code of General Laws
29. Ibid.
30. Ibid.
31. Ibid.
32. Ibid.
33. IOOF Code of General Laws
34. Ibid.
35. Ibid.
36. IOOF Code of General Laws
37. IOOF Code of General Laws
38. Ibid.
39. IOOF Code of General Laws
40. Ibid.
41. Ibid.
42. Ibid.
43. Ibid.
44. Ibid.
45. IOOF Code of General Laws
46. Ibid.
47. Ibid.
48. Ibid.
49. Ibid.
50. Ibid.

51. IOOF Code of General Laws
52. Ibid.
53. IOOF Code of General Laws
54. Ibid.
55. Ibid.
56. Ibid.
57. Ibid.
58. Ibid.
59. Ibid.
60. Ibid.
61. IOOF Code of General Laws
62. Ibid.
63. Ibid.
64. Ibid.
65. Ibid.
66. IOOF Code of General Laws
67. Ibid.
68. IOOF Code of General Laws
69. IOOF Code of General Laws
70. Ibid.
71. Ibid.
72. Ibid.
73. Ibid.
74. Ibid.
75. Ibid.
76. IOOF Code of General Laws
77. Ibid.
78. Ibid.
79. Ibid.
80. Ibid.
81. Ibid.
82. Ibid.
83. Ibid.
84. Ibid.
85. Ibid.
86. Ibid.
87. IOOF Code of General Laws
88. Ibid.
89. Ibid.
90. Ibid.
91. Ibid.
92. Ibid.

Committees
1. IOOF Code of General Laws
2. Ibid.

XVI. Sovereign Grand Lodge
1. IOOF Code of General Laws
2. IOOF Code of General Laws

3. IOOF Code of General Laws
4. Ibid.
5. Ibid.
6. Ibid.
7. Ibid.
8. Ibid.
9. Ibid.
10. Ibid.
11. IOOF Code of General Laws
12. Ibid.
13. IOOF Code of General Laws
14. IOOF Code of General Laws
15. IOOF Code of General Laws
16. Ibid.
17. Ibid.
18. Ibid.
19. IOOF Code of General Laws
20. Ibid.
21. Ibid.
22. Ibid.
23. Ibid.
24. Ibid.
25. Ibid.
26. Ibid.
27. Ibid.
28. Ibid.
29. Ibid.
30. Ibid.
31. Ibid.
32. Ibid.
33. Ibid.
34. Ibid.
35. Ibid.
36. IOOF Code of General Laws
37. Ibid.
38. Ibid.

XVIII. Joining and Maintaining Membership
1. IOOF Code of General Laws
2. IOOF Code of General Laws
3. IOOF Code of General Laws
4. IOOF Code of General Laws
5. Ibid.
6. Ibid.
7. Ibid.
8. Ibid.
9. Ibid.
10. Ibid.
11. Ibid.

12. Ibid.
13. IOOF Code of General Laws
14. Ibid.
15. Ibid.
16. IOOF Code of General Laws
17. Ibid.
18. Ibid.
19. IOOF Code of General Laws
20. Ibid.
21. Ibid.
22. IOOF Code of General Laws
23. Ibid.
24. Ibid.
25. IOOF Code of General Laws
26. Ibid.
27. Ibid.
28. IOOF Code of General Laws
29. Ibid.
30. Ibid.
31. Ibid.
32. Ibid.
33. Ibid.
34. Ibid.
35. Ibid.
36. Ibid.
37. Ibid.
38. Ibid.
39. A.B. Grosh, *The Odd Fellows Improved Pocket Manual*, 260.
40. Ibid.
41. Ibid.
42. Ibid.
43. A.B. Grosh, *The Odd Fellows Improved Pocket Manual*, 261.
44. Ibid.
45. Paschal Donaldson, *The Odd Fellows' Pocket Companion*, 175-176.
46. Ibid.
47. A.B. Grosh, *The Odd Fellows Improved Pocket Manual*, 266.
48. A.B. Grosh, *The Odd Fellows Improved Pocket Manual*, 267-269.
49. Ibid.
50. Ibid.
51. A.B. Grosh, *The Odd Fellows Improved Pocket Manual*, 126.
52. A.B. Grosh, *The Odd Fellows Improved Pocket Manual*, 261.
53. Ibid.
54. Ibid.
55. Ibid.
56. Ibid.
57. Paschal Donaldson, *The Odd Fellows' Pocket Companion*, 176-177.
58. Ibid.
59. Paschal Donaldson, *The Odd Fellows' Pocket Companion*, 183-185.
60. IOOF Code of General Laws
61. Ibid.

XIX. Branches of the IOOF

1. Sovereign Grand Lodge of the IOOF, *Journal of Proceedings of the Sovereign Grand Lodge of the Independent Order of Odd Fellows, 1999 (Volume* LXXXVII*)*, 490.
2. Ibid, 35.
3. Powley, *Concise History of Odd Fellowship*, 35.
4. Ibid.
5. Sovereign Grand Lodge of the IOOF, *Journal of Proceedings of the Sovereign Grand Lodge of the Independent Order of Odd Fellows,* 1993, 390.
6. A letter of complaint was addressed to the Sovereign Grand Lodge reporting that some Odd Fellows are performing a "spurious degree" inside IOOF lodges.
7. Sovereign Grand Lodge of the IOOF, *Journal of Proceedings of the Sovereign Grand Lodge of the Independent Order of Odd Fellows, 1870,* 4725.

References

I. Published Books

Andrews, Thomas. *The Jericho Road*. Oklahoma: William Thomas Co, 1937.

Beharrell, Thomas. *Odd Fellows Monitor and Guide*. Indianapolis: Robert Douglass, 1883.

Beharrell, Thomas. *The Brotherhood: Being a Presentation of Odd Fellowship*. Indiana: Brotherhood Publishing Co., 1875.

Beito, David. *From Mutual Aid to the Welfare State: Fraternal Societies and Social Services, 1890-1967*. Chapel Hill: University of North Carolina Press, 2000.

Blainey, Goeffrey. *Odd Fellows: A History of IOOF Australia*. Australia: Allen & Unwin, 1991.

Brooks, Charles. *The Official History ad Manual of the Grand United Order of Odd Fellows*. Pennsylvania: Odd Fellows Journal Print, 1903.

Carnes, Mark. *Secret Ritual and Manhood in Victorian America*. New Haven: Yale University, 1989.

Clark, Peter. *British Clubs and Societies 1580-1800: The Origins of an Associational World*. New York: Oxford University Press, 2000.

Clawson, Mary Ann. *Constructing Brotherhood: Class, Gender, and Fraternalism*. New Jersey: Princeton University Press, 1989.

Cooke, L. Hamel. *Democracy and Odd Fellowship*. Canada: L. Hamel Cooke, 1943.

Cordery, Simon. *British Friendly Societies, 1750-1914*. New York: Palgrave Macmillan, 2003.

Curry, Elvin James. *The Red Blood of Odd Fellowship*. Maryland: Elvin Curry, 1903.

Defoe, Daniel. An *Essay upon Projects*. London: R.R. for Tho. Cockerill, 1697.

Dennis, Victoria Solt. *Discovering Friendly and Fraternal Societies*. United Kingdom: Shire Publications, 2008.

Donaldson, Paschal. *The Odd Fellows Text Book*. Philadelphia: Moss & Brother,

1852.

Donaldson, Paschal. *The Odd Fellows' Pocket Companion*. Ohio: R.W. Carroll & Co, 1881.

Emery, George and Emery, J. C. Herbert. *A Young Man's Benefit*. London: McGill-Queen's University Press, 1999.

Ford, Henry. *Symbolism of Odd Fellowship*. New Orleans: Cornerstone Book Publishers, 2013.

Gosden, Peter Henry John Heather. *The Friendly Societies in England, 1815-1875*. United Kingdom: University of Manchester Press, 1961.

Greer, John Michael. *The Element Encyclopedia of Secret Societies*. New York: Barnes and Nobles, 2006.

Grosh, Aaron Burt. *The Odd Fellow's Manual*. Philadelphia: H.C. Peck & Theo Bliss, 1860.

Grosh, Aaron Burt. *The Odd-Fellows Improved Pocket Manual*. New York: Clark & Maynard, 1873.

Grosh, Aaron Burt. *A Manual of Odd Fellowship. New York*: New York: Clark & Maynard, 1882.

Gutmann, Amy. *Democracy and the Welfare State*. New Jersey: Princeton University Press, 1988.

Kaufman, Jason. *For the Common Good? American Civic Life and the Golden Age of Fraternity*. New York: Oxford University Press, 2002.

King, J.B. and the Grand Lodge of Ontario, IOOF. *Odd Fellowship*. Toronto: Independent Odd Fellow Print, 1907.

Macoy, Robert. *General History, Cyclopedia, and Dictionary of Freemasonry*. New York, Masonic Publishing Company, 1870.

Melling, John Kennedy. *Discovering London's Guilds and Liveries*. United Kingdom: Shire Publications, 2002.

Moffrey, Robert. *The Rise and Progress of the Manchester Unity of the Independent Order of Oddfellows*. United Kingdom: Grand Master & Board of Directors of the Order, 1904.

Moffrey, Robert. *A Century of Odd Fellowship*. United Kingdom: Manchester

Unity Independent Order of Oddfellows, 1910.

P.D. A *candid enquiry into the principles and practices of the most ancient and honourable society of Bucks*. London: C. Kiernan, 1770.

Powell, Benson. *The Triple Links*. Kansas: Ed G. Moore & Son, 1900.

Powley, Joseph. *Concise History of Odd Fellowship*. Toronto: The Grand Lodge of Ontario IOOF, 1943.

Powley, Joseph. *Concise History of Odd Fellowship (Revised edition)*. Toronto: Macoomb Publishing, 1952.

Reedy, Tom and Thurman, Nita. *Denton Lodge No.82, I.O.O.F.: A History 1859-2009*. Maine: Acme Bookbinding, 2009.

Ridgely, James Lot. *History of American Odd Fellowship: The First Decade*. Baltimore: James Lot Ridgely, 1878.

Rosenberg, Dave. *The Future of Odd Fellowship: Evolution and Change*. California: Dave Rosenberg, 2015.

Ross, Theodore. *Odd Fellowship: Its History and Manual*. New York: M.W. Hazen Co., 1888.

Smith, Joshua Toulmin. *English Gilds*. London: N. Trubner & Co., London, 1870.

Spry, James. *The History of Odd Fellowship: Its Origin, Tradition and Objectives*. London. J.R.H. Spry, 1866.

Streeter, Michael. *Behind Closed Doors*. United Kingdom: New Holland Publishers, 2008.

Stillson, Henry Leonard. *The Official History of Odd Fellowship*. Massachusetts: Fraternity Publishing Company, 1900.

Stillson, Henry Leonard. *The Official History of Odd Fellowship*. Massachusetts: Fraternity Publishing Company, 1908.

Sovereign Grand Lodge of the Independent Order of Odd Fellows. *Members Handbook: Independent Order of Odd Fellows*. Winston-Salem: Sovereign Grand Lodge, 2013.

Tinkham, George. *The Half Century of California Odd Fellowship*. Stockton, CA: Record Publishing Co., 1906.

Wallace, W.W. *The Odd-Fellows' Keepsake: A Concise History of Odd-Fellowship in the United States.* New York: Office of the Mirror of the Times, 1850.

Weinbren, Daniel. *The Oddfellows 1810-2010: 200 Years of Making Friends and Helping People.* Lancaster: Carnegie Publishing, 2012.

II. Journal of Proceedings

Sovereign Grand Lodge of the Independent Order of Odd Fellows. *Journal of Proceedings of the Right Worthy Grand Lodge of the United States, and the Sovereign Grand Lodge of the Independent Order of Odd Fellows, from its Formation in February, 1821-1846 (Volume I).* Baltimore: The Sovereign Grand Lodge of the I.O.O.F., 1893.

Sovereign Grand Lodge of the Independent Order of Odd Fellows. *Journal of Proceedings of the Right Worthy Grand Lodge of the United States, and the Sovereign Grand Lodge of the Independent Order of Odd Fellows, from its Formation in February, 1847-1852 (Volume II).* Baltimore: The Sovereign Grand Lodge of the I.O.O.F., 1888.

Sovereign Grand Lodge of the Independent Order of Odd Fellows. *Journal of Proceedings of the Right Worthy Grand Lodge of the United States, and the Sovereign Grand Lodge of the Independent Order of Odd Fellows, from its Formation in February, 1853-1857 (Volume III).* Baltimore: The Sovereign Grand Lodge of the I.O.O.F., 1884.

Sovereign Grand Lodge of the Independent Order of Odd Fellows. *Journal of Proceedings of the Right Worthy Grand Lodge of the United States, and the Sovereign Grand Lodge of the Independent Order of Odd Fellows, from its Formation in February, 1858-1862 (Volume IV).* Baltimore: The Sovereign Grand Lodge of the I.O.O.F., 1884.

Sovereign Grand Lodge of the Independent Order of Odd Fellows. *Journal of Proceedings of the Right Worthy Grand Lodge of the United States, and the Sovereign Grand Lodge of the Independent Order of Odd Fellows, from its Formation in February, 1863-1867 (Volume V).* Baltimore: The Sovereign Grand Lodge of the I.O.O.F., 1876.

Sovereign Grand Lodge of the Independent Order of Odd Fellows. *Journal of Proceedings of the Right Worthy Grand Lodge of the United States, and the Sovereign Grand Lodge of the Independent Order of Odd Fellows, from its Formation in February, 1868-1870 (Volume VI).* Baltimore: The Sovereign Grand Lodge of the I.O.O.F., 1880.

Sovereign Grand Lodge of the Independent Order of Odd Fellows.

Journal of Proceedings of the One Hundred and Sixty-Ninth Annual Communication of the Sovereign Grand Lodge of the Independent Order of Odd Fellows, 1995 (Volume LXXXIII). Winston-Salem: The Sovereign Grand Lodge of the I.O.O.F., 1996.

Sovereign Grand Lodge of the Independent Order of Odd Fellows. *Journal of Proceedings of the One Hundred and Seventy-Third Annual Communication of the Sovereign Grand Lodge of the Independent Order of Odd Fellows, 1999 (Volume LXXXVII)*. Winston-Salem: The Sovereign Grand Lodge of the I.O.O.F., 2000.

Sovereign Grand Lodge of the Independent Order of Odd Fellows. *Journal of Proceedings of the One Hundred and Seventy-Fourth Annual Communication of the Sovereign Grand Lodge of the Independent Order of Odd Fellows, 2000 (Volume LXXXVIII)*. Winston-Salem: The Sovereign Grand Lodge of the I.O.O.F., 2001.

Sovereign Grand Lodge of the Independent Order of Odd Fellows. *Journal of Proceedings of the One Hundred and Seventy-Sixth Annual Communication of the Sovereign Grand Lodge of the Independent Order of Odd Fellows, 2002 (Volume XC)*. Winston-Salem: The Sovereign Grand Lodge of the I.O.O.F., 2003.

III. Rituals

Grand Lodge of Maryland and the United States. *Lectures and Charges of the Degrees of the Independent Order of Odd Fellowship*. Maryland: Grand Lodge of Maryland and the United States, I.O.O.F., 1820.

Manchester Unity Independent Order of Odd Fellows Manchester Unity Friendly Society. *Ritual of the Independent Order of Odd Fellows Manchester Unity Friendly Society: For the Use of District Officers*. Manchester: Manchester Unity Independent Order of Odd Fellows Manchester Unity Friendly Society, 1989.

Manchester Unity Independent Order of Odd Fellows. *Lectures used by the Manchester District*. Manchester: Mark Wardle, P.G. and C.S., 1824.

Ritual of The Ancient, Mystic Order of Samaritans of the United States and Canada (Cleveland: Supreme Sanctorum, 1935).

Ritual of The Ladies of the Orient of the United States and Canada (Supreme Royal Zuanna, n.d.)

Sovereign Grand Lodge Independent Order of Odd Fellows. *Ritual of a Lodge of Odd Fellows of The Sovereign Grand Lodge of the Independent Order of Odd Fellows*. North Carolina: Sovereign Grand Lodge, I.O.O.F., 2004.

Sovereign Grand Lodge Independent Order of Odd Fellows. *Ritual of a Junior Lodge under the Jurisdiction of the Sovereign Grand Lodge of the Independent Order of Odd Fellows.* Maryland: Sovereign Grand Lodge, IOOF, 1930.

Sovereign Grand Lodge Independent Order of Odd Fellows. *Ritual of Theta Rho Girls Club under the Jurisdiction of the Sovereign Grand Lodge of the Independent Order of Odd Maryland*: Sovereign Grand Lodge, IOOF, 1975.

Ward-Stillson Co. *Ancient Ritual of the Order of Patriotic Odd Fellows: Revised and agreed to in the Grand Lodge held at London, England, March 12, 1797.* Michigan: Kalamazoo Publishing, n.d.

IV. Internet Sources

Flores, Taya. "*Fraternal, Service groups battle declining membership: Elks, Rotarians and Other Fraternal Groups Struggle to Attract Younger Members.*" *Journal & Courier*, October 11, 2014. Accessed August 30, 2017, https://www.jconline.com/story/news/2014/10/11/fraternal-service-groups-battle-declining-membership/16874977/

Hayden, Sara. "*Odd Fellows Ensure No One is Odd Man Out.*" *Half Moon Bay Review*, December 26, 2017. Accessed January 5, 2018, https://www.hmbreview.com/news/odd-fellows-ensures-no-one-is-odd-man-out/article_b6e4da60-eaa0-11e7-9421-3b5f60770def.html

Kalfsbeek, Elizabeth. "*Reborn Arbuckle Odd Fellows Revitalizing Community*". *Daily Democrat*, December 9, 2009. Accessed January 5, 2018, http://www.dailydemocrat.com/article/zz/20090209/NEWS/902099769

Lacava, Franklin, "Hopwood woman breaks mold as leader of Odd Fellows". Triblive, July 18, 2015. Accessed January 22, 2019, http://triblive.com/news/fayette/8717029-74/fellows-odd-cupp

Manchester Unity Independent Order of Odd Fellows, "*The Oddfellows Over the Years*", Accessed July 20, 2016, https://www.oddfellows.co.uk/About-us/Over-the-Years.

Manchester Unity Independent Order of Odd Fellows, "*About the Oddfellows Friendly Society*", Accessed July 20, 2018, https://www.oddfellows.co.uk/about/

Moore, Dave. "*Dallas Odd Fellows Reviving Old-school Social Network.*" *Dallas Innovates*, February 23, 2017. Accessed October 3, 2017, https://www.dallasinnovates.com/dallas-odd-fellows-reviving-old-school-social-network/

Neal, Jynnette. "*Join the Club: Old-School Networking Made Cool Again.*"*Advocate Oak Cliff*, September 26, 2017. Accessed October 3, 2017, https://oakcliff.advocatemag.com/2017/09/join-club-old-school-networking-made-cool/

Pacella, Rachael. "*Towson business owner is Odd Fellows' first female African-American leader.*" *The Baltimore Sun*, June 1, 2016. Accessed August 30, 2017, http://www.baltimoresun.com/news/maryland/baltimore-county/towson/ph-tt-darlene-parker-0525-20160526-story.html

Rosenberg, Dave. "*9 Steps to Help Resuscitate a Failing Lodge*". Davis Odd Fellows Lodge No.169, February 26, 2018. Accessed May 30, 2018, http://davislodge.org/9-steps-help-resuscitate-failing-lodge/

Ross, Robyn. "*Antiques and 'Ink Master' Play Roles in Renaissance of Fading Fraternal Order.*" *New York Times*, May 10, 2014. Accessed October 2, 2017, https://www.nytimes.com/2014/05/11/us/antiques-and-ink-master-play-roles-in-renaissance-of-fading-fraternal-order.html

Saur, Chris. "*Centennial: Odd Fellows Lodge is a Community Powerhouse.*" Davis Enterprise, June 2, 2017. Accessed October 2, 2017, https://www.davisenterprise.com/local-news/centennial-odd-fellows-lodge-is-a-community-service-powerhouse/

V. Other Sources

IOOF Code of General Laws of the Sovereign Grand Lodge of the Independent Order of Odd Fellows (2018).

louieblakesailesarmiento@gmail.com

facebook.com/louieblakesailesarmientoauthor

instagram.com/louieblakesailesarmiento

twitter.com/LouieBlake

youtube.com/IOOF1819

www.ingramcontent.com/pod-product-compliance
Lightning Source LLC
Chambersburg PA
CBHW062049270326
41931CB00013B/3002